The Sociology
of
Harry Potter

22 Enchanting Essays
on the Wizarding World
Jenn Sims, Editor

The Sociology of Harry Potter:
22 Enchanting Essays on the Wizarding World

Zossima Press
Hamden, CT

For information, contact Robert@WingedLionPress.com

Zossima Press titles may be purchased for business or promotional use or special sales.

10-9-8-7-6-5-4-3-2-1

Zossima Press

ISBN-13 978-1-936294-18-3

To Jo for creating Harry,
and to Brit for introducing me to him.

ACKNOWLEDGMENTS

This book would not have come to fruition were it not for the help and support of my family, friends, and colleagues. Firstly, to all of the contributing authors of this volume – to Rachel, Katie, Flo, Marcia, Kristen, Sher, Jelena, Daniel, Tanya, Dustin, Alice, Ty, Drew, Mya, Shruti, Meredith, Anna, Grá, Justyna, R.P., and Leo: Thank you so much for your enthusiasm and hard work during this project! Thank you for reading my long emails and indulging my nit-picky requests. I am so proud of our book and so privileged to have worked with all of you.

Second, to John DeLamater and Mustafa Emirbayer: Thank you for your support and guidance throughout every stage of this process and for your helpful feedback on my chapters. Thank you as well to Andrea Ashwood, Sung Ik Cho, Alicia Dean, Naresh Hanchate, Bridget Mahoney, Anne Marie McCabe-Morgan, Chinelo Njaka, and Trevor Young-Hyman for providing feedback on and/or proofreading my chapters. And thank you to my cousin, Varian Johnson, for your kind and patient responses to my many questions.

A very special thank you to Robert Trexler, editor and publisher of Zossima Press, for accepting this project and for your tireless efforts behind the scenes to make it a reality. Thanks also goes to Laura Damon-Moore and Crystal Schmidt for composing the Index and to Joyce O'Dell for the cover design.

Finally, I would like to blame, er, I mean thank my sister Brittany, for if it were not for her I would have never even read the Harry Potter novels in the first place. Thank you Sissy for shoving me through Platform 9 ¾, for humbly accepting responsibility for my resulting Harry Potter obsession, and most importantly, thank you for your unwavering belief in my ability to make this book a reality from the moment the idea for it apparated into my head.

To anyone I have missed thanking by name, please know it was an error of the mind not heart.

TABLE OF CONTENTS

WHY A *SOCIOLOGY* OF HARRY POTTER?

JENN SIMS

Given the global popularity of J.K.Rowling's Harry Potter novels, it was inevitable that scholars from all academic disciples would analyze, criticize, and theorize about the story, its message, and "Pottermania." Naturally, literary scholars acted first. Books like *Beacham's Sourcebooks For Teaching Young Adult Fiction: Exploring Harry Potter*[1] were hot off the presses before *Prisoner of Azkaban* could settle in on the New York Times best seller list. Other analyses of the series as a work of literature, such as *The Ivory Tower and Harry Potter: Perspectives on a Literary Phenomenon*[2], quickly followed suit. These, and subsequent books by John Granger and Travis Prinzi, offered an intriguing look into Ms. Rowling's craftsmanship as well as others' efforts at interpreting the underlying messages and themes of the story.

The arts and social sciences took a little longer to take note of Harry. In 2004, *Harry Potter and Philosophy: If Aristotle Ran Hogwarts*[3] was published; and two years later came *The Psychology of Harry Potter.*[4] Interdisciplinary books such as *Critical Perspectives on Harry Potter*[5] then sought to bring together the different academic perspectives, such as cultural and media studies, with literary and social science analyses. However, within this vast collection of Harry Potter analysis, of which the books I have named are but a sampling, there are only a few disparate chapters that attempt a sociological analysis of the wizarding world. Sociology is the systematic study of human social groups and interactions. According to C. Wright Mills (1959: 15) viewing the world through a sociological lens, which he called using the sociological imagination, provides "understanding of the intimate realities of ourselves in connection with the larger social realities." So a few years ago, I decided that it was time to focus the sociological imagination on the wizarding world.

---

1   Schefer (ed.) Beachman Publishing, 2000
2   Whited (ed.) University of Missouri Press, 2002
3   Baggett and Klein (eds.) Open Court, 2004
4   Mulholland (ed.) BenBella Books, 2006
5   Heilman (ed.) Routledge, 2008

And yet.... The absence of sociological scholarship on Harry Potter is not the only reason that I wanted to organize this book. I enrolled in my first sociology course in the Spring of 2001, about the same time that my sister, tired of my pretentious anti-establishment refusal to read the popular novels, sat down in my bedroom one day and read *Sorcerer's Stone* aloud to me. Since those simultaneous events over ten years ago, my love of sociology and my love of Harry Potter have both grown exponentially – but more importantly, they have grown together. No matter what I was currently studying in my sociology courses - class inequality, education, identity management - I always found myself relating it to some aspect of the Harry Potter book I was currently reading (or rereading!). Conversely, no matter which Harry Potter book I was (re)reading or movie I was (re)watching, I couldn't help but filter it through the lens of the theories and research I was learning in my undergraduate, masters, and now doctoral sociology courses. I feel that sociology has helped me to more deeply appreciate and love Harry, and that Harry has helped me to become a better sociologist. More than just wanting *The Sociology of Harry Potter* because philosophy and psychology, our cousin academic disciplines, had their turn, I wanted to produce this book to share with others the joy that the coupling of sociology and Harry Potter has been to me.

OUTLINE OF CHAPTERS

For this volume, I selected chapters that I hoped would represent the breadth of sociological topics of interest, from classic foci like economics, groups and social stigma to more contemporary topics like the social construction of technology and trauma memory. The book is organized into five sections: Society, Social Institutions, Groups and Identity, Stratification, and Beyond the Veil. Following this Introduction is Chapter 2, by **Rachel LaBozetta**, which introduces the main themes and concepts of the discipline using material from the wizarding world as examples. This is an excellent crash course for anyone who is unfamiliar with sociology.

The first section of the book consists of five chapters examining different aspects of wizarding society. Chapter 3 is by **Florence Maätita, Marcia D. Hernandez,** and **Kristen Kalz**. Maätita et al examine the social uses and users of space in the wizarding world. Focusing on Harry, Maätita et al. analyze the construction and function of his "safe spaces" and demonstrates how differing views regarding how he should use a space lead to users contesting the space.

In Chapter 4, **Sher Ratnabalasuriar** discusses the social construction of technology. Her thesis, that technology emerges out of culturally particular social forces and interactions, is made clear via examination of differential magical and Muggle transportation and communication technology.

Furthermore, by drawing parallels between devices and gadgets that are found in the magical and Muggle worlds, Ratnabalasuriar provides us a way to see, as Arthur Weasley attempts to do, how the technologies one currently uses are embedded in a particular time and space.

Chapter 5, by **Katie Christie,** presents the results of her quantitative research study on friendship networks at Hogwarts. Using social network analysis, Christie tests for homophily among friendship groups and the hypothesis that Harry is the central social actor within his grade.

In Chapter 6, **Jelena Marić** and I describe how the social structure of a society affects an individual's life opportunities, trajectories and outcomes and vice versa. Using Severus Snape as a case study, we examine how his early life circumstances and experiences shaped his teaching pedagogy. By looking at the intersection of his social structure and personality we can understand his choices and decisions, and how they affected the larger social structure of the wizarding world.

Chapter 7 introduces Durkheim's theory of crime and punishment along with Bourdieu's notion of the logic of fields. It is here that I put forth the seemingly backwards hypothesis that the wizarding world would in fact *not* be better off without the Death Eaters.

The second section of the book contains three chapters discussing social institutions.[6] **Daniel R. Smith** explains the morality of economic consumption in Chapter 8. Smith demonstrates that the ideas surrounding purchasing commodities, from food to brooms, shapes what a given society judges as morally worth having. Comparing the purchasing patterns and expectations of Harry, Ron, Draco and Dudley as exemplars of (ir)responsible and (non) respectable consumption, he reveals the relationship between the social order and the moral order of wizarding society.

Chapter 9 looks at wizarding families by focusing on the construction of the role of "mother." Here **Tanya Cook** contrasts Lily Potter, Molly Weasley and Narcissa Malfoy with Petunia Dursley and Bellatrix Lestrange to reveal the wizarding world's sociocultural expectations of what a good mother is/ does. Moreover, in critiquing the behaviors of Hagrid and Sirius, Cook shows that "mothering" is neither specific to women nor simply synonymous with caring for one's own or other children.

---

6   One social institution which receives a great deal sociological attention, but is noticeably absent from this book, is education. The Harry Potter books have been widely analyzed by scholars in English, Curriculum and Instruction, Education, Library Studies, and so forth. And while Sociology does have a particular disciplinary view on education as a social institution, I decided nonetheless not to re-invent (i.e., analyze) the educational wheel.

In chapter 10, **Dustin Kidd** examines institutionalized spaces such St. Mungo's, professions such as Healer and Mediwizard, and the magical pharmaceutical industry to analyze the wizarding health care system. Kidd also elaborates upon wizarding attitudes towards illness, sickness and disability and illustrates how both Harry and Voldemort can be seen as "disabled" wizards.

The third section of the book contains five chapters regarding groups and identities. In Chapter 11, **Alice Nuttall** exposes the "illusion of inclusion" in the wizarding world. Interrogating the ideas about and treatment of Hufflepuffs, students who struggle with magic and Squibs, Nuttall shows that the wizarding world is no less prejudiced than the Muggle world. What's more, through her discussion of Squibs we heartbreakingly observe that it is not just others who devalue certain groups but some within those very groups themselves have internalized the negative views from the larger society and consequently consider themselves "no use" to wizardkind.

Coined by Erving Goffman in 1959, the classic sociological concept of stigma is introduced in Chapter 12 by **Ty Hayes**. Hayes applies Goffman's framework to the wizarding world to help us understand the lives of Muggle-borns and werewolves and the various efforts of these, and their non-stigmatized counterparts, to navigate an often hostile social environment.

Chapter 13, by **Drew Chappell**, examines the structure and function of different types of social groups in the wizarding world. Through analysis of Hogwarts Houses, Quidditch teams, and various other clubs and secret societies, Chappell demonstrates the importance of group membership for personal development, interpersonal interactions, and society (magical and Muggle) as a whole.

In Chapter 14, **Mya Fisher** explains group "boundary work" by focusing on the events of the 422nd Quidditch World Cup and the reconstituted Triwizard Tournament. Regarding the latter, Fisher compares the Durmstrang and Beauxbatons students' stay at Hogwarts with Muggle students' study abroad experiences, concluding that bringing students together across boundaries is not a quick and easy process, though it is well worth the effort.

Chapter 15, on collective memory and trauma, is by **Shruti Devgan**. In this chapter, Devgan discusses how traumatic memories, far from being simply a factual objective recording of the past, are socially constructed at the group level and are intricately tied to group identity. She then looks at several memory-related creatures, tools and techniques used in the wizarding world that have the potential to allow Muggles new language to communicate about collective trauma memories.

Stratification is addressed in the fourth section. In Chapter 16, **Meredith Railton** discusses gender. However, rather that scrutinizing the attributes of individual female characters or the "(anti)feminist" messages their inclusion and plot details convey like most gender analyses of the wizarding world, Railton takes a step back and looks at gender within several wizarding institutions, concluding that Muggles have a lot to learn from their magical counterparts.

Interracial relationships are the topic of Chapter 17. While Muggles in Great Britain exhibit a low rate of interracial marriage, mixed race couples in wizarding Britain are very common – if one uses the Muggle definition of race. In this chapter, I look at various couples at Hogwarts and beyond, revealing that the differential social construction of race in magical and Muggle Britian is revealed when one considers who is / is not considered to be interracially dating in each.

Chapter 18 by **Anna Chilewska** reminds us that humans are not the only players in social life or the only ones situated within the social hierarchy. Chilewska critiques the unproblematized use (and abuse) of animals by humans in the wizarding world. She also presents three case studies of human-animal relationships, showing that the bonds that can form when one does not have a utility orientation to an animal can sometimes be even stronger and more beneficial than some bonds with other humans.

Sociological analyses of stratification have traditionally centered on the "big three" of race, class, and gender. However, sexuality has increasingly been added to this scholarly trinity. While the Harry Potter novels do not delve into the characters' sexuality directly, it is clear that the wizarding world is as hegemonically heteronormative as its Muggle counterpart. In Chapter 19, **Gráinne O'Brien** examines the life and sexuality of Tom Riddle, Jr., expounding upon her thesis that Tom's repression of both his same sex desires and (in the orphanage) his magical abilities, coupled with lack of mentoring from arguably the one person in wizarding Britain who could have offered him guidance, lead him to "grow sideways" into the infamous Lord Voldemort.

The final section of the book, Beyond the Veil, consists of three chapters that bring the analysis full circle by shifting the lens of the sociological imagination from the world within the books to the relationship between that world and our own "real" world. In Chapter 20, **Justyna Deszcz-Tryhubczak** bridges Harry's world and ours through analysis of Harry Potter fan fiction. These playfully written stories by young fans of the series show not only creativity but demonstrate young people's ability to use their sociological imaginations to critically analyze social institutions, inequality and, perhaps more importantly, propose ways to implement concrete social reforms. Deszcz-Tryhubczak then speculates about how this ability might be applied in the future as these young fans enter the real civic arena.

According to Granger (2008), the "obvious" and edifying Euro-Christian content and symbolism in the Harry Potter novels explains its unprecedented success. What, then, explains the tens of thousands of fans in Asia who do not share this cultural connection? Chapter 21 presents the findings of **Ravindra Pratap Singh**'s research investigating the roots of Pottermania in India. Surveying over 500 Indian children, Singh finds support for his thesis that it is both identifiable surface content of Indian origin and deeper, just-below-the-surface, Indian meanings and symbolism which endear the British wizarding world to readers in the East.

Finally, **Leo Ruickbie** explains in Chapter 22 that responses to witchcraft can be seen as a gauge of social strain; and in the case of the Harry Potter novels, this even applies to "fictional" witchcraft. Looking at mutli-faith, multi-denominational reactions to the Harry Potter series, from claims that it paves the way to hell to churches explicitly embracing its "good triumphs over evil" message, Ruickbie closes the book by showing that both views are guilty of distorting the series as a whole and the wizarding world within it that the previous chapters examined.

As per the standard of the American Sociological Association, all citations are parenthetical in text containing the scholar's name, year of publication, and (if a direct quotation) page number. All book citations of the Harry Potter novels are written as SS, COS, POA, GOF, OOTP, HBP, DH, TBB (*Tales of Beedle the Bard*), and FB (*Fantastic Beasts and Where to Find Them*); and the page numbers refer to the American (Scholastic) hard-cover standard editions. Citation of movies are written as HP1, HP2, HP3, HP4, HP5, HP6, HP7 part I and HP7 part II, and refer to the English language versions.

Finally, with regard to analysis of "Harry Potter," it is worth emphasizing that there is a difference between analysis of the Harry Potter books and movies as works of fiction *in our "real" world* and analysis of the wizarding world *within* the Harry Potter books and movies. Unlike other academic analyses of Harry Potter, the focus of the chapters in this book does not oscillate between these two different, though equally interesting, analytical starting points. Excepting this introduction and the three chapters of the conclusion for the pragmatic reasons indicated above, we adhere firmly to the latter approach. The chapters herein discuss the wizarding world as a real social system *sui generis*. We purposely blur the distinction between life and art with the hope that, after viewing the latter sociologically, readers might begin viewing the former in the same manner.

And now for a sociological look at the wizarding world!

REFERENCES

Mills, C. Wright. 1959. *The Sociological Imagination*. Oxford: Oxford University Press.

Granger, John. 2008. *The Deathly Hallows Lectures: The Hogwarts Professor Explains Harry's Final Adventure*. Allentown, PA: Zossima Press.

The Sociology of Harry Potter

AN INTRODUCTION TO SOCIOLOGY

RACHEL LABOZETTA

"No need to ask who you are. My father's told me all the Weasleys have red hair, freckles, and more children than they can afford… You'll soon find out some wizarding families are much better than others, Potter. You don't want to go making friends with the wrong sort" (SS 108).

The above quotation, from Draco Malfoy, is quite telling. On the surface it speaks of how highly Draco thinks of himself and his kin compared to Ron Weasley and his family. On a deeper level, Draco is also speaking of the importance of class, status, and power. His words not only address the institution of family and hint at the concept of Social Darwinism[7], but summarize his understanding of how wizarding society is run. These are all aspects of sociology.

Sociology is a very broad subject with a wide range of areas of research. This chapter contains useful definitions that will help readers who are new to sociology to better understand the subsequent chapters of the book. The goal of the book is to introduce the reader to a sociological way of thinking via a popular icon, in this case, the *Harry Potter* series. A sociological way of thinking allows one to step outside of themselves and their narrow circumstance and look at things a little more objectively, thus giving one the ability to see not only "outside the box" but to attempt to look at the "box" itself.

WHAT IS SOCIOLOGY?

At its most basic definition, sociology is the study of society, in all of its parts, focusing particularly on human groups and social life as well as on the society as a whole. Sociologists look at a combination of large scale and small scale influences, i.e., macro and micro level influences, which shape the way society works. For example, we examine large institutions such as church, school, family, government, etc. and see what occurs in these institutions that make us, as people, who we are and act the way we do. We also study how, at the individual level, humans modify these institutions over time to better suit

---

7   Social Darwinism is the view that those who are currently are the top of a society have been evolutionarily handpicked to be in that position and, therefore, they are and ought to be the dominant group. In the 19th century, this concept gave rise to the justification of white dominance and, in relation to the *Harry Potter* series, the justification of pureblood dominance.

our changing needs. Sociology, as well as anthropology, political science, and several other areas of study, are considered social sciences due to the fact that we use rigorous investigation, evaluations, and analysis in our research, not unlike the scientific methods used for studying biology, physics, or chemistry.

One area of study that is intricately related to sociology is history. History and sociology go hand in hand. Examining the past helps sociologists develop theories as well as aid us in better understanding how societies have evolved over time and, thus, gives us greater insight as to what the future may hold. For example, let's try to answer the following question sociologically: "Why are life conditions in the United Kingdom today so different from life 50 years ago?" First, we would reel our brains back fifty years, which, from the current year of 2012, takes us to 1962. In that 50 years, we could look at the changes that ensued from the Women's Liberation Movement, the American Civil Rights Movement, advances in computer technology, human and material losses from wars, just to name a few. These historical events influence the way society thinks and feels today. Sociologists use history and historical events, such as the above examples, as a framework to see how society influences our lives and to theorize about what changes may occur down the road.

SOCIOLOGICAL PERSPECTIVES

Sociology began as a response to great changes in society during the 1800s. These changes were the secularization, urbanization, and industrialization of the modern world. Early sociologists began to see the world change rapidly and wondered what chain of reactions resulted in these new outcomes. Some interesting theoretical perspectives came out of these ponderings, but three of the most famous are functionalism, conflict theory, and symbolic interactionism.

Functionalism, pioneered by the sociologists Emile Durkheim and Auguste Comte, focuses on how the parts of a society are structured to maintain the society's stability and continuity. Take a computer, for example. Computers are made of many parts such as keys, a modem, RAM, and numerous other gadgets and gizmos. Each of these parts is essential to the proper functioning of the computer. When even one does not work properly, the computer as a whole cannot work. Functionalists would argue that societies work in a similar manner. When the parts of a society do not work in harmony together the society becomes dysfunctional, which aggravates social problems such as poverty or crime. In the wizarding world, for example, the reason for the existence of the Ministry of Magic, as with all governments, is to run wizarding society with a standard set of rules and regulations to ensure the society's stability. After the infiltration of the Ministry by Voldemort's regime, wizarding society no longer functions as it was meant to, resulting in a higher rate of crime, an influx of illegal shops cropping up in wizarding villages, and a general sense of fear, loss, and confusion by wizarding society as a whole. In other words, wizarding society had become dysfunctional.

Conflict theory, on the other hand, views society as being in a continual struggle, violent or nonviolent. Founded by Karl Marx, Frederic Ingles, and Max Weber, conflict theory posits that the tension between competing groups is reflected in the social behavior and organization of a society. Conflicts stratify, or separate, a society and are often, but not always, associated with class, status, and power. They are also associated with issues such as rich versus poor or majority verses minority, where the minority can be, and is often, exploited. In other words, conflict theory focuses on the inequality within a society. In the wizarding world, for example, purebloods are considered the cream of the crop and anyone who is not a pureblood is considered a lower class. This separates the society in regards to class, thus giving purebloods greater access to better jobs and opportunities than non-purebloods, reinforcing the stratification of wizarding society.

Symbolic interactionism looks toward the formation of symbols and their meanings, interpretations, and responses that people ascribe to things. This is done by looking at the interactions of individuals through the use of language. Symbolic interactionism was established and expanded upon by George H. Mead, Charles Cooley, and Herbert Blumer. In contrast to functionalism and conflict theory, symbolic interactionism uses a micro level approach of study by looking toward individual interactions instead of focusing on a society. Through day-to-day interactions and socialization, people unconsciously assign symbols and meanings to their surroundings. People respond to things differently than one another based on the significance of the object to them. One object may seem important to one person but unimportant to another. This causes disagreements and miscommunication between individuals or groups which influences social interaction and one's own identity. For example, if someone said, "It is perfectly acceptable to enslave house-elves," the meaning would be clear because we have assigned meanings, or symbols, to every word in the statement. But the interpretation and significance by another individual is another matter. Words, essentially, in symbolic interactionism, are symbols and when people speak to one another they are exchanging symbols. If someone says the word "chair," we know, without seeing or touching one that it means an object used for sitting. If another individual says "witch," the word conjures the image of a female who can use magic. The Hogwarts Houses, for example, are very symbolic. We know that intelligent students may find themselves in Ravenclaw or those who are brave and courageous would be sorted into Gryffindor.

SOCIAL INSTITUTIONS AND OTHER IMPORTANT TOPICS IN SOCIOLOGY

One of the most important elements of sociology is the social institution. A social institution is an organization that engages the majority of the member's of a given society. Institutions consist of religion, government, the economy, education, family, the criminal justice system, the health care field, etc. These institutions provide norms and values to members of society by which they are expected to abide or be sanctioned. This means certain laws and behaviors must be followed or one faces being considered deviant or participating in behaviors deemed taboo. Everyone is a member of multiple institutions and every society's institutions may be different.

Socialization is another important topic in sociology. Socialization focuses on the learned aspect of human behavior, which begins at birth, and helps us acquire the necessary skills for living social life. There are many contributors to the socialization of a human baby. Primary socialization begins with one's relationship to one's family; eventually, as one grows, secondary socialization occurs through school, peers, church, the media, and technology. Socialization is a learning and cultural experience, and other issues come into play that shape the individual such as one's gender, geographic location, or race to name a few. The list for how one can be socialized is virtually endless. Do you think that Draco was born a pureblood extremist or did he learn this from his parents Narcissa and Lucius? On the other hand, Sirius Black did not accept his family's ideology of pureblood fanaticism. Is it up to the individuals to decide what they absorb and what they do not from their surroundings? Nature verses nurture will always be a debate among sociologists.

Status, class, and power are as prevalent in our world as they are in the wizarding world, and they are all ways in which society can be divided. Sociologically, the term "status" refers to the socially defined positions in a society and generally focuses on prestige or rank. Status can be either achieved (gained through one's own skill and efforts) or ascribed (inherited at birth). "Class" refers to a group whose members all share the same economic and social status. An example would be the upper, middle, and working classes in the United Kingdom or India's caste system. "Power" refers to authority or political influence and is often intertwined with inequality.

Inequality is another major area in sociology and consists of research on gender, racial, or class inequalities. Inequality is the unequal treatment of groups, and it often results in discrimination or prejudice against certain groups and automatic advantages for others. For clarity, because they are easy to confuse, prejudice is the negative *thoughts or attitudes* toward an individual or group and discrimination is the unfair *treatment* of an individual or group. For example, Cornelius Fudge expressed prejudice toward Madame Maxime due to her giantess blood while anti-werewolf legislation is discriminatory against werewolves. Discrimination is often based on prejudices.

Privileges are advantages, special benefits, or rights that are enjoyed by a selected few but are not available to most individuals or groups. Purebloods are a prime example of a group that is privileged. Purebloods dominate in the wizarding world with high status, class, and power over all other wizarding groups. Privileges contribute to the stratification of society, whether conscious or unconsciously. For example, Arthur Weasley, albeit a pureblood wizard, lacks "proper wizard feeling" and is considered a blood traitor due to his association with lower class citizens (i.e., Muggle-borns and Muggles) which resulted in his inability to move ahead in the workplace for years and, thus, his lack of privilege in the wizarding world (COS 223).

SOCIOLOGICAL RESEARCH

The sciences use the scientific method as a means for objectively and systematically investigating a theory, to find the causes and effects of a problem, and come up with solutions. As a brain refresher from school days past, the scientific method consists of developing a theory, question or hypothesis that is to be proved or disproved, the research and collection of data, experiment and testing, analysis, evaluation, and the final result or conclusion of the endeavor. As mentioned previously, sociology is a social science; and social sciences, like the physical and biological sciences, also use the scientific method, although their techniques do differ. Social scientists, generally, have no need to use a laboratory to perform chemical experiments and do not require the aid of microscopes. The subjects of the social sciences are people and societies not molecules or cells. Due to this, it is hard, but not impossible, to have a "control" or "controlled environment" in the social sciences because people are unpredictable and varied. This is not to say that sociologists do not run experiments nor is it to say that sociological research methods do not have merit. Sociological researchers often use quantitative or qualitative methods of research which often complement one another.

Quantitative research is the collection of empirical, theoretical data by using the scientific method. This type of research uses statistics and math to help form models and test hypotheses. Quantitative research may include the use of surveys, polls, content analysis, or experiments for the collection of data. For example, if there were magical sociologists in the wizarding world, they may ask the following quantitative research question, "What is the relationship between income levels and racism in wizarding society?" To collect data, they may make surveys, which include questions regarding how much income an individual makes per year as well as questions regarding, on a scale, how they feel about Muggle-borns, Muggles, half-breeds, etc. They would then form a statistical analysis and produce percentages, where they would analyze the data and see if there are any correlations in the findings. Gallup polls are another example of quantitative research.

Qualitative research, in contrast, seeks to understand the hows and whys in order to get an in-depth understanding of human behavior and social interactions. Unlike quantitative research which is broad and generalized, qualitative research is very personal and detail-oriented. Research is collected through participant observation (the sociologist immersing him or herself in the environment of study), in-depth interviews, discussion groups, and ethnographic research. Dolores Umbridge actually used qualitative research methods when she was Hogwarts High Inquisitor, albeit not as objectively as sociologists would have. Her purpose was to ensure the effectiveness and improve upon the standards of the teaching methods at Hogwarts. To do so, she attended classes, made notes, and interviewed students and teachers.

SOCIOLOGICAL OCCUPATIONS

There is a very wide range of jobs available for sociologists due to the broadness of our discipline and research training. Some sociologists, like the majority of the authors of this book, become researchers and/or university professors. Others may want to work for international or government agencies as analysts or policy developers. Additional jobs that may draw sociologists include race relations or social service organizations, public health outreach, non-profit organizations, and community planning and development. Sociologists interested in demographics (i.e., the study of human populations) may work for polling organizations like Gallup or their nation's Census Bureau.

WHY IS SOCIOLOGY IMPORTANT?

Sociology aids our understanding of society and human groups, which in turn teaches us about culture and cultural differences. All aspects of daily life and social interaction are key to understanding how societies work. Through this understanding, sociologists can aid in pinpointing problems in a society and help in bringing about social change or reform to better life in that society.

Sociology also has another purpose. By learning about society, how it runs, figuring out why we do the things we do, etc., we are, essentially, enlightening ourselves. Moreover, as sociology helps us to identify and define problem areas in a society, the more we learn about our society the more we may want to help change it for the better. Sociology is an enlightening experience. Through looking at society on a grand scale, we also learn about ourselves.

While sociology is important to understanding human ways of life, it isn't limited to "real" existing societies. The fictional wizarding world of Harry Potter can also be viewed sociologically. Therefore, in the following chapters, we turn the tools of sociology onto the wizarding world to examine its day-to-day life, social interaction, social groups, institutions, inequality and other various aspects of the society itself. By learning the ways in which wizarding society works, we can not only gain a deeper appreciation for that world J.K. Rowling created, but we can make connections to our real world and better understand ourselves and our ways of life.

PART I
SOCIETY

"It's the Best Place for Him"
THE MAGICAL USES OF SPACE

FLORENCE MAÄTITA, MARCIA D. HERNANDEZ AND KRISTEN KALZ

INTRODUCTION

Sociologists have addressed space in our social worlds for over a century. Some scholars consider Georg Simmel to be the first to examine the social relevance of space and the effects of space on social interactions. In his work, which centered primarily on the relationship between the big city and the mind of the individual, Simmel focused on the essential qualities of spatial forms that allow actors to turn empty spaces into something meaningful. Among these features, Simmel recognized the exclusive and unique character of the space and the possibility of changing locations. His treatise on the effects of urban space on human interactions, *The Metropolis and Mental Life* (1903/1976), was influential in the development of what eventually became the Chicago School of Sociology.

In addition to informing a major school of sociological thinking, Simmel made significant contributions to urban sociology. By examining the relationship between the city and its inhabitants, scholars highlight the relational aspects of space (Lynch 1960; Harvey 1985). Sociologists and geographers call this examination of space on our actions and interactions *spatiality*. These authors have built on Simmel's writings by identifying space as, among other things, a metaphor for safety (Bachelard 1969) and as a site of struggle (Harvey 1985; Lefebvre 1991).

Attention to spatial sociology beyond urban sociology did not emerge until the past few decades. Recent discussions of space have examined the relationships between natural space, social space, social groups and individuals, although there is debate about the arrangement of these relationships. Gans (2002: 330) contends that "individuals and collectivities shape natural and social space by how they use these, although each kind of space, and particularly the social, will also have effects on them." Thus, what is essential to Gans' approach to spatial sociology is the centrality of the *user* and the *use of* space.

In this chapter, we seek to add to the growing body of spatial sociology literature by examining the user and the use of space in the wizarding world. While notions of safety and struggle are undeniably central in the magical world, in this chapter we highlight the relationships between groups of individuals and spaces. We are interested in how inhabitants of the wizarding world (especially Harry Potter) use and interact in these physical locations. Essentially, this understanding of space entails a use- and user-centered way of examining space. First, we discuss how Harry uses space to create a safe environment for himself and his counterparts. Second, we examine how sites differ in terms of who designates its use (e.g., what/where does Harry Potter consider safe from himself and his loved ones? How might that be different from what Dumbledore or the Minister consider appropriate for Harry?). Finally, although we can consider most of these locations safe spaces for Harry, they are also contentious and can potentially leave Harry open to grave danger.

Safe Spaces in the Wizarding World

Scholars have reported on safe spaces as physical, political and intellectual sites in which marginalized groups can feel free of any prejudice and discrimination (Hyndman 2003; Stroudt 2007; Redmond 2010). We employ "safe space" here to refer to a physical, social and symbolic milieu in which Harry Potter can be removed from any threat of harm at the hands of Voldemort and the Death Eaters. Harry also uses such spaces as a way to elude other threats such as Sirius Black (until he finds out that Black means him no harm) and the Minister of Magic.

One safe space for Harry Potter is where he lives after his parents' death: 4 Privet Drive, the residence of his last surviving blood family members, the Dursleys. Here is where he gets the first (of many!) letters from Hogwarts. More significantly, Harry uses 4 Privet Drive as a safe space as he returns here for summer holiday at the end of each year at Hogwarts. This suburban habitat is one of Harry's few connections to his parents, although it is physically and symbolically removed from the wizarding world.

Arguably, the ultimate safe space for Harry Potter is Hogwarts School of Witchcraft and Wizardry, especially Gryffindor Tower. Hagrid explains to Harry why Hogwarts is so safe:

> [Lord Voldemort] was takin' over. 'Course, some stood up to him – an'
> he killed 'em. Horribly. One o' the only safe places left was Hogwarts.
> Reckon Dumbledore's the only one You-Know-Who was afraid of.
> Didn't dare try takin' the school, not jus' then, anyway. (SS 55)

Furthermore, as Hermione tells Harry, "As long as Dumbledore's around you're safe. As long Dumbledore's around, you can't be touched" (HP1). Molly Weasley echoes this sentiment two years later when she thinks that Sirius Black has escaped from Azkaban and is on his way to find and kill Harry. She says to her husband, "Well, Arthur, you must do what you think is right. But you're forgetting Albus Dumbledore. I don't think anything could harm Harry at Hogwarts while Dumbledore's headmaster" (POA 66).

Specific locations within Hogwarts are also significant for Harry in terms of the safety they provide him and his associates. For one, while at Hogwarts Harry and other students use the Room of Requirement (also called the Come and Go Room) as a safe space in a number of ways. On one hand, they use this room to hide critical magical and incriminating objects such as when Harry hides the Half-Blood Prince's potions textbook, and Tom Riddle hides Rowena Ravenclaw's diadem after he makes it a Horcrux. More important, the Room provides a safe haven for Hogwarts students who wish to learn how to defend themselves from the Dark Arts. When it becomes clear that Dolores Umbridge, their fifth year Defense against the Dark Arts teacher, will not teach them vital practical skills and information, students – who form Dumbledore's Army – take it upon themselves to find a space to learn. To open the room, Harry thinks, *"We need somewhere to learn to fight… Just give us a place to practice… somewhere [Umbridge and the Inquisitorial Squad] can't find us…"* (OOTP 389, emphasis in original).

Regardless of – or because of – Dumbledore's presence and the safety of Hogwarts, Harry feels of sense of "belonging" at the school. When Dobby implores Harry not to return to Hogwarts for his second year Harry stammers "W-what?... But I've got to go back… I don't *belong* here. I belong in your world – at Hogwarts" (COS 16, emphasis in original). Others agree that Harry belongs at Hogwarts as well. One such indication occurs when Harry is preparing to return to school for his fifth year after he was nearly expelled. His godfather, Sirius:

> put up a very good show of happiness on first hearing the news, wringing Harry's hand and beaming just like the rest of them; soon, however, he was moodier and surlier than before, talking less to everybody, even Harry, and spending increasing amounts of time shut up in his mother's room with Buckbeak. (OOTP 158)

Hermione thinks that Sirius is being selfish and counsels Harry to "Don't you go feeling guilty!" because "you belong at Hogwarts and Sirius knows it" (OOTP 158).

DESIGNATING THE USE OF A SPACE

While we must acknowledge how Harry Potter uses safe spaces, we must also address *who* designates how Harry must use them. In many cases, Harry himself is instrumental in determining how he will use a particular safe space. For example, not only is Hogwarts safe, but Harry designates the castle and its grounds as his home. Early in his first year, Harry begins to see Hogwarts as home. He remembers that he "could hardly believe it when he realized that he'd already been at Hogwarts two months. The castle felt more like home than Privet Drive ever had" (SS 170). By the end of the year, we witness Harry's increasing power to claim this space for himself. As they board the Hogwarts Express, Hermione Granger says, "Feels strange to be going home, doesn't it?" Harry responds, "I'm not going home. Not really" (HP1). Just a few months later, he asserts his even more strongly to Dobby in declaring that, "Hogwarts is my home!" (HP2). In these instances, we see that Harry himself has designated this safe space to be used as his home.

Others are also instrumental in setting the terms for how Harry should use certain safe spaces. Professor Dumbledore, for one, plays a key role in designating how Harry Potter will use spaces. We first become aware of this role when Dumbledore meets Professor McGonagall at 4 Privet Drive the evening after Voldemort killed James and Lily Potter. McGonagall expresses her concern over leaving Harry with his Muggle aunt and uncle by asking if it is safe to leave him there. Dumbledore responds, "[4 Privet Drive] is the best place for him. His aunt and uncle will be able to explain everything to him when he's older. I've written them a letter" (SS 13). Later we learn that Dumbledore set numerous magical enchantments on 4 Privet Drive making it safe for Harry as long as he was a minor living under the supervision of his mother's blood relative, his Aunt Petunia.

Even Cornelius Fudge, the Minister of Magic, designates a safe space for Harry. The summer before his third year at school Harry blows up his Aunt Marge and leaves 4 Privet Drive. When he eventually arrives at the Leaky Cauldron, thinking that he is in an immeasurable amount of trouble, he finds that Fudge wants Harry to stay in Diagon Alley until school begins. Fudge continues:

> Just one thing, and I'm sure you'll understand... I don't want you wandering off into Muggle London, all right? Keep to Diagon Alley. And you're to be back here before dark each night. Sure you'll understand. Tom [the innkeeper at the Leaky Cauldron] will be keeping an eye on you for me. (POA 46)

Later on, we discover that Fudge has designated the Leaky Cauldron and Diagon Alley as safe spaces for Harry to use because he wants to protect him from Sirius Black, who everyone thinks is out to kill Harry Potter.

CONTESTED AND CONTESTING SPACES FOR HARRY

There are cases in which other witches and wizards attempt to exercise an ability to designate if Harry can use an established particular space as a safe space. These spaces then become contested spaces. Moreover, others sometimes engage in contesting if Harry should even use a space at all.

Contested Safe Spaces

Throughout his adolescence, Dark witches and wizards attempt to make various safe spaces lose their capacity to provide protection for Harry and his counterparts. One such space is Hogwarts as there are moments during Harry and his friends' tenure in which students' safety at Hogwarts is compromised. When Lord Voldemort, via Ginny Weasley, opens the Chamber of Secrets for instance, and Muggle-born students are attacked, Dumbledore confesses that "our students are in great danger," and instructs McGonagall to tell the staff "the truth – tell them Hogwarts is no longer safe" (HP2). As the situation worsens, there is a great deal of concern over the future of the school. When their "worst fears [are] realized" and "a student [is] taken by the monster into the Chamber itself," Professor McGonagall concludes, "We shall have to send all the students home tomorrow... This is the end of Hogwarts" (COS 293). Thankfully, however, Harry and Ron (and Hermione, of course) were able to save the day.

Hogwarts ultimately is turned into an un-safe space for Harry when Professor Snape kills Dumbledore at the end of sixth year. After Dumbledore's funeral, Harry reveals to Ron and Hermione that he has no intentions of returning to Hogwarts the following year. He explains: "I'm going back to the Dursleys' once more, because Dumbledore wanted me to... but it'll be a short visit, and then I'll be gone for good" (HBP 650). This plan gives a hint of what is in store for Harry, Ron and Hermione in their subsequent adventures hunting Voldemort's Horcruxes, a time during which there is a near-absolute absence of safe spaces. Moreover, it shows Harry acknowledging, and honoring, Dumbledore's designation of Dursleys' as a safe space for him.

Like Hogwarts when the Chamber of Secrets is opened, the Dursleys' home can lose the capacity to provide protection. No. 4 Privet Drive will no longer be a safe haven for Harry or the Dursleys the instant Harry turns 17. As Harry relates to his uncle when imploring him to let the Order of the Phoenix relocate and protect the family: "...once I'm seventeen, all of them – Death Eaters, dementors, maybe even Infer – which means dead bodies enchanted by a Dark wizard – will be able to find you and will certainly attack you" (DH 35). Ultimately the Dursleys accept this plea and leave 4 Privet Drive admitting "it's not safe for us here anymore" (HP7 part I).

During the Second Wizarding War, 12 Grimmauld Place becomes the headquarters for the Order of the Phoenix. Its safety is slightly compromised, however, after Bellatrix Lestrange murders Sirius Black, her cousin, during the Battle of the Department of Mysteries. As Dumbledore explains:

> Black family tradition decreed that the house was handed down the
> direct line, to the next male with the name of 'Black.'...[And while
> Sirius'] will makes it perfectly plain that he wants [Harry] to have the
> house, it is nevertheless possible that some spell or enchantment has
> been set upon the place to ensure that it cannot be owned by another
> other than a pureblood. (HBP 50)

Upon establishing that Harry had in fact inherited the house from Sirius
and that ownership did not pass to Bellatrix Lestrange (neé Black), Harry
agrees to continue allowing the Order of the Phoenix use the space. The space
thus returns to being safe and Harry, Hermione and Ron use it as such the
next year as they begin their final quest for the remaining Horcruxes. After the
trio steals the Horcrux from Umbridge in Ministry of Magic, however, they
try to return to Grimmauld Place. Unfortunately, Yaxley, a Death Eater, grabs
Hermione as they disapparate and is still holding on when they arrive at 12
Grimmauld Place. Hermione finally shakes him off and takes herself, Ron and
Harry elsewhere because now that "Yaxley could get inside the house, there
was no way that they could return" (DH 271). This turn of events signals the
end of 12 Grimmauld Place as a contested safe space as it becomes resolutely
un-safe.

Contesting Spaces

While there are a number of cases in which a previously safe space
becomes no longer safe, there are also moments in which Harry's desired, or
designated, use of a space does not correspond with others' perspectives. At
these moments, Harry and the other witch or wizard are contesting his use of
the space. At 4 Privet Drive, for example, when Uncle Vernon decides to move
Harry's living quarters from the cupboard under the stairs to the smallest
bedroom, Dudley is furious at the loss of his toy room. "I don't *want* him in
there... I *need* that room... make him get out..." he bawls (SS 38, emphasis
in original). Dudley is contesting Harry's designated use of this space but to
no avail:

> He'd screamed, whacked his father with his Smelting stick, been sick
> on purpose, kicked his mother, and thrown his tortoise through the
> greenhouse roof, and he still didn't have his room back. (SS 38)

Hogsmeade is also a space over which Harry's desired use is often in
conflict with others' perspectives. During his third year, when Sirius Black is
believed to be looking to find and kill Harry, Lupin contests Harry's sneaking
into the village when he says, "Your parents gave their lives to keep you alive,
Harry. A poor way to repay them – gambling their sacrifice for a bag of
magic tricks" (POA 290). Another instance of someone contesting Harry's

use of Hogsmeade takes place when Harry, Hermione and Ron go to the village on their way to Hogwarts in search of the final Horcruxes. Aberforth Dumbledore comes to their rescue after they set off the Caterwauling Charm and says gruffly, "You bloody fools… What were you thinking, coming here?" (DH 559). Like Dudley and Lupin, Aberforth does not agree with Harry's use of a particular safe space.

DISCUSSION

For over a century, sociologists have sought to theorize space. Their propositions have been central to the development of the Chicago School of Sociology and urban sociology. Yet, as others continue to maintain, we still have a long way to go in advancing a sociology of space. Not only do we intend for this chapter to add to an ever-growing body of research, but we aimed to apply concepts from the Muggle literature on space to the wizarding world.

We borrowed primarily from Herbert Gans' approach to spatial sociology and its focus on the *user* and the *use of* space, although we recognize that this approach is not without its shortcomings (see Gieryn 2002 and Zukin 2002, for instance). The *user* in our examination is Harry Potter, while the *uses* and who designates these uses are complex and varied. Clearly, Harry and his friends use space primarily as a safe space, a space that provides them with a modicum of safety from harm at the hands (or wands) of Voldemort and his followers. Harry has some control over how he will use some spaces, although others – such as Professor Dumbledore and members of the Order of the Phoenix – can also establish a safe space's use. Nevertheless, the matter of agency also leads to a discussion of how Harry Potter manages contentious spaces throughout the series. This part of our analysis certainly harkens back to previous handlings on the hierarchical nature of space and wars over territory (Simmel 1903/1976; Lynch 1960; Harvey 1985; Urry 2000).

Future writings can focus on some of the questions beyond the scope of the current discussion. While we focus on safe spaces, there are innumerable alternative ways that Harry and others use space in the wizarding world. How do spaces help Harry develop an identity as a wizard and in his understanding of his roles and responsibilities? In what ways do spaces maintain and/or challenge gendered expectations throughout the wizarding world? What are the implications for different species (e.g., house-elves) and their ability to transcend place and space? Overall, we hope that this chapter will usher in a new body of discourse on the sociology of space and the wizarding world.

REFERENCES

Bachelard, Gaston. 1969. *The Poetics of Space*. Boston, MA: Beacon Press.

Gans, Herbert J. 2002. "The Sociology of Space: A Use–Centered View." *City & Community* 1(4): 329–339.

Gieryn, Thomas F. 2002. "Give Place a Chance: Reply to Gans." *City and Community* 1(4): 341–343.

Harvey, David. 1985. *Consciousness and the Urban Experience*. Baltimore, MD: Johns Hopkins University Press.

Hyndman, Jennifer. 2003. "Preventive, Palliative, or Punitive? Safe Spaces in Bosnia-Herzegovina, Somalia, and Sri Lanka." *Journal of Refugee Studies* 16(2): 167-185.

Lefebvre, Henri. 1992. *The Production of Space*. Hoboken, NJ: Wiley-Blackwell.

Lynch, Kevin. 1960. *The Image of the City*. Cambridge, MA: The MIT Press.

Redmond, Melissa. 2010. "Safe Space Oddity: Revisiting Critical Pedagogy." *Journal of Teaching in Social Work* 30(1): 1-14.

Simmel, Georg. 1903[1976]. *The Metropolis and Mental Life: The Sociology of Georg Simmel*. New York, NY: Free Press.

Stoudt, Brett G. 2007. "The Co-Construction of Knowledge in 'Safe Spaces': Reflecting on Politics and Power in Participatory Action Research." *Children, Youth and Environments* 17(2): 280-297.

Urry, John. 2000. "The Sociology of Space and Place." Pp. 416-433 in *The Blackwell Companion to Social Theory*, 2nd edition. Edited by B. Turner. Hoboken, NJ: Wiley-Blackwell.

Zukin, Sharon. 2002. "What's Space Got to Do with It?" *City & Community* 1(4): 345-348.

*"Never trust anything that can think for itself
if you can't see where it keeps its brain"*

THE SOCIAL SHAPING OF TECHNOLOGY
IN THE WIZARDING WORLD

SHERUNI RATNABALASURIAR

INTRODUCTION

The wizarding world offers a compelling site for an analysis of the ways in which various types of technologies are constructed, understood, and used in the wizarding and Muggle worlds. More specifically, the wizarding world provides an important set of case studies that can help reflect our own understandings of our own everyday technologies back to ourselves through a magical lens. To do so, this chapter provides a brief discussion of several theories in a branch of sociology focusing on the social shaping of technology (SST).

Technology is present in society in several ways and used for very different purposes. First, following the revelation of Harry Potter's status as a member of the magical community, we accompany Harry on his journey into this secret world and share his wonder at its many dazzling and strange occurrences. Throughout, we have the opportunity to compare them with the now more mundane Muggle world. Specifically, some of the more everyday types of magical artifacts such as quills show interesting parallels to the development of Muggle writing technologies. Second, Muggle technology becomes a point of reflection through Harry's journey and, at times, is illustrated through comparisons with magical technology. Finally, an important case study is found in Mr. Arthur Weasley, a wizard who attempts to bridge both Muggle and magical worlds through his fascination with magical modifications of Muggle technologies. The tension between his roles as a magical law enforcement officer responsible for regulating the use of Muggle artifacts for magical means on the one hand, and his enthusiasm for tinkering with and modifying Muggle artifacts on the other, provide yet another interesting point of reflection on our Muggle world and our own attitudes towards technology. Understanding the various ways Muggle technology serves as both a counterpoint to and augmentation of magic can help us better understand our own experiences with everyday technologies and understand how they are continually socially constructed.

SOCIAL CONTEXT AND SOCIOLOGICAL FRAMEWORK:
THE SOCIAL SHAPING OF TECHNOLOGY

Contemporary Muggle technologies are shifting, developing, and changing at an unprecedented rate. With this rapid pace, an interesting facet of technology has begun to emerge. Advanced technologies that once seemed magical to Muggles have become more mundane, diminishing much of their fantastic and magical aspects. A recent visit to the headquarters of one of the most prolific Muggle technology firms (Facebook) by United States Muggle president Barack Obama led him to comment on this lack of wonder and awe concerning the rapid pace of technological change. The president suggested this might be remedied through renewed commitments to improving science, technology, engineering, and medical (STEM) education: "I want people to feel about the next big energy breakthrough and the next big Internet breakthrough the same way they felt about the moonwalk" (quoted in Tsotsis 2011).

Devices and gadgets that once seemed the product of fantastical science fiction are now relatively ordinary occurrences. Muggle technology corporations such as Apple, Google, and Microsoft continue a tradition of releasing new products each year in large mediated press events constructed as major spectacles of technological change. However, the release of these "revolutionary products" have become such a regular occurrence (often in bi-annual or quarterly events) that much of the magic of new technologies becomes old news the moment the newest and shiniest version of a particularly piece of technology is unveiled. The Muggle world is a world in which feats such as the near-instantaneous transfer of information through one of the largest, most interconnected infrastructures in history, is shrugged off and accepted as the most mundane of everyday occurrences.

In the wizarding world, the appearance and disappearance of things (apparition and invisibility cloaks), the transformation of objects (transfiguration), the manipulation of time (Hermione Granger's use of the Time-Turner), space (the existence of platform 9 ¾), and perception (the confundus charm), all serve as the context in which the magical world operates. However, what is so compelling is the juxtaposition of the magical world against the boundaries of the Muggle world. This difference is most apparent in the contrasting ways both the Muggle and magical worlds have of enhancing everyday existence accomplished through various means. One of the most ready examples is the differences between various means of magical communication (Owls and floo powder) and Muggle communication technologies (email, telephones, etc.). It is in the colliding of these two worlds that we can most easily see differences in the construction of each type of communication method. For example, Ronald Weasley's humorous attempt to use a telephone to call Harry at his aunt and uncle's house during summer holidays is a prime example of the ways magical outsiders not socialized to use Muggle technologies encounter our world. Practically screaming into the phone, Ron misunderstands even this most commonplace Muggle technology, in turn highlighting how taken for granted this technology has become for Muggles.

This contrast can help us understand the diminishing magical quality – the banality – of technology in our own social contexts. To that end, SST can provide a powerful tool for understanding the various ways the wizarding world comments upon technology. This area of study is concerned with broadening analyses of technologies to include examinations of socio-economic and cultural patterns embedded in the development, innovation, and content of various technologies (McKenzie and Wajcman 1999; Williams and Edge 1996). As a field, SST emerged in response to and to critique popular ideas about technology which dominated much of the discourse of technology at the time. Known as technological determinism, this view is a conceptualization of technology as being an inevitable, unchangeable, almost non-controllable force that, for the most part, is treated as unproblematic. This mode of thinking about technology was most eloquently unpacked in the work of David Edge (1988). He explains that one of the key dangers of technology's determinism lies in the unproblematic acceptance of technology as a given; that technological changes effecting social, economic, and political outcomes are predetermined and unable to be influenced by anything other than what appears to be the inevitable march of technological progress. Ignoring that technology development is a phenomenon influenced and controlled by social forces is to abdicate responsibility for the ways society shapes and influences technology.

SST has drawn a large number of scholars from a diverse range of academic disciplines. There is now an extensive body of literature on the ways various types of technologies are constructed depending on their social and cultural context, as well as the various meanings assigned to different types of technology over time. The field has offered some important commentary on the ways in which technologies shift and change. It has pointed out how technologies are not only shaped by programmers, engineers, and designers, but are also shaped by their actual users within specific social contexts for various purposes, whether these align with the original intended uses or not. According to Robin Williams and David Edge (1996: 4), SST research is characterized by several key areas of investigation: "SST research investigates the ways in which social, institutional, economic and cultural factors have shaped: i) the *direction* as well as the rate of innovation; ii) the *form* of the content of technological artifacts and practices; iii) the *outcomes* of technological change for different groups in society" (emphasis in the original).

A perspective that has particular relevance for the exploration of Muggle technologies through a magical lens comes from the work of Hughie Mackay and Gareth Gillespie (1992). These Muggle sociologists explored and extended social shaping of technology by bringing new understandings of the role of appropriation of technology by users. They argue that different technologies are "open" to varying degrees. In other words, certain technologies lend themselves more easily to being changed and modified by end users than other types of technology and that this adaptability has different meanings for users. In many cases, it is precisely this lack of openness which drains innovation of its magical character.

TECHNOLOGY VS. MAGIC: OF APPARITION AND QUILLS

Once Harry's identity as a member of the magical world is revealed, he marvels at the many wonders that magical folk experience in their everyday lives as regular occurrences. When introduced to the various aspects of the fascinating magical world, Harry's encounters with various wizards and witches provide an important counterpoint to Muggle existence. And, aiding in this re-enchantment of the everyday, magical folk themselves express fascination with the various technologies that Muggles have devised in order to go about the daily business of living. In some ways, the fascination with Muggle technologies evinced by various magical folk like Rubeus Hagrid, Keeper of Keys and Grounds at Hogwarts School of Witchcraft and Wizardry, and Mr. Arthur Weasley, agent in the Ministry of Magic's Misuse of Muggle Artifacts Office, can be seen as an appreciation for the efforts Muggles make towards enacting their own type of "magic" under limited circumstances, without any type of magical power or aid. Muggle technology such as ticket takers, turnstiles, parking meters, and batteries are objects of fascination for both Mr. Weasley and Hagrid who marvel at the devices Muggles have developed to help them with the tasks of everyday life.

A Muggle historian and contributor to studies of sociotechnical factors shaping technology development who shares this fascination with everyday technologies is Wiebe Bijker. He has contributed several key works in SST that provides insight into the relationship between various social forces and their influence of Muggle technology development that can also be applied to examinations of magical artifacts. His writing, particularly his collaboration with colleagues Trevor J. Pinch and Thomas P. Hughes in their edited volume *The Social Construction of Technological Systems* (1987), as well as Bijker's own solo-authored book *Of Bicycles, Bakelights and Bulbs: Toward a Theory of Sociotechnical Change* (1995) are some of the major works in SST discussing the processes influencing the somewhat magical quality of technologies that, due to their ubiquity, seem mundane and an unchanging, taken-for-granted part of everyday life. Bijker explains that what appear to be magical devices in the realm of Muggle technology do not just apparate into existence out of thin air in a finished, pre-determined form. Instead Bijker and other SST researchers propose that there are very specific and deliberate design choices influenced by social contexts that are quite intentional that lead to the final marketed form of various technologies.

If we linger a moment on a memory from Harry Potter's school days, we can revisit that excellent yet potentially hazardous mode of magical travel, apparition. While at first apparition seems to be an everyday occurrence among magical adults, we see how complex a process it actually is as Harry, Hermione, and Ron approach the age when older Hogwarts students begin to learn how to apparate – a process akin to Muggle teenagers learning to drive an automobile. Apparition involves intention. If the proper technique is not employed – if the "user" does not maintain a clear intention of his destination, as Charlie Weasley once did not – the results can be disastrous, perhaps even landing a traveler five miles from their intended destination, on top of an old Muggle lady doing her shopping (GOF 67). Preparation and careful planning are required if one wishes to avoid ending up in the wrong place, potentially violating the statue of secrecy, which protects Muggles by requiring witches and wizards to conceal their powers. In fact, a 12 week course on apparition is offered to older Hogwarts students during their sixth year. Professor Wilkie Twycross hammers homes the importance of the three Ds of Apparition – Destination, Determination, and Deliberation in his classes (HBP 384). A particularly painful example of the complexity of the apparition process is shown in Ron's experience of *splinching* – accidently leaving a body part behind due to insufficient concentration upon the intended destination – during his escape from Voldemort's agents in their search for his Horcruxes.

Bijker also explores the importance of social forces that can shape the development of various technologies as can be seen in his excellent discussions of the historical power struggles that occurred during the development of fluorescent lighting technology. These tensions arose among companies who made the bulbs and fixtures as well as the utility companies who were developing access to electricity. Struggles emerged over the use of filament materials, current and voltage standardization, as well as a host of other factors necessary to deliver fluorescent lighting to private homes and businesses. Bijker emphasizes the importance of these power struggles and how they serve to constrain choices.

Similar struggles and choices constrain the evolution of magical techniques as well. Take the example of the use of quills in the magical world and the development of the QWERTY keyboard ubiquitous in Muggle computing technologies. The wizarding world has adopted the exclusive use of quill, ink, and parchment for most types of communication. The accessories for writing, and even the use of Owls as one of the major forms of communication, stem from the particular choice of writing implementation. We are treated to an example of this during Harry's first foray into Diagon Alley with Hagrid when each of these technologies must be acquired as part of his school supplies.

Harry, after the first of what would be many unpleasant encounters with Draco Malfoy, engages in a little retail therapy by stopping in to Scribbulus Writing Implements to get quill and parchment, and buys a bottle of color-changing ink that cheers him up (SS 79; HP2). However, as anyone who has ever attempted amateur calligraphy or ink drawing can attest, with the use of a quill nib and ink is a rather messy, slow and inefficient way of writing, but one that still holds a specific social meaning even in Muggle culture. With pen and ink, there is not so much emphasis on speed of communication, but instead on intention, clarity of the thought, and even an aesthetic quality.

Rita Skeeter of the *Daily Prophet*, that ruthless reporter/paparazzi figure who plagues Harry's fourth year at Hogwarts, displays an example of a magical "upgrade" of the traditional quill which illuminates some elements of ideas from SST. With her marvelous and mischievous Quick Quotes Quill, much to the chagrin of her interviewees, Rita Skeeter is able to conduct and record interviews, hands free, and as a result is left with a suitably embellished transcript of the interview that is practically ready for press. Rita Skeeter's quill has the ability to transcribe the words of speakers onto parchment without the use of the writer's own hand. The quill races across the page and words begin to appear. However, it appears that Rita's quill has some additional charms that render not a verbatim transcript, but Rita's embellishments of the facts that give her stories that particular quality of sensationalism that her readers either love or despise. However, we can see an interesting parallel between the ideas of Bijker and other SST scholars when we think about the social shaping of the development of Rita Skeeter's quill just as we can see the development of our own rather ubiquitous writing implement – the QWERTY keyboard.

As I muddle along communication to you through my tray of white plastic Chiclet-like keys, at what I feel is a snail's pace, stopping to correct a mistyped word here and there as a result of my ill-timed, over-eager key presses, I think about the origins of Western Latin-alphabet keyboards and, in particular, the American English language familiarity with the QWERTY keyboard layout. Why do we not use sound recording and transcription? Why not carbon copies of quill-written documents or ball point ink?

That Rita's Quick Quotes Quill not only transcribes audio dialogue and can differentiate between speakers (a feat even the most impressive

Muggle dictation software and computer cannot yet accomplish). It has an added artificial intelligence in that it can improvise and embellish dialogue, an amazing feat in and of itself. However, if we apply Mr. Arthur Weasley's admonishment to "never trust anything that can think for itself if you can't see where it keeps its brain" (COS 329), we can perhaps more easily sympathize with Harry's initial wariness of Rita's quill. Yet even the Quick Quotes Quill can be seen as an example of SST's conceptualizations of technology as emerging from the complex interactions among social, technological, economic and developmental constraints. The Quick Quotes Quill and the development of magical charms that influence its function revolve around several remaining inconveniences of writing with a quill: it must be manually operated and it requires a fixed physical intention to operate. That Hogwarts teachers assign essays in inch requirements as opposed to Muggle teachers assigning page numbers is yet another example of design constraints influencing social practices. As a teacher myself, I have often wondered if Professors McGonagall and Snape ever sighed when reading a student's particularly large, wide-spaced handwriting the way I sigh when I get to the essay typed in 13 point Courier New font in my own student papers. But I digress.

As I conduct interview research on Muggle technology use, I marvel at our own rough version of the Quick Quotes Quill – the Livescribe smartpen. The pen operates with special paper made up of tiny dots read by an infrared camera at the tip to record handwriting strokes while a tap of the pen on a printed "record" button at the bottom of the page turns on an microphone embedded in the pen to record speech and sync it to the handwritten notes. It still can't move through the air by itself though, and after a hand-cramping, three-hour interview, I still think Rita Skeeter's Quick Quotes Quill has my Livescribe pen beat!

HACKING THE MAGICAL WORLD: THE TINKERINGS OF ARTHUR WEASLEY

Mr. Arthur Weasley serves as an interesting case study to examine the ambivalence around technology and technological artifacts embedded in the wizarding world. Additionally, the case study of Arthur Weasley can also serve as a form of critique of social shaping of technology in terms of providing an example of how tinkering represents the appropriation of technology by users. Mr. Weasley's position with the Ministry of Magic involves the regulation, sanctioning, and control of any sort of magical modifications of Muggle artifacts with an emphasis on keeping dark magical items out of circulation. The office is also responsible for regulating the use of charms and other magical augmentations of Muggle artifacts for anything other than the artifact's original intended purpose. However, despite his official role in prohibiting and discouraging the use and modification of Muggle artifacts, he readily experiments with magical modifications of various types of Muggle technologies, much to the chagrin of his wife and family.

As might be imagined, Mr. Weasley's enforcement of magical law governing the misuse of Muggle artifacts is not always consistent. Displaying a more flexible conceptualization of magical law enforcement, we see Mr. Weasley enforcing the law more strictly for magical augmentation of Muggle artifacts when the witch or wizard being investigated is suspected of engaging in the Dark Arts than when he or she is not. Witness for example his multiple searches of Death Eater Lucius Malfoy's Manor compared to his quick resolution of a disturbance at the residence of Order of the Phoenix member Alastor "Mad Eye" Moody. Moody had enchanted Muggle dustbins as a sort of security device to warn against intruders, and Mr. Weasley attempts to get to the scene to diffuse the situation before Mad Eye is detained by magical law enforcement, which would delay his starting of the position of new Defense Against the Dark Arts teacher at Hogwarts. Unlike his repeated investigations of Lucius Malfoy, who he suspected of possessing Dark objects, Mr. Weasley does not conduct any further inquiries or raids of Mad Eye's property as he considered his augmentations benign.

Mr. Weasley also appears to try to subversively assert special protections and lessen restrictions on his own tinkering via written modifications to magical law within the loophole he created in the Ministry of Magic to allow the flying of his enchanted Ford Anglia. His loophole allowed for modifying the car so that it could fly only if the user does not *intend* to fly the car (COS 39). This particular exception is an interesting example of Mackay and Gillespie's (1992) ideas about the appropriation of technology and the conflicts between the intentions of designers and the end users.

Conclusion

In many ways, Mr. Weasley's fascination with all things Muggle, and particularly, with Muggle technology, are understood by him – as with all of us – only through the lens of his context and existence embedded within his everyday world. His tinkering points out that no technology is a finished product, set in stone, but instead always open to re-interpretation as new uses are found. These new uses are always driven by social, economic, cultural, and political phenomena and, as such, are highly contingent on the time and place in which users find themselves.

By reflecting our Muggle world in the magical one, perhaps we can help re-enchant the technological marvels which surround us on an everyday basis. By doing so, we open possibilities of technology ever further. When we can stop seeing technological progress as a natural, inevitable process, we can better attempt to make technology more responsive to the needs of more diverse groups of people, in varied contexts, even those the designers of such technologies might never have considered.

References

Bijker, Wiebe E. 1997. *Of bicycles, bakelites, and bulbs: Toward a theory of sociotechnical change.* Cambridge, MA: MIT Press.

Mackay, Hughie and Gareth Gillespie. 1992. "Extending the Social Shaping of Technology Approach: Ideology and Appropriation." *Social Studies of Science* 22(4):685-716.

MacKenzie, Donald A. and Judy Wajcman, eds. 1999. *The social shaping of technology.* Philadelphia, PA: Open University Press.

Tsotsis, Alexia. 2011. "Obama: I Want People To Feel The Same About The Next Internet Breakthrough As They Did About The Moonwalk." *TechCrunch.* Retrieved April 23, 2011, from http://techcrunch.com/2011/04/20/obama-i-want-people-to-feel-the-same-about-the-next-internet-breakthrough-as-they-did-about-the-moonwalk/

Williams, Robin and David Edge. 1996. "The Social Shaping of Technology." *Research Policy* 25:856-99.

"Who'd Want to be Friends With You?"

AN ANALYSIS OF FRIENDSHIP NETWORKS AT HOGWARTS

KATIE CHRISTIE

INTRODUCTION

Due to the unique setting at Hogwarts School of Witchcraft and Wizardry, an environment that serves as both school and home for the students, socialization and friendship play a large role in the daily lives of the students. It is therefore important to consider the ways in which friendships are formed and the role friendships play in the setting of Hogwarts. One way sociologists do this is by using friendship network analysis. In this chapter, I first examine research literature that relates to adolescent friendship networks, and then I present the analysis and findings of my research study of friendship networks at Hogwarts, demonstrating that wizarding networks can be analyzed using the same methods and procedures as Muggle networks.

Berndt (1982) cited three explanations for the significance of adolescent friendships. He found that biological, social, and cognitive forces are at work in shaping adolescent friendships. In early adolescence, the adolescent reaches a unique position because s/he is no longer a child, but also doesn't yet have all the responsibilities or freedoms that come along with adulthood. The majority of social interactions in this stage exist between close friends and peers, and friendships are egalitarian. Berndt also discussed the role of intimacy within friendships, and how adolescents build self-esteem by sharing feelings and information with friends. In a later study, Berndt (1995) examined the influence of friends on psychosocial development as it related to school adjustment and found that adjustment is affected by the characteristics and quality of friendships.

McPherson et al. (2001) defined the tendency for people to have more contact with people who are similar to them than to people who are dissimilar as homophily. The idea of homophily is important because it says that people are more likely to confide and share with individuals who are similar to them. When the principle of homophily is applied to adolescents, the literature suggests that teenagers tend to associate with other teenagers who are similar in terms of behavior or achievement (McPherson et al. 2001). Sources of homophily include space, family ties, and organizational – including school –

ties. Shrum, Cheek, and Hunter (1988) examined racial and gender homophily in children in association with grade level. Their findings showed that racial homophily increased as grade level increased, although the reverse was true for gender homophily. One of the most interesting and significant findings of this study was that children develop an early awareness of racial identity, and as they age, there is an increasing tendency to develop homophilous friendships.

PRESENT STUDY

Based on previous studies of adolescent friendships, several themes appear to be consistent. First, the majority of social interactions in early adolescence are between close friends/peers, and these friendships tend to be egalitarian in nature. By combining Berndts' ideas with Shrum et al.'s (1988) findings that young adolescents are more likely to spend time with members of the same gender and same race, my first research objective to examine whether or not this is true within the setting of Hogwarts, and how or if this changes over time. In other words, I will determine the extent to which homophily plays a role in the friendship ties among students in Hogwarts by examining the interactions occurring between friends who are similar in terms of gender and organization.

A second objective of this study is to determine how much power and influence Harry Potter has in his network of friends. I hypothesize that Harry will have the most connections in the network. The final and most important objective of this study is to test social network analysis procedures developed by Muggle sociologists on the friendship networks present in Hogwarts in order to set the stage for further sociological analysis of other non-Muggle social settings.

My study expands the sociological literature on adolescent friendship in that although there is a great deal of research available on cliques and group level analysis, studying of liaisons or other linking social actors, especially of non-Muggle social settings, seems to be rare. Most social network analysis includes information on cliques and isolates. Shrum and Cheek (1987) argued that examining liaisons in the social networks of adolescents, rather than focusing solely on cliques as the hub of peer relations, is important in social network analysis. They defined a liaison as an individual belonging to a social system, who serves the purpose of linking outside members to the system and clique members as participants in a close-knit group of interacting peers. They argued that distinguishing liaisons from cliques is especially important for contemporary theories of the school as a context for developing peer relations. Social networks can also be viewed as changing, adaptive processes (Cairns et al. 1995). Cairns et al. (1995) found that fluidity in the strength of friendships and group members is an important feature of social relationships. I aim to contribute to this developing area of research with this study.

RESEARCH METHODS

The data collection process of this study involved unique procedures. Two networks were examined among the students at Hogwarts School of Witchcraft and Wizardry. To begin collecting data, a pool of potential social actors was devised. Hogwarts consists of seven grades, grades one through seven, with about one thousand students in attendance in any given year (Rowling 2000). For the first set of data, or Network A, a social actor was classified as relevant and included if he or she was mentioned throughout the recently published "seven volumes on the life of Harry Potter" (TBB xvi), beginning with the first volume. A preliminary list of social actors was drawn up by examining each witch or wizard who was named during the Sorting Ceremony at Hogwarts during Harry Potter's first year. All students who attend HSWW belong to one of four Houses, which is determined in the Sorting Ceremony in their first year at Hogwarts. The four Houses are Gryffindor, Hufflepuff, Ravenclaw, and Slytherin. Twenty-three students are identified during the Sorting Ceremony for Harry's grade (SS 119-22).

The next step in the data collection process was to identify the relational ties between social actors in the Hogwarts network. From this pool of witches and wizards, relevance was determined based on who went on to be featured regularly in subsequent volumes detailing the events leading up to the Second Wizarding War. With few exceptions, the students who were identified at Hogwarts were mentioned in relation to Harry, and the vast majority of witches and wizards with regular mentions were in the same grade with him. Only sixteen students in Harry's grade played an active role at Hogwarts up to the year of Lord Voldemort's re-birth. These sixteen witches and wizards are the social actors comprising the first data set, Network A, and the relations linking these actors are ties of friendship.

During the preliminary stages of research, it was observed that friendship patterns changed throughout the students' time at Hogwarts (which is to be expected as the witches and wizards age.) However, differences in friendship ties became especially pronounced after the formation of Dumbledore's Army. Dumbledore's Army is a club by Harry Potter, Ron Weasley, and Hermione Granger for students wishing to practice using defensive spells. The first network, Network A, therefore, consists of social actors who played a prominent role at Hogwarts *and* were friends before the formation of Dumbledore's Army. Network A also represents early adolescence, as the actors in this network were between the ages of eleven and fifteen. Network B refers the ties of friendship formed after Dumbledore's Army. Of the students who joined the DA, six went on to have significant roles in the Second Wizarding War; so they were included in Network B.

The two friendship networks consist of symmetric, undirected ties and a binary scale of measurement. To measure friendship ties between nodes, the presence or absence of friendship ties is determined based on the question, "Is node A friends with node B?" A score of 1 was given for a tie of friendship, and a score of 0 was given where a tie was absent. All ties of friendship were symmetric and undirected. In other words, if actor A considered B to be a friend, B also considered A to be a friend.

The network size for the first data set, friends before Dumbledore's Army, or Network A, was found to be sixteen by performing a simple count of nodes. The network diameter was found by running the Ucinet procedure for identifying geodesic distances. Geodesic distances refer to the shortest possible path from one actor to another, usually resulting in the most efficient connections between actors. The diameter of the network was the furthest distance between actors, and in the case of friendship ties before Dumbledore's Army, the number was two. The second network, or Network B, is comprised of all of the actors present in the first network, with the addition of six actors who were not present before the formation of the DA. The network size of the friends after the formation of Dumbledore's Army was twenty-two. The diameter of this network was one. The change in the diameter between the first network and the second can be attributed to the removal of steps between social actors when more friendships were formed due to the actors' involvement in Dumbledore's Army. These results will be further explored and discussed in the next section.

Analysis and Findings

Network Size and Reachability

In order to analyze the two friendship networks at Hogwarts, basic network properties of connection and distance were first examined. A total of two measures were used relating to connection and distance: network size and reachability. To determine the size of Network A and Network B, a simple count of nodes was performed. The total number of nodes for Network A was sixteen. This means that a total of sixteen ties were possible, since the network is symmetric. In other words, by using the equation, $k*(k-1)/2$, where k is number of nodes, and plugging in the count of nodes, *16*, the total number of ties was found. It is important to establish a count of ties in order to determine the Network's density. The total number of nodes for Network B was twenty-two, and the total number of ties, therefore, was twenty-two. The difference in sizes between Networks A and B is important because as the number of nodes increases, so does the number of potential relationships. This generally means that the level of complexity increases as the size of a network increases. Figures 1a and 1b (see end of chapter) show the differences in network structure before the formation of Dumbledore's Army and after.

Reachability can be defined as the set of connections or links that exist between actors, even if those actors are not adjacent or directly connected. In a symmetric network, if actors are not reachable, the network can become divided and sub-populations can form. A division was encountered in this study: a major rift existed between the actors belonging to the Slytherin House, and all other actors. This is true for both Network A and Network B (refer to Figures 1a and 1b). For Network A, the actors Lavender Brown and Parvati Patil are not reachable to any other actors, and gaps exist between actors within the House of Gryffindor. However when Network B is examined, we see that all actors are equally reachable, and a natural block formation appears, showing the divisions between Dumbledore's Army members and non- Dumbledore's Army members.

The results from the Reachability measure lead us to the conclusion that the friendship ties that sprung up due to the formation of Dumbledore's Army led to a cohesion in the friendship network, further resulting in direct paths being formed between all actors in that group. Therefore, due to the high level of connection between members of Dumbledore's Army, we would expect the flow of information and mobilization of resources to be high[1].

Homophily at Hogwarts

The first objective of this study was to identify the presence of homophilous friendship ties by determining if young adolescents interact predominantly with friends who are similar in terms of gender and organizational association, or association with House-members. The methods used to test this procedure were fairly straight-forward. To test the hypothesis, external group ties and internal group ties were measured by running the E-I Index procedure on Ucinet. Social actors were coded separately for gender and House and were used as attribute vectors for comparing Network A and Network B.

---

1   Indeed, a perfect example of this occurred at the end of the students' fifth year. At the end of the school year, Harry was nearly attacked on the Hogwarts Express Slytherin students, Malfoy, Crabbe, and Goyle. Before they are able to attack him, however, several members of Dumbledore's Army, including Hannah Abbott, Susan Bones, Anthony Goldstein, and Terry Boot, jump to the rescue and prevent Harry's attack (OOTP 864). This example illustrates the differences that existed after the formation of Dumbledore's Army: a significant increase in camaraderie and a banding together, or higher level of mobilization, could be observed.

E-I Index was used to measure the percentage of ties being sent outward and the percentage remaining internal. The E-I Index was run for Network A and Network B, to compare the changes in homophily after the formation of Dumbledore's Army. For gender, the re-scaled E-I Index was found to be -.185. The negative value shows a weak tendency for internal ties. However, when the same procedure was run for Network B, the E-I index was found to be .083, showing a higher tendency for external ties.

The friends in Network A consist of a total of six females and ten males. The node Hermione Granger had a total of three ties, all of which were connected to males. The node Hannah Abbott had two ties, both of which were connected to boys. Both Millicent Bulstrode and Pansy Parkinson had four ties, three of which were to males, and one of which was to a female. The nodes Lavender Brown and Parvati Patil stood out: not only did they constitute a sub-division in the network, but they were tied to only each other, showing them as isolates from the rest of the network.

In the case of Network A, it does not appear that females show a tendency towards friendship with members of the same gender. However, when the males in the network were examined, there was a considerable difference. The actors Dean Thomas and Seamus Finnigan each had three ties, all of which were directed at males. Ron Weasley had a total of five ties, four of which were directed at males. The actor with the most ties, Harry Potter, had a total of seven ties, and six of these seven ties were directed towards males. Although there was a disproportionate ratio of males to females, it is clear that within Network A, there was a discrepancy between males' tendency to befriend other males and females' tendencies to befriend other females. These findings are therefore partially inconsistent with Shrum, Cheek, and Hunter's (1988) observations that gender homophily is strong among young adolescents: although males showed a strong tendency for gender homophily, females did not. Shrum et al. (1988) found females to be much more likely to associate with same-gender friends beginning in early adolescence, and the reverse appears to be true for females at Hogwarts.

When ties were measured for house membership, Network A was shown to have an E-I Index of -.852, representing a strong tendency towards internal ties. The results were even stronger for Network B, which had an E-I Index of -1. However, this can be attributed to formation of Dumbledore's Army to not have external ties.

The Chosen One

In order to determine if Harry Potter was the most central and powerful actor in Network A and Network B, Freeman's measures of closeness centrality and betweenness centrality were calculated. The idea behind closeness centrality is that actors who are closer to others have greater power. Betweenness centrality is the idea that actors who serve as intermediaries between other actors have the most power. According to Freeman's closeness centrality measure, the most powerful actors in Network A were Harry Potter, Ron Weasley, and Ernie Macmillan. The weakest actors were Parvati Patil and Lavender Brown. However, when the same measure was performed for Network B, all members of Dumbledore's Army had the same amount of closeness centrality, which was substantially more than the non-members. The change from Network A to Network B can be attributed to the decreased distance between actors from Network A to Network B. In other words, all actors were at an equal distance from one another, so no one actor had a greater amount of power.

Freeman's betweenness centrality measure yielded very interesting results between Network A and Network B. In Network A, the most powerful actors for betweenness were Harry Potter, Ernie Macmillan, Justin Finch-Fletchley, and Ron Weasley. All other actors had the same amount of betweenness power. However, when these results were compared to Network B, it was found that no actors had betweenness power: all actors had a betweenness power of 0. The reason for this is that the creation of Dumbledore's Army removed intermediaries, neutralizing the power of Harry Potter and the other formerly powerful nodes. It should also be noted that the actors who were not a part of Dumbledore's Army had the same amount of power between actors because they also had no intermediaries: all actors were the same distance, a distance of 1, from other actors. The results of Freeman's centrality measures show that Harry Potter did have the most power in terms of betweenness and closeness prior to the formation of Dumbledore's Army, but that power was voided after the formation of Dumbledore's Army.

DISCUSSION AND CONCLUSIONS

The first objective of this study was to test existing theories about homophily, specifically the idea that adolescents are friends with those who are similar to them in terms of race, gender, and organization. This was accomplished by comparing changes in friendship patterns before Dumbledore's Army, when the students were between the ages of 11-14, and after, when they were 15 and older. The results of this study showed a decrease in gender homophily between friends over time, further supporting Shrum, Cheek, and Hunter's (1988) findings that gender homophily decreases over time. However, in contrast to their research, these findings showed that males were more likely to be friends with other males prior to the formation of Dumbledore's Army, whereas females exhibited many cross-gender ties. Organizational homophily was not shown to have a significant change over time, but a strong tendency towards internal ties was discovered, suggesting that the placement of students into Houses played a heavy role in the friendships those students formed. At Hogwarts, students are required to share dormitories and common rooms, attend classes, and eat lunch with members of the same House; so it is not surprising to find that ties of friendship within Houses are stronger than ties of friendships outside Houses.

The unexpected finding in this study that among early adolescents, males were more likely to exhibit gender homophily than the females had one notable exception. Until the formation of Dumbledore's Army, Hermione Grainger did not have friends of the same gender in her grade. She spent the majority of her time with Harry and Ron. Although I did not measure the intensity of friendship ties, or examine the social dynamics between close friends or "best friends," this would be an interesting avenue for future research. The witches and wizards Dean Thomas and Seamus Finnigan, Lavender Brown and Parvati Patil, Harry, Ron, and Hermione, and Malfoy, Crabbe, and Goyle, are understood to be best friends; and an analysis of the similarities between those dyads, or triads, could further support sociological studies pertaining to the nature of adolescent friendship. Another useful study that could be conducted in the future would be to examine the break-down of gender in the friendship networks at Hogwarts. There are a disproportionate number of males to females within the friendship networks studied, and a comparison study could be drawn up between Hogwarts and Beauxbatons or Durmstrang.

The second objective of this study was to determine if Harry Potter, the boy who lived, the Chosen One, wielded the most power and influence within his social network. Although I did prove my hypothesis that Harry held the most power and connection in his friendship network as a young adolescent, it was interesting to discover that the level of power dispersed as Harry lost his position as an intermediary. Future research could place more emphasis on the power of intermediaries in social networks, perhaps using Bonacich's power measure as a basis for determining actors' power.

This study analyzed witches and wizards and their social network of friendship ties in Hogwarts as one would do any Muggle social network with basic properties and characteristics. The study examined friendship ties during Harry's first four years at Hogwarts, and compared them to friendship ties after Dumbledore's Army, which was formed in Harry's fifth year. The primary objective of this study was to highlight the similarities that exist between witches and wizards friendship networks and recent sociological studies on Muggle population on the same subject. Contrary to the belief of some within each world, wizards and Muggles are not so different after all. Adolescence is a difficult time and, magic or Muggle, friendship is definitely "something worth fighting for." (HP5)

FIGURE 1A. FRIENDSHIP TIES BEFORE DUMBLEDORE'SARMY

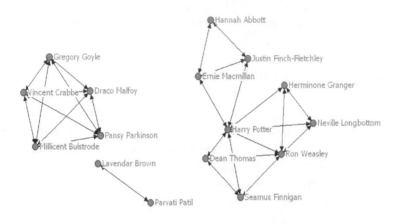

FIGURE 1B. FRIENDSHIP TIES AFTER DUMBLEDORE'SARMY

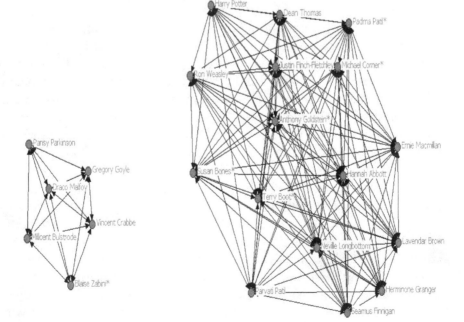

REFERENCES

Berndt, Thomas J. 1982. "The Features and Effects of Friendship in Early Adolescence." *Child Development* 53:1447-60.

Berndt, Thomas J. and Keunho Keefe. 1995. "Friends' Influence on Adolescents' Adjustment to School." *Child Development* 66: 1312-29.

Cairns, Robert B., Man-Chi Leung, Lisa Buchanan, and Beverly D. Cairns. 1995. "Friendships and Social Networks in Childhood and Adolescence: Fluidity, Reliability, and Interrelations." *Child Development 66*: 1330-45.

Crosnoe, Robert. 2000. "Friendships in Childhood and Adolescence: The Life Course and New Directions." *Social Psychology Quarterly* 63: 377-91.

De Nooy, Wouter. 2001. "Stories and Social Structure: A structural Perspective on   Literature in Society." *The Psychology and Sociology of Literature*: 359-75.

Griswold, Wendy. 1993. "Recent Moves in the Sociology of Literature." *Annual Review of Sociology* 19: 455-67.

McPherson, Miller, Lynn Smith-Lovin, and James M. Cook. 2001. "Birds of a Feather: Homophily in Social Networks." *Annual Review of Sociology* 27: 415-44.

Rowling, J. K. 2000. Scholastic.com Interview

Shrum, Wesley and Neil H. Cheek, Jr. 1987. "Social Structure During the School Years: Onset of the Degrouping Process." *American Sociological Review* 52: 218-23.

Shrum, Wesley, Neil H. Cheek, Jr., and Saundra MacD. Hunter. 1988. "Friendship in School: Gender and Racial Homophily." *Sociology of Education* 61: 227-39.

*"I can teach you how to bottle fame, brew glory,
and even stopper death – if you aren't as big of a
bunch of dunderheads as I usually have to teach"*

PEDAGOGY OF THE HALF-BLOOD PRINCE

JELENA MARIĆ AND JENN SIMS

Albus Dumbledore once said that "it matters not what one is born but what one grows to be" (GOF 708). Yet sociology, particularly the sub-field of social psychology, reminds us that far from being solely based on personal choices, many larger factors, over which we have little control, have a profound impact on what we grow to become and even what we are *able* to become. As explained by Karl Marx (1851: 329):

> Men [sic] make their own history, but they do not make it just as they please; they do not make it under circumstances chosen by themselves but under circumstances directly encountered, given, and transmitted from the past.

A branch of social psychology called Social Structure and Personality studies the influence that social structures have on the individual and the impact that individuals have on the broader social order. This chapter will examine the teaching pedagogy of Hogwarts professor Severus Snape as a case study to demonstrate how society shapes a person's personality and traits and how an individual, in turn, can also affect the social structure. Structure is not fate, however. As will be explained below, in his family Severus learned that a woman is an object – not person to be respected – to abuse. Instead, he dedicated his life to a woman that he never had: A little red-haired girl named Lily, who he loved until the very end.

LIFE AND LIES OF SEVERUS SNAPE

> "Cruel, sarcastic, and disliked by everybody except the students from his own house (Slytherin), Snape taught Potions.... He was a thin man with sallow skin, a hooked nose, and greasy, shoulder-length black hair" (COS 77-78).

Severus Tobias Snape was the only child of Tobias Snape, a Muggle, and Eileen Prince, a witch. Severus' parents were poor and this was reflected his appearance and dress. As a "sallow, small, stringy" boy "his black hair was overlong and his clothes were so mismatched that it looked deliberate: too short jeans, a shabby, overlarge coat that might have belonged to a grown man, an odd smock like shirt" (DH 663). Furthermore, his parents had an abusive relationship. Tobias would yell at a cowering Eileen right in front of their son (OOTP 592). From an early age Severus dreamed about Hogwarts as a shelter from his impoverished and violent home life.

When he was nine or ten years old he met his best friend, Lily Evans. Severus was aware of his magical powers, but to Lily, a Muggle-born witch, it was all very strange and new. It was Severus who told her everything about the wizarding world and Hogwarts. While Petunia, Lily's older sister, looked down on Severus, judging him based on his poor appearance and residence (DH 665), Lily was always kind to him.

From a young age, Snape had an affinity for the Dark Arts. It was remembered that: "Snape knew more curses when he arrived at school than half the kids in the seventh year" (GOF 531). He was sorted in Slytherin House and according to Sirius Black became "part of a gang of Slytherins who nearly all turned out to be Death Eaters" (ibid). Even before he was a fully trained wizard he was not only a gifted potion maker, but he was also able to make his own spells (e.g., Sectumsempra). Isolated in his youth, Severus Snape thought that he had finally found a place where he belonged at Hogwarts and friends in the Death Eaters.

Severus was befriended by Lucius Malfoy and other powerful Slytherins; nevertheless, within his own grade he was abused by two golden boys from Gryffindor – James Potter and Sirius Black. They named him "Snivellus" and took every chance they got to make school a living hell for him. They were making fun of him because he was unattractive, because he was poor, because he had old robes, because he studied hard. They hated everything about Severus, especially the fact that he was Lily's friend.

By the time Snape graduated from Hogwarts, Lord Voldemort had risen to power. Voldemort was obsessed with pureblood ideology, and he started to kill Muggles and Muggle-borns. In the beginning, Snape was one of the most passionate of Voldemort's supporters. Having lived his entire life as lower economic class and lower social class, among Voldemort's inner circle Snape was respected and, for the first time in his life, held high status. While he must have enjoyed the experience of being atop the social hierarchy for once, everything started to change after he heard the famous prophecy of Sybil Trelawney:

> The one with the power to vanquish the – Dark Lord approaches...
> born to those who have thrice defied him, born as the seventh month
> dies... and the Dark Lord will mark him as his equal, but he will have

power the Dark Lord knows not... and either must die at the hand of
the other for neither can live while the other survives... (OOTP 841)

At first, Severus didn't realized what he had heard. He ran to his Master
and told him about prophecy. Voldemort interpreted the prophecy to mean
that the new born son of Lily and James Potter was "The Chosen One" and
decided to kill them. Having loved Lily "for nearly all his life" (DH 740),
Severus asked Voldemort to spare her life; but when he realized that she might
be killed anyway, he turned against Dark Lord and became Dumbledore's spy.

After Lily's death and Voldemort's fall, Snape lived in a shadow. He
became Potion Master at Hogwarts (Dumbledore couldn't let him teach
Defence against Dark Arts, because of "old sins"), and he dedicated his life to
protecting Lily's son, Harry Potter. Snape never liked Harry; actually he hated
him because he was so like James. Nevertheless, even from Harry's first year at
Hogwarts, Snape worked to protect his life.

During Harry's sixth year, Snape finally reached his career goal: He
became Defence Against Dark Arts Teacher. Concomitantly, though as
Dumbledore's spy, he was also one of Voldemort's, who had returned to power,
most trusted Death Eaters. After Dumbledore's orchestrated death, Snape
became a Headmaster of Hogwarts. He died during the Battle of Hogwarts,
killed by Nagini on Voldemort's order as the latter, erroneously, believed
it necessary in order to take possession of the Elder Wand. His last words,
whispered to the boy that he hated so much: "Look...at....me... You have your
mother's eyes" (DH: 658; HP7 part II). Snape died immediately thereafter,
staring into the eyes of the love of his life.

PEDAGOGY OF HALF-BLOOD PRINCE

Relationships with students

Every teacher (in both the Muggle and wizarding world) has his/her own
style of relating to the students and specific pedagogy / teaching methodology.
So does Severus Snape. As a teacher, Snape's style could be described as being
mean, cruel and unfair. It was not Snape's style to treat his students equally. To
some he was intimidating and abusive while to others he showed favouritism.
Some students he simply ignored.

Professor Severus Snape had a perverted need to intimidate some students
by degrading and humiliating them. The best example of this sadistic practice
can be seen in his treatment of Neville Longbottom. For example, Snape
tried to poison Neville's frog, Trevor, with his own improperly brewed potion.
When Snape realized that Hermione helped Neville, he punished them both.
Neville was so afraid of Snape that his Boggart looked like Snape. Often,
Snape called Neville an "Idiot boy" (e.g., SS 139).

Snape was downright abusive to other students whom he disliked, in particular Harry. Harry recalls of his first year at Hogwarts that "At the start-of-term banquet, [he] had gotten the idea that Professor Snape disliked him. By the end of the first Potions lesson, he knew he'd been wrong. Snape didn't dislike [him] – he *hated* him." (SS 136, emphasis in original). It wasn't until Harry's fourth year that Snape directly told him how he felt saying "To me Potter, you are nothing but a nasty little boy who considers rules to be beneath him" (GOF 516).

Rather than just intimidating and humiliating Harry as he did to Neville, Snape purposely was nasty to Harry, in and outside class, and wasn't afraid of losing his job because of mobbing him at school. When Harry did something correctly in Potion class, Snape would break his bottle so that Harry would receive no marks for the assignment. Snape also loved to put Harry into detention, for instance making him clean his cabinet. But the most malicious detention was in Harry's sixth year, when Snape made him copy (without magic) the list of the records of other Hogwarts wrongdoers and their punishments. When Harry saw his father's and godfather's names, he "felt the familiar boiling sensation in the pit of his stomach" (HBP 532). Snape knew how he would feel, so he coldly sneered: "It must be such a comforting thing that, though they are gone, a record of their great achievements remains" (ibid). In fact, several times, and only half joking, Snape actually threatened to poison Harry, like it was the funniest thing in the world.

In stark contrast to this treatment, Snape was perfectly genteel to other students. Naturally, the main condition was that one is in Slytherin, and that one has some deal of intelligence. In Harry's generation, Snape's pet was Draco Malfoy, probably more likely because of his friendship with Draco's father, Lucius Malfoy, than because Draco was a naturally gifted potion maker[1]. In third year he made Ron cut Draco's roots while Draco was pretending to still be suffering from Buckbeak's attack. In fourth year Snape didn't punish him when his (Draco's) spell enlarged Hermione's teeth. However, when he realized that Draco was supposed to kill Dumbledore, they became very rough with each other. Snape recognized that Draco was too "weak" and had promised Narcissa to help him; and Draco believed that Snape had betrayed Lucius and was now trying to encroach upon his, Draco's, moment of glory.

As Dumbledore pointed out to Harry, "indifference and neglect often do much more damage than outright dislike" (OOTP 834). As a professor, some students Snape liked, some he hated, and some he just ignored. Hermione Granger was one of the students whom he preferred to pretend did not attend

---

1   Actually, Snape never believed that any of the students were talented in his subject. Hermione was brilliant, but even she couldn't make the perfect potion when the instructions need improvisation (HBP 190-191; 194).

his classes. Hermione was a brilliant student, a "borderline genius" (Rowling 1999). There was no question that she could give the right answer. Sometimes, this habit could be annoying to teachers; and it was especially so to Severus Snape. For instance, he ignored every right answer she gave; he even used to deduct points from Gryffindor for her being an "insufferable know-it-all," (POA 172). When she would help other students such as Neville, he punished her for "showing off" as well. Were he to accept that she answered a question correctly, he was dismissive of the achievement. In response to providing the correct benefit of using silent spells Snape replied, "An answer copied almost word for word from The Standard Book of Spells, Grade Six... but correct in essentials" (HBP 178-179). To him, Hermione just had a great memory, not a truly magical gift.

Methodology

With regard to Snape's actual teaching methods, he favoured a rigorous, but loosely guided, approach. He disliked the way every DADA professor taught that class. He had his own vision of how that subject should best be taught. Concerning the difficultly level of the material, he stated that Professor Lupin was "hardly overtaxing" the students, adding that he would "expect first years to be able to deal with" what Lupin was covering in their third year course (POA 171). Yet despite his view that more difficult material should be covered, Snape's teaching methodology involved little explanation of new material once it was introduced. Snape didn't explain anything. Students had to manage lessons in their own way. For instance, as Potions Master he would often simply list the ingredients and directions on the board and expect the students to figure it out themselves within an allotted amount of time. During a DADA lesson, he told the students to divide into pairs to practice a spell; but unlike Professor McGonagall, Professor Flitwick or even the imposter Professor Moody, Snape did not first demonstrate the spell to show the students the correct way to perform it.

Snape always used to give students hard and long essays for homework. He assigned anywhere from two full rolls of parchment (POA 173) to twelve inches of parchment (OOTP 234). Moreover, whereas other professors like Binns gave students a week or more to turn in a long essay (COS 148), Snape's were almost always to be handed in the very next class meeting, just two or three days after it was assigned. When it came to students whom he did not like, he found it very appropriate to punish them by giving them extra homework, i.e., another longer essay (e.g., OOTP 364). With regard to grading homework, Hogwarts grades were unique from O.W.L. and N.E.W.T. scores. In fifth year, Snape decided to evaluate their homework essays based on the exam grading system. He concluded that "[t]he general standard of this homework was abysmal. Most of you would have failed had this been your examination. I expect to see a great deal more effort for this week's essay on the various varieties of venom antidotes, or I shall have to start handing out detentions to those dunces who get a D^2."(OOTP 309).

In conclusion: Snape never explained how to make a potion or do a spell, but he was always unfair, cruel and strict when he was giving grades to students. It is our opinion that he never wanted to be a teacher and that he never enjoyed his job. He didn't appear to like children or working with teens. However, he stayed because when Harry came to Hogwarts he could fulfil his mission: abuse the boy, make him miserable, and save his life.

MAKING OF THE MAN

Social Structure and Personality

The core theme of the social structure and personality paradigm is that one's position in the social structure affects individual-level experiences and characteristics such as attitudes/opinions, personality, interpersonal relationships, and life's choices and achievements. Stryker (1980)[3] argued that the structure of a society could influence individual interactions in three ways. First, the structure largely determines who interacts with whom on a daily basis. This is clearly evident with regard to Houses within Hogwarts. Members of a given House eat, sleep, study, socialize, etc. with primarily members of their own House. In this way, it is the organizational structure of the institution that determines, for example, who will become friends rather than just whose personalities "click." Lavender Brown and Parvati Patil were as close as can be and had many things in common; yet were it not for their shared structural location (Gryffindor House) they would not have had the opportunity to form such a tight friendship.

Second, the social structure determines which symbols and cultural materials people can use and understand. For example, due to their position within the wizarding world, only witches and wizards would have perfectly understood Mr. Weasley's explanation to the Dursleys of how and why he connected No. 4 Privet Drive to the Floo Network to collect Harry. Like Harry's relatives, other Muggles would likewise not "understand a single word of this" (GOF 45) due to their differential social location (i.e., outside, and unaware, of the wizarding world). The reverse is true as well. When Dean Thomas yelled "Red card ref!" during a Quidditch match, the other spectators did not understand what he meant (SS 188). "Red card" refers to the referees

---

2   Grades are as follows: O for 'Outstanding,' E for 'Exceeds Expectations,' A for 'Acceptable,' and then P for 'Poor,' D for 'Dreadful' and T for 'Troll.' (OOTP 237)

3   Thank you to Matt Mohr for providing the summary of Stryker's (1980) theory.

in the Muggle game of football/soccer expelling a player for committing an "open and revolting foul" (ibid). Dean, because of his structural location as a Muggle-born who lived until two months prior exclusively in the Muggle world, had learned to associate fouls with receiving the red card.

In addition to symbols, one's social position also equips one to be able to effectively use cultural materials that differentially located others cannot manage. For example, at the 422nd Quidditch World Cup, Hermione had to show Mr. Weasley how to use matches, a Muggle fire-starting tool he could not figure out how to work (GOF 85). These cases of knowledge as a function of location in the social structure are explained by the concept of people having "cultural tool kits." According to Swindler (1986), members of different cultures have at their disposal different "symbols, stories, rituals, and world-views" (277) in their tool kits that provide "resources out of which individuals and groups construct strategies of action" (281).

Physical location in the social structure is not the only thing that determines the contents of one's tool kit; temporal location does as well. The generation in which a person was born and the world events that occurred during that time period also influence what one can understand. For example, at the World Cup, Harry was ignorant of the significance of the Dark Mark because he spent most of his life to that point in the Muggle world; yet Ron had grown up in the wizarding world and he too was confused about "what that skull thing was" (GOF 141). Harry and the younger Weasley children did not know why its appearance was "such a big deal" because, as Mr. Weasley explained, they were "too young" (GOF 142). The full weight of the terror of the Dark Mark is a part of older generations of witches' and wizards' cultural tool kit. Thus only Mr. Weasley and Bill, the eldest, could appreciate the magnitude of the situation (though see chapter 15 for an explanation of how Hermione's reading about the Dark Mark in *The Rise and Fall of the Dark Arts* led her to have the same reaction that night as those who actually lived during the First Wizarding War).

Finally, Stryker's third argument is that our internal identities are arranged into hierarchies, and the ordering of our identities follows the status hierarchy of a society. A Hogwarts student's identity as a House Quidditch team member would be expected to be higher on her/his internal identity hierarchy than that of a choir member because the European wizarding community values Quidditch players more than singers (except maybe in the case of the Weird Sisters). Through these three mechanisms – available interpersonal interactions, available symbol referents via one's cultural tool kit, and identity organization – Stryker argues that the social structure influences individual level experiences and characteristics – including a professor's teaching methods and how s/he relates to students.

Structural Influences on Snape's Relationships with Students

Snape's structural location in Slytherin House means that he only had sustained interpersonal interactions with one quarter of the students at Hogwarts. As such, it is easy to see why he favoured students from his own House. They were the only ones his structural social position allowed him to really get to know and develop a relationship with. Moreover, while Professor McGonagall may have seen Neville studying dutifully, Professor Snape only saw Draco, Pansy, and other Slytherin students' outside the classroom efforts, making it easier to give his students the "benefit of the doubt" when they did not perform up to par.

Snape's past interpersonal interactions structured his relationships with students as well. As a child, Severus witnessed his parents' fights and his father abusing his mother. Sociological studies with Muggles from impoverished circumstances like Snape's report that "it's strange what [witnessing domestic violence] does to you, seeing that as a kid. You'd think you'd be like, 'wow, I'm never gonna treat someone like that, I'm never gonna be violent with a girl, I'm never gonna dominate someone.' But that ain't the way it works" (MacLeod 2009: 342). Bandura et al (1961) explains "the way it works." Results of this classic social psychological lab experiment showed that the children who witness aggressive behaviour in adults were more like to copy that behaviour than the children who did not witness such events. This is not to say that people automatically and unthinkingly do what they see others doing; but it demonstrates that repeatedly witnessing a behaviour places it in one's cultural tool kit, and thus it becomes a ready option for one's own future behaviour. Returning to Professor Snape's relationships with his students, he clearly drew upon these aggressive and abusive behaviours in his interactions with Harry, Neville and other students he did not like.

Snape's cultural tool kit also contained a symbol that was widely recognized by all in his temporal location: Lily Potter's bright green eyes. Everyone in this generation and older, upon meeting Harry, commented that he has his mother's eyes, so often in fact that Harry "found it a bit wearing" (HBP 69). What's more, this comment was usually followed with a declaration of how talented and/and or kind Lily was (HP3; HBP 70). For Snape, however, Lily's eyes don't just symbolize her talent and kindness, but also, painfully, his lost friendship with and unrequited love for her. During Snape's interactions with Harry, upon seeing this painful symbol, he reached again for the familiar behaviour he witnessed his father using: abuse.

Professor Snape, like all witches, wizards, and Muggles, was many things. He was a Potions Master, Head of Slytherin House, Dumbledore's spy, and a (faux) Death Eater to name a few. With regard to his identities within Hogwarts as an educational institution, his position as Potions master and as a Head of House were the most salient. As a Head of House was a position of leadership, only one of four at the entire school, we can expect that in the status hierarchy of the wizarding world, this position would be ranked higher than that of regular professor. Remember that Stryker (1980) theorizes that people organize their internal identities into hierarchies that reflect the broader social views; therefore, we can expect that being Head of Slytherin House was more important to Snape than being Potions Master. This ordering of importance was visible not just in his favouritism of Slytherin students, but also in his ignoring of brilliant students like Hermione. His identity as a professor, as one who embraces learning and helps satiate students' curiosity, was second place; and ignoring students who would foreground it allowed him to keep it that way.

Structural Influences on Snape's Teaching Pedagogy

As with his relationship with students, Snape's structural location, past and present, heavily influenced his teaching. With regard to one's location structuring interpersonal interactions, we can note that *lack* of interpersonal interactions due to one's structural location has an effect on individuals as well. Given that Snape knew so many spells upon arrival at Hogwarts, it can be assumed that he studied and taught himself. Moreover, as an unpopular student, it can be assumed he continued studying alone during his tenure at Hogwarts as well. Limited interpersonal interactions with others with regard to learning, therefore, may be an explanation for his "hands off" approach to teaching his students. Having learned with little help himself, he expected others to do the same. His temporal location influenced what interactions he had as well. As a student of Horace Slughorn's he would have attended Potions classes taught in the same manner that he himself later conducted the class: ingredients listed on the board or in the book, students working independently, professor walking around the room observing but not offering guidance (HP6).

His position in the wizarding social structure also determines which cultural materials Snape used in the classroom. In particular, he was fond of assigning long essays, sometimes to be completed in as little as two days. However, this method is more a reflection of his position as a Hogwarts teacher than as whatever it was Ron called him that made Hermione say "Ron!" (POA 173). As the students' surprise at Lupin's practical lessons and exams demonstrates, Hogwarts' teachers usually rely on essays as their main pedagogical tool. Professors Binns, Burbage, McGonagall, Sinistra, Sprout, and Vector all assign essays. Even Lupin, who all the students (excepting maybe the Slytherins) loved, sometimes made them summarize readings and write essays (POA 139; 277). So while the length and due dates of Snape's essays may be reflective of his surly attitude (Professor Binns gave ten days for an essay shorter than one Snape assigned to have been due to two days), his use of this particular pedagogical tool in general was a reflection of his structural location not as a professor but as a specifically Hogwarts professor.

Finally, Professor Snape's teaching was influenced by his internal identity organization which mirrors the hierarchy of positions in the wizarding world at large. As mentioned above, one's position as a regular teacher does not accord the same status as that of Head of House or Deputy Headmistress. In fact, any work in the educational field isn't very prestigious in the wizarding world. Wizarding parents like Mrs. Weasley hope their children will work for the Ministry after graduation; and students who hold this aspiration for themselves must receive top marks. Being a professor, however, was not as valued. Dumbledore, for example, baffled people with his contentment as a professor; such talent, it was thought, belonged in top positions at the Ministry (SS 64-65). That is because talent was recognized in the wizarding world. Order of Merlin was awarded for great deeds, and discovering new potions or magical properties, not for having one's students' ace all their N.E.W.T.s. With regard to Snape, then, we can expect his identity as a skilled potions maker to have been higher on his internal identity hierarchy than other less prestigious identities like professor. To maintain his reputation and identity as a Potions Master, therefore, it was pertinent that no one surpass him in knowledge or skill. His rigorous curriculum coupled with a hands off teaching methods ensured that the students were prepared enough for their O.W.Ls and N.E.W.T.s while simultaneously protecting his identity as Potions Master by not allowing the possibility that someone could become a better potions maker than he was.

CONCLUSION

We mentioned in the opening of the chapter that the Social Structure and Personality paradigm also explains how an individual can affect the social structure. To "[t]hose familiar with the history of the most recent wizarding war" (TBB xvi), Snape's personal effect on the social structure of the wizarding world is obvious. Were it not for Snape's love of Lily and request that the Dark Lord spare her life, she would not have had the choice to step aside or continue shielding Harry. This is significant, because it was her wilful sacrifice that provided Harry, first, with magical protection and, ultimately, the strength to do "what [his] mother did" (DH 738), which of course led to the final destruction of Lord Voldemort. In this manner, the life of Severus Snape is an exemplar of both directional paths of Social Structure and Personality paradigm.

Dumbledore may be correct that our choices are more important than our abilities; however, he also understood that one can only make choices amongst the available options – which are determined partially by one's structural location (i.e., "what one is born") and experiences in society. Prior to his death, when discussing Voldemort's mother's "choice" of death rather than to live for her child, he counseled Harry "do not judge her too harshly... She was greatly weakened by long suffering and she never had your mother's courage" (HBP 262). Snape, like Merope, was greatly affected by the poverty, abuse and generally harsh circumstances of his early life. They both did what they what they could to the best of their limited capacity: Merope did not choose to live for her son, but her dying act was to secure a safe place for him to live after she was gone. And while Snape was by no stretch of the imagination ever nice to Harry, he kept his pledge to protect Lily's son literally until his dying day.

We must understand that Snape's father ruined his childhood; James ruined his youth; and Voldemort took his one happiness in life when he killed Lily. Miserable childhood, unhappy youth, lousy job, a life dedicated to the woman he could never have and a boy that he hated. Sociology reminds us that "the biographies of men and women, the kinds of individuals they variously become, cannot be understood without reference to the historical structure in which the milieu of their everyday life are organized" (Mills 1959: 158). Using the Social Structure and Personality paradigm, one can see how the wizarding social structure shaped Snape's personality and made him the man and type of professor that he became. Mills (1959) said this knowledge is both a terrible lesson and a magnificent one. We agree. And while past suffering, even understood, does not excuse individuals like Snape from often cruel treatment of others, it allows us, as it did Harry, to have compassion and forgiveness for a great man: Severus Tobias Snape.

REFERENCES

Bandura, Albert, Dorothea Ross, and Sheila A. Ross. 1961. "Transmission of Agression through Imitation of Aggressive Models." *Journal of Abnormal and Social Pyschology*, 63: 575-582.

Mark, Karl. 1851. The Eighteenth Brumaire of Louis Bonaparte. Pp. 329-355 in *Karl Marx: Selected Writings, Second Edition*. Edited by D. McLellan. Oxford: Oxford University Press.

MacLeod, Jay. 2009. *Ain't no makin' it: Aspirations and attainment in a low-income Neighbourhood*. Updated Third Edition. Boulder, CO: Westview Press.

Mills, C. Wright. 1959. *The Sociological Imagination*. Oxford: Oxford University Press.

Rowling, J. K. 1999. Interview with The Connection (WBUR Radio), 12 October, 1999.

Stryker, Sheldon. 1980. [2002] *Symbolic Interactionism: A social structural version*. Caldwell, NJ: Blackburn Press.

Swindler, Ann. 1986. "Culture in Action: Symbols and Strategies." *American Sociological Review, 51*, 273-286.

"Or Dear Bellatrix, who likes to play with her food before she eats it."

WHY THE WIZARDING WORLD NEEDS DEATH EATERS

JENN SIMS

"NOT ALL WIZARDS ARE GOOD"

The Death Eaters, Harry Potter learns after the mayhem at the 422nd Quidditch World Cup, are some of those wizards about whom Hagrid was speaking when he said that "not all wizards are good" (HP1). The atrocities committed by the Death Eaters are infamous. They destroyed the Millennium Bridge in London (HP6), tortured the Longbottoms to the point of insanity, and killed Muggles and Muggle-born witches and wizards just for entertainment. Based on this, one would assume that the wizarding world would be a much better place without them. After all, had there been no Death Eaters then countless deaths would be prevented, there would be no First or Second Wizarding Wars, and Harry and Neville would each have grown up with two loving parents....

Sociologists, however, would argue that, despite their misdeeds, or indeed *because* of them, the Death Eaters are a vital and needed element of the wizarding world. While definitely not "good" for society, the existence of crime and criminals, and the system of trials and punishment to which they are subjected, is "normal" and "functional" for a healthy society. This chapter will discuss the, at first glance, outrageous claim that "something repugnant may nevertheless have a useful reason for existing" (Lukes 1982: 32).

"THAT'S ILLEGAL!"

Functionalism, as summarized in chapter two, is a classic theoretical perspective in sociology. Developed by Emile Durkheim, the major premise is that society is composed of interrelated "parts" that must work together to make the whole function properly. Each part (e.g., the family, schools, health care, government, culture, etc.) has a role to play. If one doesn't perform well, the whole suffers. Yet what contributing role could heinous crimes and hardened criminals possibly play to ensure the smooth functioning of society? Durkheim addresses this conundrum with his theory of crime and punishment.

Across several books and essays, Durkheim explains that crime and punishment are both normal and functional. Regarding normality, he theorizes that crime is normal because it exists in every society. "By virtue of the fact that we each have our own organic constitution and occupy different areas in space," he writes, "it is impossible for everyone to be alike," (Lukes 1982: 100). Crime, actions that receive punishment for offending strongly held moral sentiments, is therefore inevitable. There will always be some witches, wizards and Muggles who do not share the dominant view of their society and consequently whose behaviors offend others.

Durkheim's theory also states that crime is functional for society in so far that by collectively punishing criminals "not only are moral boundaries of the community clearly demarcated, but the strength of attachment to them is reinforced" (Reiner 1984: 180). Moreover, punishing crime "strengths social solidarity through the reaffirmation of moral commitment among the conforming population" (ibid). Finally, Durkheim postulates that crime is "positively beneficial" for society (Reiner 1984: 181). In so far that the conforming population must continually respond to criminal activities, crime can be seen as "the precondition for a society's capacity for flexibility in the face of essential change" (Reiner 1984: 181). Durkheim's theory of crime and punishment, then, is that it is normal because it is inevitable, and it is positively functional because, in punishing crime, society's norms and values are revealed, moral and social boundaries are created, these are reinforced via punishment rituals that provide social solidarity among conformers, and innovation and social change are made possible (Kidd 2007). This theory allows us to understand that, evil as they are, the Death Eaters nonetheless serve a vital function in the wizarding world… to a point.

While the existence of some crime may be functional, "excessiveness is pathological" (Lukes 1982: 98). There can come a point when, if it reaches a certain level, criminalized deviance becomes detrimental to the current social order and may even destroy it entirely. However, despite acknowledging that at a certain level crime becomes detrimental, Durkheim's theory "gives us no ready recipe for calculating" what level is functional and what is destructive (Reiner 1984: 182). Subsequent theorists have sought to extend the theory to address this gap. To understand how crime becomes pathological, we will turn in the latter part of the chapter to Pierre Bourdieu, whose thinking was greatly influenced by Durkheim, and his theory of the conflict over the "logic of the field."

"THEY'RE HIS TOO-- HIS FOLLOWERS"

Norms

The first premise of Durkheim's theory of the functionality of crime is that it "defines the norms of a society" (Kidd 2007: 70). According to Durkheim, crime is, at its simplest definition, an "action that offends certain collective feelings which are especially strong and clear cut" (Lukas 1982: 99). Commonly referred to as "morality," the existence of these deeply ingrained norms, values and feelings are vividly brought to light when they are offended; as such, the best way to learn what norms society values most is to examine the offenses that it considers most egregious. In the wizarding world, the three "Unforgivable Curses," popular among Death Eaters, are the "most heavily punished by wizarding law" (GOF 212).

Barty Crouch Jr., disguised as Professor Alastor Moody, introduced the Unforgivable Curses to Harry Potter and his classmates in their grade four Defense Against the Dark Arts class. The first curse discussed was the Imperious Curse, which involves "total control" of another as explained by the impostor Moody (GOF 213). He demonstrated the curse on spider, making it dance around to the amusement of the class; but the laughter subsided when he made the students see the severity of it. With total control of another, you can make them hurt, even kill, themselves or others. As such, the Imperious Curse is illegal because it offends against the collective sentiment that individuals should be autonomous. In Europe, the ideology of respect for individual autonomy arose during the Enlightenment period, admittedly though at first focused on the rights of the masses against stifling control by institutions such as the government and the church. The Imperious Curse, therefore, violates the liberalist norm to respect individual's "freedom of expression and action" (Blackburn 2005). The strength of this norm can be seen in efforts, such as Harry's and Barty Crouch Sr.'s and Jr.'s, to fight being controlled by another.

Another Unforgivable Curse is the Cruciatus Curse which causes the target agonizing pain. The impostor Moody's demonstration of this curse on a second spider caused Neville much distress as his parents subjection to it 13 years prior had led to their insanity and his, essentially, being an orphan. The illegality of Cruciatus Curse shows that the wizarding world has a norm to not harm others. However, as Bellatrix explained to Harry after his failed attempt to curse her for killing Sirius, "You need to really want to cause pain – to enjoy it – righteous angry won't hurt me for long" (GOF 810). In this way, we can see that wizarding morality distinguishes not only between the intentionality of the one causing harm (i.e., justified or for pleasure) but also among the moral standing target (i.e., guilty or innocent) as well. Only harming others in and of itself, for no other purpose than to hurt them, is morally offensive; and only harming those who have done nothing wrong is morally offensive. Harry was angry at Bellatrix, but because it was righteous anger and she was guilty of committing a grave offense, the curse only "knocked her off her feet, but she did not writhe and shriek with pain" (ibid). Therefore, via the Cruciatus Curse, we can see that for witches and wizards it is morally wrong to specifically harm innocent[1] others for pleasure.

The third and final Unforgivable Curse is Avada Kedavra – the killing curse. The norm and value that this curse violates is obvious: respect for human life. Respect for human life is so valued that killing is explicitly outlawed in almost every society on earth; unlike torture, for example, which is legal in some places and under certain circumstances. In the wizarding world, killing is considered "the supreme act of evil" (HBP 498). It is "rips the soul apart" which is considered "against nature" (ibid). Moreover, unlike righteously causing pain to the guilty, which the Cruciatus Curse's lack of effectives on those who have committed evil acts shows is morally acceptable, killing even the guilty is considered morally reprehensible. In many modern nation states the Death Penalty – the killing of criminals deemed especially dangerous – has been eradicated. This shows the depth of societies' commitment to respecting human life, *all* human life. Harry, too, values human life to this extent. In the final showdown with Voldemort Harry asked him to "try for some remorse" (DH 741). This, he knows, is the only way to mend and save his soul, and thus his life (DH 103). After all the suffering that Voldemort had caused him personally and the wizarding world in general, Harry still did not commit the act against nature and kill Voldemort. In the end, Voldemort's own backfired Avada Kedavra curse killed him instead.

Boundaries and Rituals

Crime not only makes explicit society's norms and values, but it "establishes social boundaries" (Kidd 2007: 70). Criminals serve as an out-group against which the rest of the law abiding members of society use to define their social identify. Social psychologists theorize that there are multiple foundations for identity including role, group (i.e., social), and personal. Social identities are:

> based on a person's identification with a social group (Hogg and Abrams 1988). A social group is a set of individuals who share the

---

1   "Innocent" here does not mean guilty of *no* crime, but being innocent of a grave offense. When Amycus spat in Professor McGonagal's face he was not "innocent;" but Harry was nonetheless able to successfully harm him with the Cruciatus Curse (DH 593). This is likely because of the difference in the severity of the offense of killing someone versus disrespecting them, with anger for the latter being less "righteous" than the former and thus allowing one to produce an effective Cruciatus Curse.

view that they are members of the same social category. Through a social comparisons and categorization process, persons who are similar to the self are categorized with the self and are labeled the ingroup. Correspondingly, person who differ from the self are categorized as the outgroup. (Burke and Stets 2009: 118).

The general magical population needs the existence of crime and criminals like the Death Eaters in order to see themselves as a law abiding group; and the Death Eaters need "blood traitors" and other groups in order to form their social identity. In other words, there can be no "we" without a "them." Crime's ability to establish social identities by separating criminals from others is further evidence that it is functional for society.

It would be prudent to take a moment here to assure the reader that sociologists are not attempting to justify crime or laud criminals. As Durkheim explains, "if it is normal for crimes to occur in every society, it is no less normal for them to be punished. The institution of a system of repressions is as universal a fact as the existence of criminality, and is no less indispensable to the collective well-being" (Lukes 1982: 32). In other words, we must remember that "[crime] serves only when reproved and repressed" (Durkheim 1897: 362). The social institution responsible for defining and enforcing the laws of a society is called the criminal justice system.

In the wizarding world, the criminal justice system consists of courts, trials, law enforcement organizations and prisons. Remembering that punishing criminals "strengthens social solidarity through the reaffirmation of moral commitment among the confirming population" (Reiner 1984: 180), we can view court trials and public sentencing to prison as providing "rituals that helps build solitary" (Kidd 2007: 70), the third premise of Durkheim's theory. Rituals are social ceremonies. The trials of Death Eaters after the First Wizarding War were rituals that publicly reaffirmed the societies' norms, reinforced social boundaries and identities, and created solidarity among the law abiding magical public. Similarly, public sentencing to prison is also a ritual. It is symbolically and literally erecting social boundaries between groups, law abiding versus not, by sending the criminal away from the general population.

While the use of an unforgivable curse is "enough to earn a life sentence in Azkaban" (GOF 217), these curses are actually not, as the imposter Moody claimed, the most heavily punished offenses in the wizarding world. Life imprisonment is nowhere nearly as horrifying as the Dementor's Kiss, a punishment that is "nearly unbearable to witness" (HP3) which involves the removal of one's soul from her or his living body. The Kiss was used, prior to the re-constituted Ministry, as a punishment for only one offense: escape from prison. If, as stated above, the best way to learn what norms society values most is to examine the offences that it considers most egregious, why would escape from prison be more offensive to the collective sentiment than abuse, torture or murder? Moreover, what boundaries would it form or groups would it give solidarity to? The answer lies in what breaking out of prison can be seen to represent. Having been judged, by due process or not, to be unfit for general society, Azkaban escapees commit the ultimate offense when the leave – refusing to recognize the existence of the social contract.

The "social contract" is a concept which states that humans create societies by agreeing to abide by established rules and roles, even if it means giving up a few personal freedoms, in exchange for mutual benefit and protection (Rousseau 1762). Breaking the rules of the contract is one thing; but refusing to recognize the existence of the contract is another. It is the latter, I believe, that breaking out of Azkaban seems to entail. In other words, the escapee is offending against, not just one person as with even the most gruesome murder, not just "society" as whole or against particular values, but against the very *idea* of social living. The offense of complete disregard for the idea of the collective is the most egregious human ontology.

Most importantly, however, the Dementor's Kiss is a ritual. By carrying out this ritual (i.e., ordering or authorizing the dementors to perform the Kiss) members of society are able to collectively re-affirm their decision to be socially cooperative (i.e., to be a society rather live in a Hobbesian "war of all against all" state of existence) by banishing, not the just the body, but that most human essence, the soul, from the one who has symbolically violated the premise on which society rests. In that regard, the Dementor's Kiss, more so than any other ritualized punishment, gives wizardkind a sense of solidarity.

Innovation and Social Change

There is a maxim among American Muggles that "necessity is the mother of invention." Sociologists would say that crime is too. Durkheim wrote that crime "directly pre-paves the way for change" and that criminals' activities are "useful for prosperity" (Lukes 1982: 102). The final premises of his theory, therefore, are that "crime produces innovation" and "can provide the necessary impetus for social change" (Kidd 2007: 70-71). Innovations resulting from responses to crime include new laws, protocols, and technology. For example, in response to Dark wizards interfering at Hogwarts, the students created a new organization, Dumbledore's Army, to counteract the negative affect that this illegal activity was having on the school. The DA's meeting notification coins, which were designed by Hermione and instrumental in alerting fellow students during the Battle of the Astronomy Tower and the Battle of Hogwarts, were modeled on the Death Eaters' Dark Mark.

Moreover, because of the Death Eaters' crimes Harry, Ron and Neville made significant improvements to Auror's department, thereby better protecting the wizarding community from future harm. Due to the crimes committed in the name of pureblood ideology, such as torturing Muggles/ Muggle-borns, it was finally recognized that pro-pureblood laws needed to be abolished – which Hermione eventually accomplishes during her career at the Ministry of Magic.

Crime can also lead to smaller, personal changes. The Malfoy family for example, having witnessed – and (some coercively) participated in – the Death Eaters' activities began to recognize the how dangerous their ideology could be. It was this recognition that led Draco to pretend he did not recognize Harry, Ron, and Hermione when they were brought to Malfoy manner by Snatchers and that led Narcissa to lie to Voldemort about Harry being dead in the forest. Were it not for the Death Eaters' horrific crimes, these new laws and ever-so-slight changes of heart would not have been possible.

"THEY ARE COMING"

There came a point, however, right before the beginning of the Second Wizarding War, when the Death Eaters' actions went beyond the utility to society outlined above. Their actions were not only disrupting the wizarding world, but spilling over and negatively affecting Muggles and the Muggle world as well. It is at this point that their criminality ceased to contribute to the functioning of society and began to disrupt it. The climax occurred on the day of Bill and Fleur's wedding when a coup d'état felled the Ministry of Magic. The Minister was killed, The Burrow (and other wizarding houses and communities we can assume) were raided and their occupants searched and interrogated. This was a moment of societal disarray; rules, norms, values, authority, social structure, everything was temporarily in flux. Pierre Bourdieu theorizes about such a change in the structure of society with his concept of the transformation of fields. He explains that "fields" are a way of viewing society as a set of structural locations that have a given relationship with other positions, regardless of the individual people who currently occupy the positions. Conflict over control of the logic of the field – control over defining what is valued, important, what functions as social capital for social mobility, how different positions relate to one another, etc. – is an inherent feature as "occupants of these positions seek, individually or collective, to safeguard or improve their positions and impose the principles of hierarchization most favorable to their products" (Bourdieu and Wacquant 1992: 101). While some conflict is always present in fields, Bourdieu points out that when one group "[manages] to crush and annual the resistance and reactions of the dominated," then a "totalitarian regime" is reached; however in practice, this is "a limit that is never actually reached." (Bourdieu and Wacquant 1992: 102). What typically happens is that one group, and their logic of the field, is overthrown and replaced by another, as happened during the Second Wizarding War, and conflict continues.

Following the fall of the Ministry, the Death Eaters seized power and a new regime was established. Pius Thicknesse (under the Imperius curse) became Minister for Magic, and new committees were formed and new protocols were implemented at the Ministry. Snape was installed as headmaster of Hogwarts and new curriculum was instituted. The Death Eaters' norms, values and ideologies now held power and currency in society; theirs was now the logic of the field. For example, number of O.W.L.s or N.E.W.T.s someone received no longer mattered as cultural capital for career advancement; it was now "all about the kind of service [Voldemort] received, the level of devotion he was shown" (HBP 151). Most importantly, Voldemort and his Death Eaters now defined what was legal and what was illegal; and so it was not their behavior that was criminalized, but those of dissenters like the Order of the Phoenix and Dumbledore's Army. And like the Death Eaters before them, the new criminals and this new form of criminal activity were as necessary to the functioning of new social order as the old criminals and crimes were to the old order.

While the British wizarding world was under Voldemort's control, previously acceptable behaviors became criminalized. For example, while in the past few witches and wizards did so out of fear and remembrance of the horrors of the First Wizarding War, it was never actually illegal to say Voldemort's name until he came to power again during the Second Wizarding War. Criminalization of saying Voldemort's name demonstrates that in the new order there was a norm that Voldemort was to be given respect. At Hogwarts, attendance was previously voluntary; but under the new regime it became illegal *not* to attend if one was pure or half-blood and became illegal for Muggle-born witches and wizards *to* attend. These new crimes illustrate which social boundaries and identities mattered most in the new order. Also with regard to Muggle-borns, it was illegal to fail to register with newly formed Muggle-born Registration Committee. Committing the crime of not presenting oneself to the commission highlighted not only the new ruling norms and social boundaries of the society, but prevented an important social ritual: the interrogation and sentencing to prison of Muggle-borns for "stealing" magic. This "trial" served the same purpose for the new order as the trying and sentencing Death Eaters did under the old order. The ritual publicly affirmed what the society valued, symbolically and literally removed those who violated it (by actions or just existing) from the rest of the population, and built solidarity among the new ruling class. Witches and wizards breaking of this law, and that of Hogwarts compulsory attendance, led to occupational innovation in that the new job of Snatcher was created.

However, as with the Death Eaters before them, once crime reached a certain level it resulted in chaos rather than contributing to the functioning of society. Harry (DH 444-445) and Xenophilius Lovegood (HP7 part I) used Voldemort's name, breaking norms of respect. Muggle-borns like Hermione and Ted Tonks refused to present themselves to the Muggle-born Registration Commission, undermining social boundaries and identities and preventing solidarity rituals from taking place. Neville, Ginny, Luna and other students at Hogwarts continually found innovative ways to break the new rules and continue thwarting the Carrows' "education" efforts. By the time of the Battle of Hogwarts, the wizarding world was once again a society in structural limbo. During those epic hours, there was no collective consensus on right versus wrong, over who held valid authority, or what the hegemonic cultural values were. Resolution of this chaos – Harry's defeat of Lord Voldemort – resulted in social change. The dynamics of the field were solidified and the former (albeit soon to be improved) order, along with the former notion of crime, was reestablished.

NO FLAW IN THE PLAN

Most of the Death Eaters were the type of bad wizards Hagrid warned Harry about over dinner in the Leaky Cauldron. No sociologist would argue differently. However, in any given society crime will exist. It is a function of the fact that in no society do all members agree on everything. But as we have seen, crime ensures clearly defined norms and group boundaries, provides rituals to affirm these, and leads to innovation and social changes. What's more, we have seen that the functions of crime remain the same regardless of *what* is considered criminal. As a result, criminals are not a parasitic element on a healthy society but, quite to the contrary, are actually a normal and functional feature of one. So, in a way, we should thank dear Bellatrix and the other Death Eaters ... while sentencing them to Azkaban.

References

Blackburn, Simon. 2005. *Oxford Dictionary of Philosophy: New Edition*. Oxford: Oxford University Press

Bourdieu, Pierre and Loïc J. D Wacquant. 1992. *An Invitation to Reflexive Sociology*. Chicago, IL: The University of Chicago Press.

Burke, Peter. J. and Jan E. Stets. 2009. *Identity Theory*. Oxford: Oxford University Press

Durkheim, Emile. 1895. *The Rules of Sociological Methods*. Pp. 31-166 in *Durkheim: The Rules of Sociological Methods and selected texts on Sociology and its Method*, Steven Lukes (ed.) W.D. Halls (trans.) 1982. New York, NY: Free Press

Durkheim, Emile. 1897. *Suicide: A study in sociology*, George Simpson (ed.) John A. Spaulding and George Simpson (trans.) 1951 [1979]. New York, NY: Free Press

Kidd, Dustin. 2007. "Harry Potter and the functions of popular culture." *The Journal of Popular Culture, 40* (1): 69-90

Reiner, Robert. 1984. "Crime, law, and deviance: The Durkheim legacy," Pp. 175-201 in *Durkheim and Modern Sociology*. Edited by S. Fenton. Cambridge: Cambridge University Press

Rousseau, Jean-Jacques. 1762 [1968]. *The Social Contract, Or Principles of Political Right*. Baltimore MD: Penguin Books.

PART II
INSTITUTIONS

"I suppose your parents will go hungry for a month to pay for that lot"

RECIPROCITY, RECOGNITION AND MORAL WORTH IN THE WIZARDING ECONOMY

DANIEL R. SMITH

PREMISE – "LITTLE TYKE WANTS HIS MONEY'S WORTH"

In both the Muggle and wizarding worlds there are assumptions about how to be good people. Harry's Cousin Dudley's reaction to his birthday presents is a good example of what can be perceived as moral worthiness. When Dudley realises that he has been given two less presents than the previous year, he is petulant and acts like the spoilt eleven-year-old brat that he is. Aunt Petunia's reaction to her son's distress and outrage is to pander to him, "we'll buy you another *two* presents while we're out today" (SS 21). Many would agree that this is bad parenting. As a sociologist I ask myself, why is Dudley's insistence to having more presents treated like it is? Why does Uncle Vernon say the "little tyke wants his money's worth, just like his father" (SS 22)? I propose that it has to do with what people in society believe is their moral worthiness to receive gifts and, in sociological terminology, what are called "commodities" (Marx 1976). Going shopping is, we shall see, much more about recognising someone's worth as a person, not merely wealth but their place in the social world they inhabit.

In this chapter we will discuss what it means to be good people and what counts in the eyes of others as praise worthy or shameful behaviour through shopping and the use of commodities in our everyday life. The Muggle consumer economy is a huge topic for sociologists and it has received widespread attention in the Muggle world. In the following sections I shall demonstrate how these issues taken up by sociologists of Muggle society are also evident and important to the wizarding world. We shall discuss that what one is really buying in shops is not so much magical stuff but also ideas about what is morally worthy for a wizarding society. A discussion of broomsticks can reveal all sorts of interesting assumptions within the wizarding world. So too can a visit to Gringotts bank.

INTRODUCTION: SOCIAL ORDER IS MORAL ORDER

Ever since it became a professional discipline, sociology has played the role of the diagnostician of social ills. Sociologist Emile Durkheim noticed that the problem with his society, 19th century France, was that it was susceptible to a social malaise created by a lack of social cohesion and solidarity. The emergence of industrialism and capitalism resulted in the radical re-organisation of society. For example, people now lived in nation-states, not the small political communities of the past. They lived further apart, meaning that trains were used instead of walking. Postmen delivered your messages instead of your next-of-kin. People didn't believe in the same God, and some did not even think there was a God. Contracts were used to tie people in relationships instead of kinship and family obligations. Indeed, the whole way of keeping people together was fragile. But as Durkheim was keen to point out, this so-called "modern age" developed a moral economy just as it developed an industrial economy (Durkheim 1933).

Durkheim argued that contractual ties and obligations between corporations are able to develop a new way of binding people together to keep society together. It was called "the cult of the individual." People were seen as individuals with rights, a basic sense of dignity and a sense of worthiness to liberties of civil life. Today our "cult of the individual" is more often the right to go shopping and reap the benefits of our economy's output (Davis 2008). Consumption is part of the moral fabric of our Muggle lives and a lot of the time, consumption is about recognition of self-worth interceded by our duty to other people.

CONSUMPTION IN THE WIZARDING WORLD

American sociologist Talcott Parsons (1951 and 1964), who followed in Durkheim's footsteps, stated the cult of the individual had important implications for what people said and did, and why they said and did them. Parsons analysed what sociologists call "reciprocity" (exchanges between people of "good morning" is an example of reciprocity) and recognition ("Well done, Mr. Potter!" is an example of recognition). These two things hold society together. What is behind these notions is a shared understanding of obligations people have to other people. But it is also an assumption about the moral worth we place upon other people. Harry is a person who is morally worthy of praise in wizarding society (and not just for saving the wizarding world). We can find examples of these reciprocities and recognition in his and others' acts of shopping.

Certainly, when it comes to going shopping, one is never shopping simply for oneself. Most consumption in everyday life comes from daily provisioning. Social anthropologist, Daniel Miller's (1995) study of shopping found that people's shopping lists consisted of fulfilling other people's needs: Knowing what your child's favourite flavour of Bertie Bott's Every Flavour Beans becomes less about the nice taste, more about making sure you're a good mother and you don't give your child ear wax flavour! Alas, says Dumbledore. Not supplying your family with provisions, it could be suggested, can be seen as an act of callousness and be seen as morally repugnant in the eyes of others. Poor Aunt Petunia's spoiling Dudley so much, thus making him into the brat he is, can be understood as a sign she is worried about being a bad mother.

Another thing about our shopping activities is that we make choices based not only on what we think about ourselves but, increasingly, on what others may think of us. In the early twentieth century, American sociologist Thorstein Veblen's book *The Theory of the Leisure Class* (1994) hypothesised that our buying choices all stem from what he called "pecuniary canons of tastes." What Veblen meant was that classes of people have the obligation to "keep up with the Joneses." Looking at suburbia, Veblen observed that seeing your neighbour as your equal means that if your neighbour buys a nicer car than yours, it puts you in shame about your own car and, more importantly, shame about yourself. Mr. and Mrs. Dursley constantly worry about their front lawn and keep it pristine for this very reason! Reciprocities in our buying choices are also a way of judging how good someone is. A good example of this is the case of the Weasleys and the Malfoys.

MALFOYS VS. WEASLEYS: THE MORALITY OF CONSUMPTION

An encounter at Flourish and Blotts exemplifies the fact that the laws of shopping are also the laws of social esteem and moral worth. When Draco Malfoy sees the Weasley family in the Flourish and Blotts, he responds to Ron's snarl of "Bet you're surprised to see Harry here, eh?" with the statement "Not as surprised as I am to see you in a shop, Weasley … I suppose your parents will go hungry for a month to pay for all those" (COS 61). The Weasley family is not very well off, and it's common knowledge that they struggle to make ends meet. Malfoy's comments highlight a key aspect of the sociology of consumption: If money is spent in one place, it cannot be spent anywhere else. He is therefore saying Ron's parents will be going hungry simply because they've entered a shop. Draco assumes the Weasleys will have to forego food in order to buy school books.

Malfoy's joke is an evil one precisely because he questions the Weasleys' ability to get by in life, thus linking consumption to one's ability to provide for ones dependents. Lucius Malfoy is similarly mean-spirited not just because he's a Death Eater but because he shows that the lack of social estimation he gives Mr. Weasley is related to, what he believes, is his failure to "be a good wizard." When Lucius makes jibes about Mr. Weasley's poor pay, it stems from his belief in his failure to be a good wizard. As he says, "Dear me, what's the use of being a disgrace to the name of wizard if they don't even pay you well for it" (COS 62). We see this opinion firmly related to consumption practices. Mr. Malfoy begins his interacting with Ron by commenting on how the Weasley's clothes are all hand-me-downs and books are second hand: "... red hair, vacant expressions, tattered second hand books, you must be the Weasleys" (HP2). Here we see illustrated the problem of consumption being not just about getting useful things. It's also about getting recognised as being worthy of respect and our ability to provide for ourselves and others. So money and consumption becomes sociologically translated into ones moral worth.

Lucius Malfoy has informed Draco's ideas about the wizarding world's status hierarchy. During one of their first encounters, Draco introduces Harry to the social hierarchy of the wizarding world. Just as his father had seen status stemming from appearance, Malfoy comments to Ron, "No need to ask who you are. Red hair and a hand-me-down robe. You must be a Weasley" (HP 1). He then turns to Harry and remarks, "You'll soon find that some wizarding families are better than others" (ibid). Harry has come right up against the status order through consumption of clothing. Harry makes his moral judgement clear, saying he can figure out "the wrong sort for myself thanks" (ibid). Harry rejects what social theorist Jean Baudrillard (1998) called the "order of signs." Seeing robes as a mark of esteem and moral worth is to view people through arbitrary signs, Baudrillard would argue. Harry clearly rejects Malfoy's ideology of the choice of clothes as a sign of moral worth.

Within this ideology, since consumption choices translate money into moral worth, they can be used to assert moral superiority over others. At the Quidditch World Cup, Draco brags to the Weasleys that "Father and I are in the Minister's box" (HP4). Lucius swiftly stabs him with his walking cane and spits, "Don't boast, Draco. There's no need with these people" (ibid). Not only are the Weasleys poor, they do not deserve acknowledgement.

Understanding our consumption as also moral worth is to understand what is considered a legitimate claim to participate in society. To be a wizard or a witch is to be a wand bearer. What marks wizards out from other magical creatures, such as Goblins, is that they use magic through their wands. Buying a wand is buying your claim to participate in wizarding society. When it came to the horrific trials conducted by the Death Eater controlled Ministry of Magic, the stripping of a Muggle-born wizard of their wand becomes a ritual of dramatic social exclusion. It denies one's claim to be a member of the wizarding world. On trial, Mary Cattermole states, "I didn't take it ... I bought it when I was eleven years old. It *chose* me" (DH 260, emphasis in original). Mary's statement is a claim to legitimate membership: You can't buy a wand that doesn't choose you! But Umbridge denies her: "Wands only choose witches or wizards. You are not a witch" (DH 261).

We have seen that consumption is a moral order whereby we sustain recognition of ourselves, or lack of recognition, with the example of the Weasleys, Malfoys, and Mary Cattermole. But what then do these reciprocities count for? How do we become recognised as well-regarded, esteemed and honoured members of society? A good example comes from shopping for broomsticks.

HARRY VS. DRACO: RECOGNITION IS MORAL WORTH PROVED

When Harry gets his Nimbus 2000 he soon learns that he's a fantastic flyer and even better Seeker. It's in his blood, as Hermione tells him. We can take from Harry's flying skills that he's able to contribute to the Gryffindor team and contribute to winning matches against other Houses. Harry's reciprocity is Seeking, he finds the snitch; Fred and George "stop him from getting blooded up" (HP1) as Beaters; Katie, Angelina and Alicia score goals as Chasers; and Wood, as Keeper, defends his teams' hoops against the opponents' Chasers. They all have a status on the team and a role to play. Harry's broomstick, while advertised as a wonderful, exciting commodity (like all Muggle daily appliances in the home and on TV), is essential to his being a good seeker. Harry's broomstick, not simply his seeker skills, gains him recognition as worthy of being on the team.

As we have seen, the sociologist Thorstein Veblen is responsible for observing that everyday objects can be symbols of wealth and gain us recognition from our peers, but also they can assert ferocity. Speaking of the Victorian walking-stick, Veblen (1994: 162) turns it into a barbaric weapon so people can recognise the gentleman as worthy of deference and respect:

> The walking-stick serves the purpose of an advertisement that the bearer's hands are employed otherwise than in useful effort, and it therefore has utility as an evidence of leisure. But it is also a weapon, and it meets a felt need of barbarian man on that ground. The handling of so tangible and primitive a means of offence is very comforting to anyone who is gifted with even a moderate share of ferocity.

We could argue that broomsticks in the wizarding world can be seen as evidence of this "predatory" element of wizard culture. While they're used in a barbaric game, as Hermione might view a game of wizard's chess, they're essential to be seen as a person of respect and being recognised as such. Harry's Nimbus was a symbol of his ability to prove his pre-eminence on the pitch, his prowess as a player.

Yet we encounter an interesting case of fraudulent consumption in Harry's second year when, to everyone's surprise, Draco Malfoy enters the Slytherin team as their new seeker. How did Draco manage this? He bribed the

Slytherin Quidditch team with the Nimbus 2001s. We could say that Malfoy misunderstood the walking-stick as symbol that wealth had been earned, that broomsticks are the mark of a good flyer. He thought it was the means to gain prowess and status, but really it *proves* it. Malfoy thinks the *broomstick itself* will outdo his peers. As Marcus Flint says, "Very latest model. Only came out last month....I believe it outstrips the old Nimbus Two Thousand series by a considerable amount" (COS 111). Flint too engages in what Karl Marx called the "fetish of commodities" (1976:163ff): People mistake the consumer product as having value as a part of its very nature, when in reality the broom itself is just a lump of wood. Instead we have to remember that the broomstick's brilliance comes from the brilliance of the wizard using it. As the perceptive Hermione puts it, "At least no one on the Gryffindor team had to *buy* their way in … *They* got in on pure talent" (COS 112, emphasis in original). Malfoy's broomstick does not show his prowess as a great wizard of the Quidditch pitch, rather his bribery. It was a fraudulent thing to do.

Hermione, clever as always, understands that people can't just buy their moral worth and social status, as sociologists have been able to tell us. Hermione's judgements also tell us something important about the morality of buying things: That we can't buy everything (no matter how many lovely sweets Honeydukes has on offer).

HARRY VS. DUDLEY: MORAL RESPONSIBILITY IN CONSUMPTION

The places in which we Muggles do our shopping are overloaded with fantastic trinkets and offerings. They have been said to be so exciting that they've been labelled "cathedrals of consumption" (Ritzer 1999). They offer such wonderful promises, and we imagine ourselves using them as we gaze upon them. As sociologist Georg Simmel (1989) observed, the money economy of modern society allowed unrestrained freedoms in man's will. Harry isn't exempt. Upon witnessing the Firebolt, Harry knew that he shouldn't buy it "when he had a very good broom already....but he returned, almost every day after that, just to look at [it]" (POA 52). Harry also encounters his fellow Gryffindor's, Dean and Seamus, in the shop later on "ogling the Firebolt" (POA 55). The broomstick is a fantastic piece of consumer dreams and fantasies (Campbell 1987), but it is also understood as costing too much money.

Harry understands that buying the broom is a big investment and that he shouldn't waste money on something he doesn't need. What is sociologically important is that too high a level of shopping is damaging to social order and the reciprocities we are engaged in – how would Harry afford all his school books if he spent his money on a Firebolt (especially since the price of this broomstick isn't even disclosed !)? (POA 51).

The sociologist understands these thoughts as indicative of a socially shared morality. This is a morality which is preached in Diagon Alley itself. As Harry enters the wizard bank Gringotts and goes down to the vaults, he sees upon a silver door a message of warning:

> Enter, stranger, but take heed
> Of what awaits the sin of greed,
> For those who take, but do not earn
> Must pay most dearly in their turn ...
> (SS 72).

Explicitly here, the guardians of the wizarding world's monies are employing a moral judgement about rightful senses of social justice. It makes clear that legitimate and sanctioned acts of shopping are to be morally justifiable not just to oneself, but also to society. If one is greedy, or even a thief, he or she jeopardises the foundations of social order and reciprocities. Going shopping every day leads to an inability to perform as a regular member of society, and therefore, Parsons would label overspending as a form deviance. What turns Fred and George from tricksters who, in Mrs. Weasley's eyes, overindulge in Zonko's Joke Shop products, is their transformation into savvy businessmen who contribute to society (even during the dark times of Voldemort's second rise).

It seems clear that the best candidate for the irresponsible, deviant consumer is Cousin Dudley. Recall his inability to appreciate his parents' gifts, demanding more and more presents than the previous year. Remember also that Harry used to live under the stairs due to the fact that the Dursley's spare room was Dudley's toy room! A whole devoted room to the vertiginous, needless spending his parents had put upon him. Dudley is in dire need of a modern day Muggle lifestyle specialist, one of the wise aunties who try to tame the shopaholic. Dudley's over-consumption is subversive and, as warned by sign at Gringotts, he "must pay most dearly" for his over indulgences (i.e., "the sin of greed") (SS 72). If we recall the actions of Hagrid when Dudley scarfs down Harry's 11th birthday cake while he's not looking, we see society's sense of justice being acted out through the wand: Hagrid's swift flick of his wand gives Dudley a curly pig's tail that pokes out the back of his trousers, revealing him for the very animal over-consumption has made him.

CONCLUSION

The lessons that the sociology of consumption are able to reveal is that a clear set of moral judgements and processes of recognition are at work in the most mundane acts. Choosing what is worthy to buy (get your book list first, and just fantasize about the broomstick), displaying the products in front of your peers (and the social failure of buying the broomsticks to bribe people) all highlight this moral order. Of course, simply being a good member of society through earning what you buy, and not being a greedy pig like Dudley, is a valuable lesson. Investigating what people, Muggle or wizard, do with things is a good way to answer questions of what is morally worthy to us.

Sociologists who study consumption are always asking these questions. A classic study of "tastes" for consumer goods is Pierre Bourdieu's *Distinction* (1986). It tells us that what is being negotiated when we Muggles listen to certain types of music, eat certain types of food or even play tennis on holiday is actually a sense of the proper ways to do things. Playing tennis wearing a Lacoste t-shirt and Bermuda shorts becomes, sociologically, a struggle over defining the right and wrong ways of doing things and, in so doing, creates social divisions and exclusive places for exclusive people. All through the arbitrary classifications of the world of consumer goods!

Buying things is often about upholding moral worth in society. By looking at consumption patterns in the wizarding world, we Muggles are able to better understand our own.

REFERENCES

Baudrillard, Jean. 1998. *The Consumer Society: myths and structures*. London: Sage.

Bourdieu, Pierre. 1986. *Distinction: a social critique of judgement and taste*. London: Routledge.

Campbell, Colin. 1987. *The Romantic Ethic and the Spirit of Modern Consumerism*. Oxford: Blackwell.

Davis, Mark. 2008. *Freedom & Consumerism*. Aldershot: Ashgate.

Durkheim, Émile. 1933. *The Division of Labour in Society*. New York, NY: Free Press.

Marx, Karl. 1976. *Captial, Volume 1*. London: Penguin.

Miller, Daniel. 1995. *A Theory of Shopping*. Cambridge: Polity.

Parsons, Tallcot. 1951. *The Social System*. London: Routledge.

—. 1964. *Social Structure and Personality*. London: Free Press of Glencoe.

Ritzer, Georg. 1999. *Enchanting a Disenchanted World*. Thousand Oaks, CA: Pine Forge.

Simmel, Georg. 1989. *The Philosophy of Money*. London: Routledge.

Veblen, Thorstein. 1994. *The Theory of the Leisure Class*. Mineola, NY: Dover Publications.

"You Have Never Treated Harry as a Son"

THE POLITICS OF MOTHERHOOD
IN THE WIZARDING WORLD

TANYA COOK

"Dumbledore paused, and although his voice remained light and calm, and he gave no obvious sign of anger, Harry felt a kind of chill emanating from him and noticed that the Dursleys drew very slightly closer together. 'You did not do as I asked. You have never treated Harry as a son. He has known nothing but neglect and often cruelty at your hands. The best that can be said is that he has at least escaped the appalling damage you have inflicted upon the unfortunate boy sitting between you" (HPB 55).

INTRODUCTION

During his visit to No. 4 Privet Drive Harry's penultimate summer with his aunt and uncle, Dumbledore finally sanctions the Dursleys for their terrible treatment of Harry. Uncle Vernon responds defensively but Petunia is described as being "oddly flushed" after Dumbledore's reprimand. As self-centered (or shall we say Dudley-centered) as she can be, Petunia demonstrates an awareness that she has failed as Harry's adoptive mother. Furthermore, Dumbledore indicates that she has failed her biological son, Dudley, through a pathological over-mothering. This encounter highlights just one of the many examples of what I call "the politics of motherhood." The role of "mother" in the wizarding world carries with it specific sociocultural expectations of what a mother is or should (or should not) be.

In this chapter I focus on the mothers Harry encounters and demonstrate the pervasiveness of norms related to motherhood. Three mothers: Lily Potter, Petunia Dursley, and Molly Weasley can be viewed as illustrating best, worst, and second-best case scenarios for mothering, respectively. I will illustrate the concept of social roles as an interactive social construction. Drawing on West and Zimmerman's (1987) concept of "doing gender," I argue that through "doing motherhood" the women listed above are variously constrained and enabled by their mother role performances. The role of mother is further shown to be a re-constructed and re-negotiated one as Harry's generation grows into adulthood. Finally, drawing on the concept of othermothers (Hill Collins 1990) and Ruddick's *Maternal Thinking* (1989), we see exactly how social the role of mother is in that "mother" does not have to equal biological mother or even woman.

SOCIAL ROLES AND SOCIALIZATION

Sociologists developed the concept of socialization in order to explain how individuals internalize norms or guidelines for behaviors that are socially accepted. Borrowing from the language of the theater, social roles are parts individuals play out in society that are governed by norms. Role performances are then subject to judgment and criticism by other members of society based on how well one adheres to normative behavioral guidelines as was illustrated in the example which began this essay (Bankston et al. 2000). Individuals possess many roles which may be encompassed in a role set (Merton 1957). Roles have been described as "the dynamic aspect of status" (Linton, quoted in Turner 2001). Here, status is the position; and role is the performance or behavior that is expected of an individual in that position. A given individual will have multiple roles within their repertoire on which to draw in a specific, context-influenced interaction. Some roles, however, "...are more dominant than others" (Zurcher 1983: 230), and as such will be arranged hierarchically with certain roles carrying precedence over others. For example, the role of mother trumps other social roles in various interactions that Harry observes.

Roles link what are sometimes called the macro and micro levels of sociological analysis. The individual (micro level) acts out a role performance that is structured or defined in some ways by larger social institutions (macro level). The individual's performance may in turn affect the larger social institution in which it takes place. I draw on West and Zimmerman's (1987) concept of "doing gender" and Ruddick's (1989) theoretical argument for a kind of thinking defined by motherly activities to highlight the dynamic, interactive, and pervasive characteristics of the mother role as exemplified by the mothers Harry knows.

"MOTHER" AS ROLE PERFORMANCE

The mothers Harry encounters are almost always seen by him as performing a "mother" role, not as women, wives, or workers. For example, Molly Weasley demonstrates her status as mother by performing her role in a way that corresponds to normative expectations of mothers as responsible for most of the feeding work done by families. When Ron and his twin trouble-making brothers Fred and George rescue Harry from a sort of house arrest imposed by the Dursleys, they use their father's illegally bewitched flying car to do so. They then attempt to sneak into The Burrow without their mother noticing, although she catches them in the act. After scolding the boys for taking the car and leaving without asking, Molly insists that they all, especially Harry, sit down and eat breakfast. The boys sit down to eat, are joined by their brother Percy, and as Molly continues to cook and serve breakfast, her husband Arthur Weasley arrives. Arthur asks who Harry is and then asks when he arrived. Molly answers while still standing at the kitchen stove: "This morning. Your sons flew that enchanted car of yours to Surrey and back last night" (HP2). She has already scolded the boys but looks to Arthur for further reprimand, implying that although mothers hand out discipline along with breakfast, the father's authority takes precedence over hers. Arthur asks the boys, "Did you really? How did it go?" (ibid). Molly then hits him on the arm, a physical punishment for Arthur's failure to perform the fatherly disciplinarian role to her satisfaction. He then reprimands the boys, albeit weakly.

There are many interesting things happening in this interaction. Firstly, Molly and Arthur demonstrate understanding and empathy for the reasons behind their children's rule-breaking. Molly's scolding makes the boys feel shame for their actions but is largely symbolic. Although she understands (along with Arthur) the reasons why they did what they did, as a "good" mother she still must reprimand them according to sociocultural expectations that parents are responsible for their children's behavior and must discipline rule-breaking in order to appropriately socialize them. Secondly, Molly reinforces motherhood as a performed role when she serves everyone breakfast and continues to stand in service while the other family members (excluding Ginny who is hiding from Harry) eat. Thirdly, Molly's behavior demonstrates the "social" in social role. Her role is carried out via interaction with others who are also performing social roles – Arthur as father and husband, Ron, Fred, George and Percy as sons and Harry as guest. Social theorist Simmel labeled this aspect of social roles "reciprocity"[1] and argued that roles have meaning through interaction (Levine 1971).

Lending further support to the idea of motherhood as a social role performance is the evidence that mothers are judged by broader society not only for what they do but for who their children are. Returning to the quote at the start of this chapter, Dumbledore was judging Petunia's (and Vernon's) parenting based on Dudley, the object of their parenting. Petunia, as mother to Dudley and Harry is either hot or cold. She either over-mothers or under-mothers. Dumbledore's comments indicate that over-mothering in this case, judging by the final product, is worse. Harry is a better person than Dudley.

What is interesting is that Dumbledore himself indicates that he has known about the abuse Harry suffered under the Dursleys' roof all along and

---

1   While there is some overlap, the word reciprocity, as used here and by Simmel, refers to the defining of social roles and meaning via interaction, not the Parsonian concepts of exchange and social order that were presented in the previous chapter.

yet he abdicates responsibility; after all, *he wrote them a letter.* The Dursleys were tasked with the unexpected burden of a raising a second child who scared the wits out of them. This is not to defend the Dursleys' cruel and unusual treatment of Harry; instead it is to point out the differences in behavioral expectations based on the role one occupies. Dumbledore in his role as Headmaster was performing perhaps beyond expectation; and there is the matter of the blood kin protection which he explains to McGonagall who objects to Harry's placement as a baby and finally to Harry shortly before his death. But we expect better from the Dursleys, particularly Petunia in the mother role because, after all, good mothers do not lock their children in cupboards under the stairs or allow others to do so.

EXPANDING SOCIAL ROLES INTO DYNAMIC INTERACTION

West and Zimmerman (1987: 127) in their influential paper "Doing Gender," argued that role as a concept may be too limiting in that it "...obscures the work that is involved in producing gender in everyday activities." Looking at the mothers Harry encounters, I would make a similar argument for mother as a situated activity that an individual performs in interaction with others. The status of an individual as mother also "...is created through interaction and at the same time structures that interaction" (131). West and Zimmerman's analytical shift helps to expand the concept of roles and make them more dynamic in that performance in a role can also change and challenge the meaning of the role itself. Mothers are mothers not because of who they are but because of what they do in social contexts with other social actors. The focus shifts to role as *inter*action versus internalized value system that guides behavior. West and Zimmerman are also making the argument that gender is more expansive than a static role concept because gender overrides the boundaries of a given social context. For example, women engineers are never judged simply as engineers but always first as "women" acting in a socially-accepted (or not) feminine way. Similarly, Molly Weasley is never seen outside of her role as mother. Motherhood, like gender, pervades, bleeding through the context-boundaries of other role performance spaces. Molly, a member of the Order, tries to screen off the Order's activity from Harry despite the fact they are staying at Order headquarters and despite the fact that Harry's godfather, Sirius Black, objects to keeping him out of the loop. Molly's status as a mother changes the interaction and further she displays "motherly" protective behavior in opposition to Sirius who wants to treat Harry as an autonomous decision-making adult. Molly, in wanting to act as a good mother should, interacts with the other members of the Order in specific way; and her behavior then reflexively defines what a "good" mother is. Furthermore,

Molly's role as mother not only extends beyond the boundaries of her home into another social setting (her membership in the Order), it also extends beyond the relationships with her own biological children to the orphaned Harry. Molly's interactions with the other members of the Order are both structured by and structure her role performance as mother. Her status as mother cannot be left at the door of The Burrow but instead affects all of her other interactions.

Gladstein (2004) argues that the wizarding world represents a world in which the goals of liberal feminism are achieved and one finally witnesses true equality between genders. From Gladstein (2004: 59): "Each [witch or wizard] is judged individually by what kind of person he or she is, and each [witch or wizard] is given the opportunity to be either good or evil..." As I have argued, however, mothers are judged differently than women. Harry may be subject to abuse by both villains and villainesses (e.g., Umbridge, Lestrange) but none of the latter are mothers; however, when Petunia abuses Harry she is specifically judged by her social role of adoptive mother.

This conceptualization of motherhood as an expanded, interactive role is supported by social science research on the "motherhood penalty." Correll et al. (2007) found in an a lab experiment that varying only parental status between pairs of similar resumes correlated with lower offered starting salaries for mothers versus non-mothers and for mothers versus fathers. Test resume evaluators offered mothers an $11,000 lower starting salary than they offered non-mothers and a $13,000 lower starting salary than they offered fathers. By contrast, in addition to being offered a higher starting salary than mothers, childless women were offered a higher starting salary (by $4,000) than was offered to childless men and only $2,000 less (compared to mothers' $13,000 less) than fathers. The authors explained the results as a conflict between sociocultural expectations of worker versus mother due to lower perceptions of competence and commitment for mothers. The juxtaposition of the social role of worker versus member of the female gender category (West and Zimmerman 1987) posed no such conflict.

In a follow up study, Benard and Correll (2010) found that female testers rated mothers who were presented as committed and competent workers as less likable and warm than their non-mother counterparts. Male participants, however, rated successful mothers more highly on interpersonal variables than female testers did. This difference may suggest a greater internalized prioritization of the mother role for female testers and therefore harsher judgment for women who are perceived to have chosen the professional over the mother role. The authors argue that this experiment shows evidence of prescriptive stereotyping of mothers. In other words, when mothers fail to conform to the role performance expectations of mother and instead succeed in role performances as workers, they are still socially sanctioned (judged) by their mother role (Benard and Correll 2010). The results of these studies support the idea of motherhood as a pervasive social role.

In theory it would be possible to assess the activities of the mothers Harry knows separate from their status as mother; however, as we have seen, mothers' behavior/actions in any context are judged according to broader values of what a mother is and what a mother does. For example, although Narcissa Malfoy may be on the wrong side, she displays her dominant role of mother when she implores Severus Snape to help protect her son, Draco. Narcissa "crumpled, falling at [Snape's] feet, sobbing and moaning on the floor. 'My only son... my only son...'" (HBP 35). Her sister, Bellatrix, on the other hand chastises her saying: "You should be proud!... If I had sons, I would be glad to give them up to the service of the Dark Lord!" (ibid). Narcissa's performance of the mother role is in stark contrast to Bellatrix's statement that she would willingly sacrifice her children (sons). Here Narcissa acts according to expected norms of what a mother does – she protects her children, even if it means defying Voldemort, and in so doing reinforces the notion that good mothers will risk their own lives to protect their children. Narcissa becomes an even more sympathetic witch when she lies to Voldemort about Harry being dead. Her role as mother wins out in the conflict between her role as mother and role as Voldemort supporter, further supporting the conceptualization of motherhood as a pervasive role.

HARRY'S GENERATION AND CHANGING MOTHERHOOD ROLES

Through enactment of social roles, individuals change and evolve their role performances and redefine what it means to be an occupant of a status position (dynamic). In her critique of West and Zimmerman (1987), Deutsch (2007) points out that by focusing on the production of gender as a verb in nearly every interactional context, the authors do not sufficiently focus on how structural changes affect "(un)doing gender." Also, although some social conservatives advocate a return to the family values of the 1950s with its normative male breadwinner and female homemaker division of labor, this ideal did not apply to non-white and non-middle class families. Motherhood, then, is a social role that is structured by the institutions of class and race (Hill Collins 1990). Molly Weasley's role as a poor wizard mother entails very differently daily activities than Narcissa Malfoy's role as a rich wizard mother. Molly does not have the luxury of house-elf labor to rely on and she must perform magic spells to facilitate keeping up on housework.

Harry, having been born in 1980, encounters mothers who for the most part do not work outside of the home. Currently in the U.K., however, 68%

of women with dependent children work in the paid labor market (Office for National Statistics 2008) and anti-labor force discrimination and sexual harassment laws represent significant structural change. This generation of currently working mothers is reflected in the re-defining of the mother role for Harry's female contemporaries. For example, both Ginny and Hermione work outside of the home after marrying and having children (Rowling 2007). Gladstein (2004) argued that the co-ed population of professional Quidditch players suggested gender equality. When Ginny becomes a mother, she retires from a successful career as a professional Quidditch player in order to work as a sports reporter for the *Daily Prophet*. Perhaps Ginny's motivation for job change reflects what many women experience as role conflict and time constraints between the role of mother and the socially-expected duties that go along with it (housework, care work, feeding work, etc.), termed the "Second Shift" by sociologist Arlie Russell Hochschild, and the role of professional. In Hochschild's (2003) study, women often cut back on their work hours outside of the home perhaps in order to accommodate second shift duties. U.K. Labour Force Survey (Office for National Statistics 2008) results indicate that 38% of women with children versus four percent of men with children work part time suggesting support for Hochschild's (2003) findings.

Hermione and Ginny may represent "transgressive" versus "transformational" change in that although individual women may challenge gendered norms the overall gendered distribution of power remains unchallenged (Deutsch 2007). While it is certainly normal and normative for childless women to work outside of the home there is a lag between large percentages of mothers working outside of the home and normative acceptance of this trend (Correll et al. 2007, Benard and Correll 2010). This is sometimes called the "stalled revolution" (Hochschild 2003). We would need to look for evidence of the "undoing" of gender (Deutsch 2007) and shifting definitions of motherhood as more women continue to pursue post-secondary degrees.

Harry Potter and his OtherMothers

Theoretically, we can label anyone a "mother" who performs the mother role (Ruddick 1989). Indeed, Harry is the object of "mothering" by various "othermothers," people who may or may not be biologically related to the children for whom they provide some child care responsibilities (Hill Collins 1990). Perhaps the person who comes first to mind is Harry's othermother Petunia Dursley. Harry also receives othermothering from Molly Weasley and Professor McGonagall who care for his physical and emotional needs at various times. Care from Harry's othermothers demonstrates that what is lacking in Petunia's care for Harry is the love and emotional attachment we expect from someone in the mother role.

Othermothers need not be women, however. As Ruddick (1989: 17) expresses: "To be a 'mother' is to take upon oneself the responsibility of child care, making its work a regular and substantial part of one's working life." It is the social expectation of responsibility and an individual's response of taking on the goals of preservation and growth via acceptable methods that makes a person a mother (Ruddick 1989). From Bruce (1999: 22): "We expect mothers to behave in maternal ways to display appropriately maternal sentiments. We prescribe a cluster of norms or rules that govern the role of mother." One non-female othermother figure for Harry is Rubeus Hagrid. Hagrid routinely feeds and expresses concern for Harry and his friends' well-being. In fact, Hagrid's mothering extends beyond the boundaries of humanity to various, often dangerous magical creatures (e.g., Norbert, Aragog).

While Hagrid can be seen as one of Harry's othermothers, Sirius Black, although caring deeply for Harry, cannot be called a mother. Sirius treats Harry as more of a friend or companion than a child, which Harry at times greatly appreciates. Sirius encourages rebelliousness in Harry and argues in favor of treating Harry as an autonomous adult, capable of making decisions about putting himself in harm's way. Also, unlike Hagrid or McGonagall, Sirius does not "do motherhood" in that he does not physically provide for or discipline Harry. In this way, Sirius fails to conform to normative expectations of mother as protector, sheltering children from an unsafe and dangerous world. As pointed out previously, it is Molly Weasley and also perhaps Minerva McGonagall who perform the mother role in this sheltering dimension.

LILY POTTER - THE PERFECT MOTHER?

While Molly is perhaps the "best" mother Harry knows, Harry's own mother, Lily Potter, is the epitome of what a mother "should" be about – love and sacrifice. In giving her life for her son, Lily performs the ultimate sacrifice and does the most any mother can ever do for her child. Her sacrifice ends up saving the world because if Lily had not chosen to die for Harry, Voldemort would not have been defeated. Lily's example, while noble, is difficult to aspire to. It is arguably harder to live for your children than to die for them. Lily does not have to "do" the oftentimes tedious daily chores of motherhood role performance. She does not have to pick up Harry's dirty socks or listen to him complain about what she prepared for dinner. She will never make him treacle tart for his birthday.

What does it mean for understanding the meaning of motherhood as a social role that this level of sacrifice on Lily's part is expected and revered or at least not questioned? If Lily had stood aside or if she had shown hesitation we would judge her harshly. Furthermore, Lily's perfection is not limited to her unselfish final act. Harry never encounters evidence that Lily was anything but a model witch and never hears someone speaking ill of her – except for Petunia who is jealous of what Lily *is,* not necessarily critical of what she *does.* While glimpses into Snape's memory reveal James, Harry's father, to have had a reckless and sometimes cruel streak, Lily is remembered as Snape's defender and Horace Slughorn's favorite student. Indeed, Lily is so loving that her love not only saves her son, but she forever endears herself to Snape who despite hating Harry's father is fundamentally motivated by his love for the girl, Lily, who was kind to him. In society we expect different behaviors from women than from men; and even before they are mothers, or even if they never become mothers, women are expected to demonstrate compassion and protectiveness of the weak and the marginalized. Lily perfectly embodies this expectation. This expectation of gender-based compassion for children is also what makes Umbridge and Lestrange, who fail to demonstrate it, so despicable.

If Lily's sacrifice, bravery, and protectiveness are what define her as a "good" mother in terms of taking her role performance in service of societal norms to its logical conclusion, then her motherly analog is Narcissa Malfoy. As mentioned previously, Narcissa shows bravery and protectiveness of Draco in her interactions with her husband, Snape and later Lord Voldemort. Narcissa defies Lucius' wish that Draco attend Durmstrang and instead insists he be sent to Hogwarts (GOF 165). She asks Snape for help despite the Dark Lord forbidding her to speak of Draco's mission. At the Battle of Hogwarts she is completely unarmed due to giving her wand to Draco to use since he had lost his to Harry during the Skirmish at Malfoy Manor (DH 628). Through her actions she demonstrates that, despite being a Voldemort supporter, she loves her son as much as Lily loved Harry. Narcissa and Bellatrix's relationship to Draco is similar to the complementary good/bad mother pair of Lily and Petunia with respect to Harry. Bellatrix and Petunia, although biologically related to Draco and Harry, respectively, fail to live up to sociocultural expectations of what a good mother or othermother is/does. Bellatrix has no problems with Draco being in harm's way; Petunia treats Harry as more of a burden than a son. Dichotomizing good/bad mother of Lily/Petunia and Narcissa/Bellatrix illustrates Simmel's (1971) concept of "dualism." It is through the bad examples that we understand what behaviors constitute the appropriate role performance of the good mother and vice versa.

Conclusion

Examining the mothers Harry knows dramatically illustrates a sociological understanding of motherhood as a dynamic social role performance. Motherhood as a social role is shown to be dynamic in two ways. Firstly, mothers' interactions with Harry and others allow them to be evaluated based on their role performance. Secondly, the definition of motherhood as a role changes over generations while continuing to imply norms and values that constrain and enable the actions of mothers. Motherhood as a social role is pervasive in that individuals who are mothers are not viewed independently of their role, irrespective of context. Finally, motherhood as a role is social in that one does not have to biologically be a mother or even a woman to perform the mother role.

REFERENCES

Benard, Stephen and Shelley J. Correll. 2010. "Normative Discrimination and the Motherhood Penalty." *Gender and Society* 24 (5): 616 - 646.

Bruce, Steve. 2000. *Sociology: A Very Short Introduction.* New York, NY: Oxford University Press.

Correll, Shelley J., Stephen Benard, and In Paik. 2007. "Getting A Job: Is there a Motherhood Penalty?" *American Journal of Sociology* 112: 1297-1338.

Deutsch, Francine. 2007. "Undoing Gender." *Gender and Society* 21 (1): 106-127.

Gladstein, Mimi. 2004. "Feminism and Equal Opportunity: Hermione and the Women of Hogwarts," Pp.49 – 59 in *Harry Potter and Philosophy: If Aristotle Ran Hogwarts,* edited by David Baggett and Shawn E. Klein. Chicago, IL: Open Court.

Hill Collins, Patricia. 1990. *Black Feminist Thought: Knowledge, Consciousness, and the Politics of Empowerment.* Sydney, Australia: Allen and Unwin.

Hochschild, Arlie Russell with Anne Machung. 2003. *The Second Shift.* New York, NY: Penguin.

Merton, Robert K. 1957. "The Role Set: Problems in Sociological Theory." *British Journal of Sociology* 8: 106-120.

Office for National Statistics. 2008. "Labour Force Survey, Q2 2008."

Rowling, J.K. 2007. US Book Tour (http://bibliophilists.wordpress.com/2007/10/22/highlights of-jk-rowlings-us-book-tour/).

Ruddick, Sara. 1995. *Maternal Thinking: Toward a Politics of Peace.* Boston, MA: Beacon Press.

Levine, Donald. 1971. "Introduction." Pp. x-ixv in George Simmel's *On Individuality and Social Forms.* Edited by Donald Levine. Chicago, IL: University of Chicago Press.

Stryker, Sheldon. 2001. "Traditional Symbolic Interactionism, Role Theory, and Structural Symbolic Interactionism: The Road to Identity Theory" Pp. 211 - 232 in *Handbook of Sociological Theory.* Edited by J. H. Turner. New York, NY: Kluwer Academic/Plenum Publishers.

Turner, Jonathan. 2001. "Sociological Theory Today." Pp. 1-17 in *Handbook of Sociological Theory.* Edited by J. H. Turner. New York, NY: Kulwer Academic/Plenum Publishers.

Turner, Ralph. 2001. "Role Theory." Pp. 233-254 in *Handbook of Sociological Theory.* Edited by J.H. Turner. New York, NY: Kluwer Academic/Plenum Publishers.

West, Candace and Don H. Zimmerman. 1987. "Doing Gender." *Gender and Society,* 1(2): 125-151.

Weber, Ann L. 2000. "Role Conflict and Role Strain" Pp.400-405 in *Sociology Basics Vol 2*. Edited by C. Bankston III. Hackensack, NJ: Salem Press.

Zurcher, Louis. 1983. *Social Roles: Conformity, Conflict, and Creativity*. Beverly Hills, CA: Sage.

"She'd Have Been Locked Up in St. Mungo's for Good"

MAGICAL MALADIES AND MEDICINE

DUSTIN KIDD

INTRODUCTION

When Albus Dumbledore's brother, Aberforth, finally explained to Harry, Ron and Hermione the mystery surrounding Ariana Dumbledore's life and sad death, the story he told was dark and foreboding. Six-year-old Ariana had been innocently performing the magic that came so naturally to her when three Muggle boys spied her through a hedge. Curious, they asked her to show them how to perform the tricks. As a young witch, lacking in magical education, she wasn't able to repeat her magic and this angered them enough that they attacked her. According to Aberforth, "they got a bit carried away trying to stop the little freak doing it" (DH 564). How exactly the boys get carried away is not clear, and the language that Aberforth uses leaves open some terrifying possibilities; but the attack is so brutal that Ariana went mad inside, and would explode with frightening bursts of magic thereafter.

Surely in such a moment the wizarding world would offer help and aid to heal Ariana's physical and mental anguish. But the Dumbledore family chose a more secretive path. Ariana's father attacked the boys, landing himself a cell in Azkaban, and refused to explain his motivations to the authorities. Why? "[S]he'd have been locked up in St. Mungo's for good. They'd have seen her as a serious threat to the International Statute of Secrecy" (DH 564).

How could a six-year-old girl be seen as both a freak and a threat, and why would her family have so much fear of the hospital? The goal of this chapter is to examine what injury and disease mean in the magical world, and to see how wizards and witches treat illness and disability with their own magical medical institutions. Three medical spaces exist in the wizarding world. The first and most institutionalized space is St. Mungo's Hospital for the Care of Magical Maladies. A second space of medical care, only somewhat less institutional, is Madame Pomfrey's Hospital wing at Hogwarts. The third medical space is outside of institutions altogether. This is the treatment of injuries in the home and other private spaces by other witches and wizards, or by the injured themselves. After the introduction of some useful sociological concepts for thinking about embodiment, maladies and medicine, this chapter will tour through those spaces to examine the meanings and consequences of illness and disability in the magical world before turning to the story of Voldemort to see what his rebellious powers might tell us about the meaning of magical illness.

BASIC CONCEPTS

Disability and illness are concepts that we associate with the body. Although we usually think of our bodies as biological entities, the *meanings* that we associate with the body are socially produced. Our religious ideals, philosophical approaches, and our experiences with social institutions shape how think about the body generally and about our own bodies specifically. Studies of the body as a social idea often discuss the "Cartesian split." This refers to Rene Descartes's statement "I think, therefore, I am." This short phrase made a powerful philosophical leap by associating human experience with thinking, and separating thinking from embodying. Descartes created a mind/body binary that has strongly influenced modern Western conceptions of both the body and human civilization. This binary is at times mapped on to other systems for thinking about the body such as gender and race. The racial version of the Cartesian split associates White privilege, power, and supposed cultivation with the thinking man, and justifies the oppression of seemingly less cultured societies by treating them as baser and associating them with the body (and not the mind). The gender version of the Cartesian split treats men as thinkers who supersede their own bodies while it treats women as emotional reactors who are limited by the needs of their bodies (through hormones, through menstruation, through pregnancy, etc.). Sociology's focus on the body has sought to undermine the Cartesian split and to emphasize that all human experiences are embodied.

MEDICINE

Peter Conrad, one of the major sociologists who studies the history and meanings of medicine, defines medicalization as "defining a problem in medical terms, using medical language to describe a problem, adopting a medical framework to understand a problem, or using a medical intervention to 'treat' it" (Conrad 1992: 211). Some of the most striking work in this field focuses on ailments that are initially not viewed in medical terms but which come to be understood through a medical framework at specific points in history. Attention Deficit Disorder (ADD), for instance, refers to behavior that presumably occurred among children for most of human history but which only came to be "medicalized" when a) the social life of children conflicted with that behavior, and b) the medical field was able to understand and treat the behavior.

One of the key issues then in studying illness is to understand the medical field itself. Although health practitioners can be found in many societies and across time (including healers, witchdoctors, and modern surgeons) only in the modern era are those practitioners part of a distinctly medical field. In pre-modern times, these healers were often part of the religious system and no medical system was present. Having a medical field has required the development of medical education, the credentialization of doctors, and the creation of a profession through organizations like the British Medical Association and the American Medical Association. In the magical world, Healers are the leaders of the medical institution. When Harry and his friends go through career counseling at the end of their fifth year, they learn that Healing requires "at least an E at N.E.W.T. level in Potions, Herbology, Transfiguration, Charms, and Defense Against the Dark Arts" (OOTP 656). It is not clear what additional training is required after Hogwarts for pursuing this career, but credentialed healers are distinguished by the lime green robes they wear.

Another medical professional in the wizarding world is that of Mediwizard. The Mediwizards appear frequently during the Quidditch World Cup to assist the exhausted players in the grueling match between Bulgaria and Ireland, including the young Bulgarian seeker Viktor Krum. The mediwizards seem to be distinct from Healers and may focus only on medical emergencies, although that is not clear from the text.

In the magical world, the Muggle medical system is referred to as "complementary medicine." Arthur Weasley experiments with this alternative Muggle medicine, with the help of a Trainee Healer named Augustus Pye, after he is attacked by Nagini. It becomes clear that Muggle remedies do not work on magical maladies, and are the sort of thing that only Trainee healers would dabble with. When his family and friends visit him in St. Mungo's Arthur Weasley is on the lookout for Healer-in-Charge Hippocrates Smethwyck in hopes of a proper magical treatment for his wounds, since Muggle stitches were of no use. It is interesting to note the skepticism with which the magical world eyes Muggle treatments, as the Muggle world in which we live is known for associating alternative medicine and homeopathy with the fringes of society and even with witchcraft!

In the wizarding world two important distinctions are made regarding medicine. First, they distinguish magical maladies from ordinary ones. Second, they distinguish magical remedies from Muggle remedies. Magical remedies – referred to as remedial potions and charms by a St. Mungo's healer – are used on both magical and ordinary maladies. The most common ordinary malady is the broken bone, which is usually healed magically. When Neville broke his wrist during broomstick lessons, Madame Pomfrey "mended it in about a minute" (SS 156). This was Neville's second trip to the Hospital Wing in the early days of his first year at Hogwarts. The first trip resulted from a magical malady that occurred in Snape's potions class. While making a potion to *cure* boils, Neville missed one item in the directions and actually gave himself boils when the potion melted his cauldron.

One other note about institutionalized medicine in the magical world: wizards appear to have their own pharmaceutical industry. Skele-Gro, a potion that restores the bones in Harry's arm after Lockhart accidently removed them, is made by Rubens Winikus and Company Inc. (HP2). Another commercial potion is Dr. Ubbly's Oblivious Unction, which Madam Pomfrey uses to heal Ron's arm (OOTP 847).

While potions such as these are made and sold on a pharmaceutical market, other potions are homemade; and not always by professional healers. All students study potions at Hogwarts under Professor Severus Snape and later under Horace Slughorn, and are likely to make potions throughout their lives, although only a handful of students continue the study of potions after taking their O.W.L.s. For example, Snape produced a Wolfsbane Potion to help ease Professor Lupin's discomfort during his werewolf transformation.

INSTITUTIONALIZED MEDICAL CARE

Wizards and Witches at Hospital

St. Mungo's Hospital for Magical Maladies and Illnesses was founded by Mungo Bonham, a Black British wizard who lived from 1560 to 1659 and was a famous healer in his time (Rowling 2005). St. Mungo's seems to be the only magical hospital in Britain, though that should not be a problem with so many forms of magical travel

When Harry and his friends met Neville in the long-term residents ward, they were on the second of two visits to St. Mungo's that give us the best glimpse we have inside the hospital. When they first visit St. Mungo's to see Arthur Weasley, after he is bit by Nagini, they travel by subway across the city of London. St. Mungo's is in London, situated in a busy shopping district which allows sick witches and wizards to go unnoticed as the spectacle of consumption dominates the attention of the shoppers. St. Mungo's is hidden within a department store called Purge and Dowse Ltd., which is permanently "closed for refurbishment." To enter, visitors lean against the glass window and tell the mannequin the name of the patient they are visiting. Once approved for access, they are able to step through the glass and directly into the waiting room of the hospital where the Welcome Witch directs patients and visitors to the various wards. A sign on the wall gives a rough guide to the hospital's six floors. The various floors are further divided into a multitude of wards, such as the "Dangerous" Dai Llewellyn Ward, for serious bites, where Arthur Weasley is kept after his confrontation with Nagini.

While in St. Mungo's, Hermione, Harry, Ginny and Ron run into Gilderoy Lockhart, who now lives there after losing his memory from his own backfired Memory Charm in the Chamber of Secrets. They are told that he has not had any visitors. Although most people who knew Lockhart personally before his accident disliked him, he was nevertheless a famous bestselling author who we might expect to have visitors. Perhaps the stigma of being a permanent resident in the hospital has kept his fans away.

As discussed in detail in Chapter 12, stigma is an attribute that causes one to lose social standing. That sense of stigma seems especially apparent when Harry spots Neville visiting his parents in the long-term ward. Harry seems to know instinctively that Neville might feel embarrassed to be seen there, so Harry tries to find a way to distract the others. Harry likely would not do that if there were no stigma to mental illness and hospital residency. Harry fails to distract his friends and Ron calls out to Neville, leading to an interaction with Neville and his grandmother. Neville's grandmother quickly discovers that Neville has not told his friends about his parents' residency in St. Mungo's – a result of a Cruciatus Curse from Bellatrix Lestrange that caused permanent brain damage. Neville's grandmother accuses him of being ashamed of his parents when he should instead feel proud. Although Neville declares he is not ashamed, he does so "very faintly" and refuses to make eye contact with his friends. Neville's response is not a consequence of any character flaw on his part; rather, he is simply acknowledging the social reality of the stigma against disability and mental illness in the magical world (OOTP 514).

Sickness and Healing at Hogwarts

Whenever students at Hogwarts become sick or injured, they are sent to see Madam Pomfrey, the school nurse. It is not clear what training is involved in becoming a nurse or how nurses differ from healers. Madam Pomfrey operates the Hogwarts hospital wing, which includes a ward of white-linened beds and the nurse's office. Harry and his friends spend a lot of time in the hospital wing over the years. At times, they end their harrowing adventures with a visit to Madam Pomfrey, as Harry did at the end of his first year at Hogwarts. At other times, the hospital wing is the scene of the adventure itself, as we see when the hospital wing is the site where Hermione gives her Time-Turner three turns so that she and Harry can rescue Buckbeak and Sirius Black.

But the hospital wing is otherwise a place for rest and healing. Madam Pomfrey is very protective of her patients' rest, though usually stern in her delivery of that protection. Her treatments are often as abrasive as her demeanor, but they nearly always work – except for one occasion when Madam Pomfrey was unable to help Marietta Edgecombe with the pimples that spelled out SNEAK across her face after she told Dolores Umbridge about Dumbledore's Army (in violation of an enchanted list of DA members). Although Professor McGonagall is transferred to St. Mungo's after she is hit by four stunning spells, most patients are successfully treated at Hogwarts by Madam Pomfrey.

Healing at Home

In the wizarding world there are many moments of injury when wizards and witches heal themselves and each other. Mrs. Weasley often heals her children's and their friends' injuries. For example, she attempts to heal Hermione of a bruised face caused by a trick telescope made by Fred and George. Part of the trick, though, is that the bruise cannot be easily removed. Mrs. Weasley relies on a home remedy book *The Healer's Helpmate*, referencing a chapter on "Bruises, Cuts, and Abrasions". The existence of such a book indicates that the medical field includes the publication of self-healing books.

Fleur plays the role of home healer as well, attempting to nurse both Griphook and Ollivander back to health at Shell Cottage after the skirmish at Malfoy Manor. Their injuries take much longer to heal and include the use of Skele-Gro for Griphook's broken legs. Keeping them at Shell Cottage is a necessity of both the dangerous times and Harry's need for both as he formulates a plan for the next stage of his battle with Voldemort.

DISABILITY

Sociologists think about disability in a unique way that is very different from how disability is often understood, especially in the media and in public discussions. The usual understanding of disability is that it refers to a physical or intellectual impairment that causes suffering and merits medical treatment. This is called the medical model of disability because it understands disability primarily through a medical framework. The medical model does not ignore the negative social experiences associated with disability, but it does treat them as consequences of physical and intellectual conditions.

Sociologists and other social scientists who study disability often examine disability through a lens known as the social model. The social model treats disability as a consequence of social inequalities and understands the concept of disability as a form of social construction. This social construction approach, put simply, claims that the meaning of social life is not inherent to our experiences but rather is constructed in ways that are fluid, often ambiguous, and usually quite powerful. So what it means for someone to be disabled depends on how society constructs and approaches the idea of disability, and how society selects which kinds of physical experiences determine who is disabled. The problem that sometimes occurs with the social model is that it can go so far as to ignore physical conditions and even ignore the body altogether. However, sociologists like Carol Thomas, the director of the Centre for Disability Research at Lancaster University in the UK, are working to transform the social model so that it is capable of acknowledging physical conditions. Thomas defines disability in a way that focuses on the social condition of people with impairments. "[O]nce the term 'disability' is ring-fenced to mean forms of oppressive social reaction visited upon people with impairments, there is no need to deny that impairments and illness cause some restrictions of activity – in whole or in part" (Thomas 2004: 579).

Disabilities cause social restrictions in the magical world as well. St. Mungo's contains a closed ward for permanent residents within the Spell Damage wing located on the fourth floor. This is Ward 49, also called the Janus Thickey Ward, after a wizard who is discussed in *Fantastic Beasts and Where to Find Them*. These patients have been removed from society almost entirely and have only limited human contact through healers and the occasional visitor. Witches and wizards treat the long-term resident ward with a mix of fear and disdain. It was fear of the social isolation of this ward that persuaded the Dumbledore family to keep Ariana at home after her attack. Even the Welcome Witch of St. Mungo's treats the long-term residents with ridicule. When a visitor asks to see the patient Broderick Bode, he is told "you're wasting your time.... He's completely addled, you know, still thinks he's a teapot" (OOTP 486).

Voldemort and Harry as Disabled Wizards

Voldemort is a doubly-disabled wizard. The combination of his seven-part soul and the disablement that occurs in his confrontation with baby Harry cripple his mind and his body. We can say then that Voldemort experiences both mental and physical disability. His accomplishment of transforming his soul into more Horcruxes than any other wizard could achieve makes him both a freak and a savant. Sociologist Fiona Whittington-Walsh (2002) has reviewed tropes like these in an article published in the journal *Disability & Society*. She discusses the trope of the freak through an analysis of Muggle filmmaker Tod Browning's 1932 film *Freaks*, which features a murderous battle between two groups of circus performers – one group made up of people with disabilities performing as circus freaks, and one group made up of non-disabled people who perform other roles in the show (the starlet, the strong man, etc.). The freaks in *Freaks* may have bodies that seem to stray from the mainstream, but they also have a very strong sense of identity and solidarity.

They show no shame in their disabilities and they are fiercely protective of their social world. This is true also of Lord Voldemort, who sees the division of his soul as his greatest accomplishment. In that sense he also fits the trope that Whittington-Walsh calls the savant, because his disability is a path to success.

The term savant is used at times to describe individuals who have exceptional expertise in a particular area, and idiot savant has been used to describe people with developmental disabilities who nonetheless have tremendous talent. Whittington-Walsh identifies several examples from film, including Dustin Hoffman's character in *Rain Man*, an autistic man with extraordinary abilities at mathematical calculations. Voldemort is an exceptionally powerful wizard who is often compared to the likes of Albus Dumbledore. But Dumbledore has none of the physical encumbrances that Voldemort faces with his divided soul and dismantled body.

But the wounds he suffers from his battle with young Harry, inflicted really by the love that Lily Potter holds for her son, diminish his body almost to nothing and introduce two other tropes that Whittington-Walsh refers to as violence, and isolation and pathology. Disability is often framed as a motivation for extreme violence, and that appears to be partially the case with Voldemort. His path to violence began long before the fated night in Godric's Hollow, but the wounds he suffered that night gave him a particular hatred for Harry Potter and help to explain why his attempt to return to power is so entwined with the need to destroy Harry.

The decade that Voldemort spends rebuilding his strength and eventually his body is a time marked by extreme isolation. Even when Voldemort's body is rebirthed and his Death Eaters have returned to him, he never seems to trust or love any of them. As Dumbledore says, "Lord Voldemort has never had a friend, nor do I believe that he has ever wanted one" (HBP 277).

But if Voldemort is a villainous disabled wizard, then his affinity with Harry Potter makes Harry a heroic disabled wizard. Harry, too, suffers after his early confrontation with Voldemort and the Avada Kedavra killing curse that he (alone in history) survives leaves him with wounds that are deeper than the lightning shaped scar on his forehead. Harry's success with magic takes on savant-like qualities that defy his mediocre performance at school; and like Voldemort, he is often drawn towards isolation. But his choices set him on a very different path than the one taken by Voldemort. Although Harry struggles with the darkness within him, his choices are shaped more by the protective love of his mother's sacrifice than by the link to Voldemort that formed in the moment of that sacrifice. Voldemort may be one model of the disabled life in the magical world, but Harry Potter's triumphant life offers a magical model of its own.

CONCLUSION

The presence of sickness, disease, disability, and stigma in the magical world is a potent indicator that even wizards and witches are subject to the confines of the body as well as the confines of the social world. Magic may create many possibilities that are unimaginable to Muggles, but these possibilities are not entirely limitless. The wizarding world has found ways to overcome some of the limitations of the body – not through magic though, but instead through social institutions. Hospitals, Healers and Mediwizards are all examples of social structures in the magical world that enable wizards and witches to find health and healing, even as they continue to struggle with the constraints of the body and the constraints of social stigma.

REFERENCES

Conrad, Peter. 1992. "Medicalization and Social Control." *Annual Review of Sociology* 18: 209-232.

Rowling, J. K. 2005. Wizard of the Month Archive: Mongo Bonham 01/03/05 www.jkrowling.com.

Thomas, Carol. 2004. "How is disability understood? An Examination of Sociological Approaches." *Disability & Society* 19: 569-583.

Whittington-Walsh, Fiona. 2002. "From Freaks to Savants: Disability and Hegemony from The Hunchback of Notre Dame (1939) to Sling Blade (1997)." *Disability & Society* 17: 695–707.

PART III

GROUPS & IDENTITY

"Said Hufflepuff: "I'll teach the lot/
And treat them just the same'"

THE MAGICAL ILLUSION OF INCLUSION

ALICE NUTTALL

At first glance, the wizarding world seems to be a fairly inclusive society. Upon his arrival at Hogwarts, Harry moves from an outsider in the hostile Muggle world to a fully accepted and cherished member of the wizarding community. Considering the wizarding world as a whole, one notices that good wizards show equal respect to those from Muggle, half-blood, or wizarding backgrounds, while only Voldemort and his allies attempt to exclude people based on strict criteria of "purity." In the eyes of most of the wizarding world, prejudice against Muggles is as distasteful as overt racism is in the Muggle world, something underlined by the fact that the despised Death Eaters bear a strong resemblance to the Muggle hate group the Ku Klux Klan. Class prejudice is also condemned; the Malfoy family's contempt for the hard-up Weasleys identifies them as dark wizards long before their hatred of Muggles and devotion to Voldemort is revealed. It is clear that Hogwarts, and other official organisations such as the Ministry of Magic, do not exclude people on the basis of such arbitrary facts as their parentage or income – except when they are controlled by Voldemort's minions, as we see during the Second Wizarding War. However, in peacetime, there appears to be no obvious attempt to deal with another form of prejudice: discrimination against people with little or no magical ability.

SORTING

Each year, the new arrivals at Hogwarts are sorted into four Houses by the Sorting Hat. At the beginning of the ceremony, the Sorting Hat describes the character traits that it considers when deciding where a new student should be placed:

> You might belong in Gryffindor,
> Where dwell the brave at heart
> ...
> You might belong in Hufflepuff,
> Where they are just and loyal

...
Or yet in wise old Ravenclaw,
If you've a ready mind
...
Or perhaps in Slytherin
You'll make your real friends
These cunning folk use any means
To achieve their ends.

Witches and wizards from Gryffindor are known for their "daring, nerve, and chivalry" (SS 118). Many of the most prominent figures who stood against Voldemort in the First and Second Wizarding Wars are Gryffindors; they make up the majority of the Order of the Phoenix, and can be found on the front lines of nearly every battle. Professor McGonagall stays at the Death Eater-controlled Hogwarts to protect the students from the Carrows, and, during Umbridge's time as Headmistress, takes several Stunning spells to the chest when she attempts to defend Hagrid. Remus Lupin infiltrates the werewolf community to try and win support away from Voldemort, even though this brings him into close contact with Fenrir Greyback, the sadistic werewolf who targeted and bit him as a child. He and Sirius die fighting Death Eaters, while James Potter is killed trying to buy time for his wife and child to escape from Voldemort; similarly, Lily Potter gives her life to save Harry. Almost all of Voldemort's Horcruxes are destroyed by Gryffindors: Dumbledore, Ron, Hermione, Neville, and Harry himself.

Gryffindors do not only display courage in battle, but in everyday life. Harry goes out of his way to face his fear of dementors and stand up to manipulative adults such as Umbridge, Fudge and Scrimgeour. The all-Gryffindor Weasley clan consistently choose, as Dumbledore would put it, to do what is right rather than what is easy. It is strongly implied that Mr. Weasley has been passed over for promotion because he does not hide the fact that he likes Muggles, or his disapproval of the more hypocritical actions of the Ministry. The rest of the Weasleys support him, despite the fact that promotion and the accompanying pay rise would mean an easier life for all of them – they put integrity before their own comfort. Even Percy, who for several years supports the Ministry's policy of enforcing all laws, even those that are unjust, eventually swallows his pride and admits he was wrong – a very difficult task for such an ambitious over-achiever. Arriving in the Room of Requirement prior to the Battle of Hogwarts, he exclaims to his family "I was a fool!...I was an idiot, I was a pompous prat, I was a – a-"; and as Percy is lost for words Fred offers "Ministry-loving, family-disowning, power-hungry moron." Percy swallows and replies "Yes, I was!" (DH 487).

Similarly, although the Sorting Hat considered placing Hermione in Ravenclaw because of her intelligence, she proves herself to be a textbook Gryffindor. Not only does she fight alongside Harry, she campaigns for house-elf rights despite being ridiculed, and stands up to her friends even at great emotional cost to herself – for example, when Harry and Ron refuse to speak to her after she suggests to Professor McGonagall that Harry's Firebolt may be booby-trapped.

The cunning and ruthless Slytherins seem to be natural villains; the placement of the bigoted Draco Malfoy in Slytherin confirms this. Malfoy's actions throughout most of his school life are as reprehensible as his opinions. In his third year, he succeeds in having Buckbeak sentenced to death by milking the injury he received after insulting the Hippogriff. This petty vengeance is aimed more at Hagrid, whom Malfoy despises because of his class, than at Buckbeak himself. Draco torments his Gryffindor peers, particularly Harry, whenever possible. His actions range from the antagonistic – for example, when he plays up his injured arm to make Harry and Ron do his work in Potions – to the near-sociopathic. In a Quidditch game in their third year, for example, he and his cronies dress as dementors to frighten Harry, despite knowing that in an earlier game Harry's fear of dementors caused him to fall off his broom at a height that would have been fatal had Dumbledore not intervened. Surprisingly, Malfoy's worst actions – his attempts to kill Dumbledore and open a way into Hogwarts for the Death Eaters – are a result of his being manipulated by Voldemort, rather than the fanatical devotion to the Death Eater cause displayed by people such as his aunt. However, even when he and his parents become disillusioned with life under Voldemort, Malfoy makes very little attempt to mend his ways. His only possible heroic action throughout the entire Second Wizarding War is his refusal to confirm Harry's identity when he is brought to Malfoy Manor by the Snatchers.

Like a mirror of the Order of the Phoenix, who are mostly Gryffindors, all but one of the Death Eaters are Slytherins – Wormtail, despite his cowardice and weakness, is placed in Gryffindor. Voldemort himself is, of course, not only a Slytherin, but a descendant of the founder of the House, Salazar Slytherin himself, and fulfils all of the Slytherin ideals apart from blood purity. He is utterly ruthless, using any means to achieve his ultimate goal of immortality: drinking unicorn blood, attempting to steal the Philosopher's Stone, and murdering people in order to split his soul and produce Horcruxes. He is also cunning, manipulating both his followers and his enemies; he wins Ginny Weasley's trust completely in her first year, and later exploits his connection with Harry rather than going after the prophecy himself.

However, not all Slytherins are villains, although their motives for doing good are never selfless. For example, although Slughorn reluctantly agrees to teach in Harry's sixth year, it is clear that he does this because of the protection Hogwarts will offer, and as a way to "collect" Harry. As we see from Bellatrix's exchange with Snape in Spinner's End (HBP 25-31), many Death Eaters view working for Dumbledore as taking a stand against Voldemort, and it is unlikely a coward like Slughorn would risk being perceived this way without a guarantee of protection. Similarly, although giving up the Horcrux memory could be seen as brave – it is, after all, the key to defeating Voldemort – Slughorn only does so after some heavy emotional blackmail from Harry.

Snape uses his Slytherin qualities of cunning for good, acting as a double agent in order to undermine Voldemort. He protects Harry on several occasions and is eventually killed in the line of duty. His actions make him arguably the most heroic figure of the Second Wizarding War; and many years after the war is over, Harry describes him to his son Albus as "probably the bravest man I ever knew" (DH 758). However, unlike other self-sacrificing figures such as Dumbledore, or indeed Harry himself, Snape does not act for the greater good, or out of a belief that Voldemort's plans are evil; after all, as a young student he was clearly drawn to the Dark Arts and the company of future Death Eaters. Instead, Snape is motivated by his love for Lily Potter, and his wish to avenge her death by bringing down the wizard who killed her.

This brief overview of the lives and actions of notable Gryffindors and Slytherins is given to demonstration that next to these protagonists, antagonists and anti-heroes, the students of Ravenclaw and Hufflepuff often become secondary figures – and even here, Hufflepuff seems to lose out. Ravenclaw, the House renowned for the intelligence of its students, provides several of Harry's most useful allies. Through her father's newspaper, Luna Lovegood provides Harry with an opportunity to tell the story of Voldemort's return, thwarting Umbridge and the Ministry's draconian attempts to silence him. She also not only joins Harry and the otherwise all-Gryffindor rescue team in the Battle of the Department of Mysteries, but solves the problem of how to get there by suggesting the Thestrals. Even more importantly, when Harry, Ron and Hermione arrived at Hogwarts in search of the final Horcruxes, it was Luna who suggested the diadem of Ravenclaw, an option even Dumbledore had not considered. Luna's Ravenclaw ability to think laterally, combined with her own open-minded approach to the world, enabled her to help her friends even without full knowledge of the situation. Other Ravenclaws likewise stand out from the crowd at Hogwarts: Cho Chang and Padma Patil are renowned for having beauty as well as brains, as is Roger Davies, the Ravenclaw boy whom Fleur Delacour takes to the Yule Ball. Even the Ravenclaw ghost is more significant than her Hufflepuff counterpart; although the Fat Friar is often seen at the feasts, it is the Grey Lady – Helena Ravenclaw – who provides Harry with a vital clue to finding and destroying one of the Horcruxes.

By contrast, although Hufflepuffs are described as hardworking, "just and loyal," these are traits they share with Gryffindor and Ravenclaw; loyalty to one's friends, family and cause is something common to all but the darkest of wizards. Furthermore, memorable students from Hufflepuff are few and far between and the House as a whole "very rarely got any glory" (GOF 293). The most notable Hufflepuff of Harry's generation is Cedric Diggory; he is handsome, a skilled Quidditch player, and, had Barty Crouch Jr. not interfered, would have been Hogwarts' sole Triwizard Champion. This suggests that Cedric was also a very able wizard, which would have made him a valuable asset in the Second Wizarding War – had he not been killed before it began. Cedric's example suggests that it is far rarer for a Hufflepuff than for a student of any other House to stand out from the crowd.

The second significant Hufflepuff, who, unlike Cedric, survives long enough to become a key figure in the Second Wizarding War, is Nymphadora Tonks. As an Auror, a dangerous career that demands great skill, Tonks seems to prove that Hufflepuffs can achieve things that would pose a great challenge even to their Gryffindor, Slytherin, and Ravenclaw counterparts. However, as Harry soon learns, Tonks' success is not just down to hard work. She explains:

> I'm a Metamorphmagus...It means I can change my appearance at will...I was born one. I got top marks in Concealment and Disguise during Auror training without any study at all, it was great. (OOTP 52)

This natural advantage makes up for the natural disadvantage of Tonks' clumsiness, something she freely admits: "I only qualified a year ago. Nearly failed on Stealth and Tracking. I'm dead clumsy, did you hear me break that plate when we arrived downstairs?" (OOTP 52). The implication is that, had she not been a Metamorphmagus, Tonks may not have made it as an Auror; her greatest asset derives from a fortunate accident of birth. Furthermore, although she is a prominent figure in the early stages of the Second Wizarding War, she is pushed into the background once her pregnancy is announced – although admittedly, this is more because of Lupin's horror of how anti-werewolf prejudice will affect his new family. Tonks returns to Hogwarts for the final battle against Voldemort, but out of Hufflepuff loyalty rather than Gryffindor bravery – it is clear that her priority is not to fight with the Order, but to find Lupin because she was "anguished" and "couldn't stand not knowing" if he was okay (DH 624).

Many of the deaths of Harry's allies are moments of great drama and significance, from the self-sacrifices of Dumbledore and Snape to the shocking, senseless killing of Cedric and Fred. Tonks' death is not dramatic; Harry does not even see her die. Instead, her death is one of the many that occurs at

Hogwarts in the final battle, part of a tally that increases with the carnage of that night. Tonks' death is tragic because it is simply one among many, an example of the horrors of war more than anything else.

NATURE'S HUFFLEPUFFS

Although Tonks and Cedric make significant achievements, it is implied that students in Hufflepuff generally have less magical, sporting or academic ability than their peers – for example, there is no record of Hufflepuff having won the House or Quidditch Cups – and can expect futures that reflect this. Professor Sprout is an expert Herbologist, but she is the only apparent Hufflepuff who leads in her field and holds a position of authority. It may be that the perception of Hufflepuffs as quiet and hardworking leads others to assume that they lack the go-getting traits more commonly associated with the other Houses, and so may face the wizarding equivalent of the glass ceiling.

The most obvious example of prejudice against Hufflepuff comes from Draco Malfoy, who, during his first conversation with Harry, comments "Imagine being in Hufflepuff, I think I'd leave, wouldn't you?" (SS 77). If opinions like these only came from unpleasant, bigoted witches and wizards such as Malfoy, it would suggest that prejudice based on magical ability is a negative character trait, in much the same way as prejudice against Muggle-born witches and wizards. However, it is not only the Malfoys of this world who are prejudiced against those of little magical ability, as we see from the early treatment of one of the Second Wizarding War's most heroic figures, Neville Longbottom.

Neville Longbottom is a complex wizard. As a child, he is a gawky, awkward student who struggles to fit in with his peers. In many ways, he is even more of a fish out of water than Harry; although he has insider knowledge of the wizarding world, he is clumsy, forgetful, and struggles with almost every subject taught at Hogwarts, excelling only at Herbology. Neville is bullied for his lack of magical ability, not only by students like Draco, but by teachers, particularly Snape. Draco's bullying is, of course, an indication of his unpleasant character; however, his attitudes do not only reflect his family's prejudices, but also biases that permeate the wizarding world – in this case, the criteria for Sorting. During their first year at Hogwarts, Draco tells Neville that he is "not brave enough to be in Gryffindor" (SS 218) and later says "Longbottom, if brains were gold you'd be poorer than Weasley, and that's saying something" (SS 223). By implication, Neville is not brave enough for Gryffindor, not clever enough for Ravenclaw, and certainly not ambitious or ruthless enough for Slytherin. This suggests that, according to the biases of the wizarding world, Neville – at least, the young Neville – is one of nature's

Hufflepuffs. Like Tonks, one of his most pronounced character traits is his clumsiness. While most flying-related injuries take place during Quidditch matches, which are renowned for being dangerous, Neville injures himself during an ordinary flying lesson – it is unsurprising that he never even tries out for the Gryffindor Quidditch team. Indeed, Neville has recently revealed that he asked the Sorting Hat to place him in Hufflepuff, as he himself believed he wasn't brave enough to live up to the Gryffindor standard (Pottermore 2011).

During his time at school, Neville grows tremendously in confidence and ability. His potential for courage emerges at the end of his first year, when he attempts to prevent Harry, Ron and Hermione from getting into further trouble by leaving the Gryffindor common room at night; as Dumbledore notes, "It takes a great deal of bravery to stand up to our enemies, but just as much to stand up to our friends" (SS 306). Throughout his time at Hogwarts, Neville's successes often surprise his peers. For example, during a meeting of Dumbledore's Army, there is a moment where Neville successfully disarms the Death Eater mannequin, causing the entire group to stop what there are doing and stare. Two years later, when real Death Eaters search for Harry on the Hogwarts Express, the other students cower in fear, but Neville stands up and says "Hey, losers – he's not here" (HP7 part I). By the end of the Second Wizarding War, Neville has made the transition from timid observer to brave sidekick to hero in his own right. We learn that Neville led the student resistance movement when Hogwarts is being run by Voldemort's followers, a role that would undoubtedly have been Harry's had he been attending the school at that time. Furthermore, Neville is the only person to continue fighting when all appears lost and Harry is pretending to be dead. As a result of this act of bravery, he is able to perform a feat that "only a true Gryffindor" could manage: "He drew from [the Sorting Hat's] depths something silver, with a glittering, rubied handle…With a single stroke, Neville sliced off the great snake's head" (DH 733).

The powerful, defiant Neville we see in this final battle is a far cry from the tearful boy on the train who had lost his toad; however, it is his latent Gryffindor qualities that helped him reach his full potential. Even a Gryffindor who struggles with magic can rise to become a hero who not only challenges the greatest force of evil in his world, but impresses Voldemort so much with his courage and tenacity that he offers him a place by his side – unlike the talented Cedric Diggory, who is killed in a perfunctory manner within moments of encountering Voldemort.

Harry's most prominent allies are from Gryffindor, Ravenclaw, and, albeit secretly, Slytherin; the Hufflepuffs mainly keep to the background. Although Harry and his companions defeat Voldemort using a combination of the traits assigned to each House – courage, intelligence, loyalty, and cunning – the necessity of Sorting is rarely questioned, and even then, not directly. At one point, Dumbledore muses to Snape, "Sometimes I think we sort too soon…" (DH 680); however, he does not suggest that Hogwarts could be stronger if the students were not Sorted at all. Neville may have become a hero in an attempt to live up to the Gryffindor stereotype, which suggests that Sorting is beneficial; but this also implies that, had Neville been placed in Hufflepuff, he would have had no incentive to develop in this way.

Perhaps, in an unsorted Hogwarts, students would be inspired to emulate the best attributes of all four founding members. After all, the school was founded as a result of their cooperation, and, as the Sorting Hat reveals in one of its songs, it was the competition between the Houses that caused the rift between Slytherin and the other founders (OOTP 206). Although the Sorting Hat states "Though condemned I am to split you/Still I worry that it's wrong" (ibid), no witch or wizard seems to share this view. Therefore, at least for the time being, future generations of witches and wizards, like Albus Potter, must face the nerve-racking ordeal of being studied, judged and Sorted.

Squibs

While Hufflepuffs and people of lesser magical ability such as Neville are often overlooked in the wizarding world, any negative treatment they suffer pales in comparison to the treatment of Squibs. Prejudice against Squibs – non-magical people born into wizarding families – is another complex issue. Ron's 107 year old Auntie Muriel suggests that Squibs are treated much more fairly than in the past:

> In our day Squibs were often hushed up…[they] were usually shipped off to Muggle schools and encouraged to integrate into the Muggle community…much kinder than trying to find them a place in the wizarding world, where they must always be second class… (DH 155)

This is clearly what has happened to Harry's neighbour in Little Whinging, Mrs. Figg. At first, Mrs. Figg seems to be nothing more than "a mad old lady…[whose] whole house smelled of cabbage and…[who] made [Harry] look at photographs of all the cats she'd ever owned" (SS 22). However, her true identity is revealed after the Dementor attack on Harry and Dudley: "I'm a Squib, as Mundungus knows full well, so how on earth was I supposed to help you fight off dementors?" (OOTP 20).

Harry soon learns that Mrs. Figg has done everything within her limited power to help in the fight against Voldemort. She has watched over Harry ever since he arrived at the Dursleys'; this is incredibly brave, particularly after Voldemort's return. Voldemort and his followers have proved on many occasions that they have no qualms about killing people who attempt to protect

Harry, and Mrs. Figg has no way to defend herself against such powerful wizards and witches – she could not even escape by Disapparating.

Not only does Mrs. Figg watch over Harry, but she defends him publicly when he is tried by the Wizengamot. This is a different, but equally significant, kind of bravery; the Ministry of Magic represents the official stance of the wizarding world, and therefore the opinions that have led to Mrs. Figg living a rather drab existence amongst Muggles. By giving evidence for Harry, she exposes herself to the prejudices she has arranged her life to avoid; there is a strong implication that certain members of the Wizengamot do not hold the word of a Squib equal to that of a witch or wizard. Fudge, "eyeing her closely," remarks, "A Squib, eh?... We'll be checking that. You'll leave details of your parentage with my assistant Weasley. Incidentally, can Squibs see dementors?" (OOTP 143). Of course, Fudge is attempting to downplay the significance of Mrs. Figg's evidence because he hopes to find Harry guilty – after she has spoken, he comments "Not a very convincing witness" (OOTP 145). However, he cannot discredit a true wizard – Dumbledore – in the same way. While this may be because Dumbledore commands such respect in the wizarding world, the fact remains that the word of a wizard is valued over the word of a Squib.

More disturbingly, Mrs. Figg seems to have internalised this idea of inferiority. Following the dementor attack, she snaps at Harry "Don't put your wand away, boy, don't I keep telling you I'm no use?" (OOTP 21). This is far from true; not only has she protected Harry for fifteen years without blowing her cover, but she is not entirely helpless, as Mundungus Fletcher learns to his cost when she "raised the arm from which her string bag dangled and whacked [him] around the face and neck with it; judging by the clanking noise it made it was full of cat food" (OOTP 23). However, the issue is that she believes herself to be useless in comparison to those with magical ability.

Mrs. Figg is one example of how a Squib may turn out, but she spends most of her time in the background; there is a much more prominent example in the Hogwarts caretaker, Argus Filch. Filch is not a person with whom one can empathise. While Mrs. Figg protects Harry, Filch is ranked firmly among Harry's enemies, as we see in his slavish devotion to Dolores Umbridge and his dedication to stopping Dumbledore's Army. His life seems to be a constant battle to impose draconian limits on the students' power and agency. Not only does he try to confiscate the majority of jokes and toys bought by the children, he is an ardent supporter of Dolores Umbridge, whose methods of punishment are no less than torture. All students are aware that Filch would leap at the opportunity to carry out torture himself.

However, as Ron notes, Filch's hatred of students is a result of his bitterness at being a Squib (COS 145); and considering his position in the school, this bitterness is understandable. He spends most of his working life cleaning up after the students, a job he clearly does not enjoy. Additionally, Filch is given what seems to be the most uncomfortable accommodation Hogwarts has to offer. Harry noted his room was "dingy and windowless, lit by a single oil-lamp dangling from the low ceiling" and that "[a] faint smell of fried fish lingered about the place" (COS 125).

It is clear from the attitudes of many people in the wizarding world – not only Ron's Auntie Muriel – that having a Squib in the family is considered shameful. The fact that everyone who knew the Dumbledore family assumed that his sister Ariana was confined to the house because she was a Squib, rather than a traumatised girl who could not control her magic, suggests that this was another common way of dealing with a non-magical child. As a young girl in the late 19th century, her incarceration for what was assumed to be an absence of magical ability mirrors the way children with physical and mental disabilities were often dealt with in the Muggle world at that time – they were isolated from a society that found their condition disturbing.

Although the treatment of Squibs has improved since that time, there are many indications that having a Squib in the family is still considered shameful – most strikingly evidenced by the actions of Neville's family before his magic manifested. He remembers:

> [T]he family thought I was all Muggle for ages. My great-uncle Algie kept trying to catch me off my guard and force some magic out of me – he pushed me off the end of Blackpool pier once, I nearly drowned – but nothing happened until I was eight. Great-uncle Algie came round for tea and he was hanging me out of an upstairs window by the ankles when my great-aunt Enid offered him a meringue and he accidentally let go. But I bounced – all the way down the garden and into the road. They were all really pleased. Gran was crying, she was so happy. (SS 125)

The fact that families are willing to risk their children's lives and safety in order to "force" any latent magic to expose itself, rather than simply accepting them as non-magical, shows that prejudice against Squibs is still rife.

Conclusion

Although violent prejudice and totalitarian politics are the prerogative of dark wizards and Death Eaters, it is clear that even without Voldemort the wizarding world is far from an inclusive place. As in the Muggle world, there is a spectrum of bigotry and bias throughout wizarding society, from the Malfoy family's generalised racism and classism to Snape's deeply personal loathing of Harry because he is a reminder that Lily chose James. For Harry, joining the wizarding world is an escape from persecution for being different; however, for people who are "different" by wizarding standards, the wizarding world is not always such a welcoming place.

Fortunately, there is hope for the future. In her career at the Ministry of Magic, Hermione revises exclusionary policies with the same dedication to fairness and equality that inspired her to advocate for house-elves' rights, (Rowling 2007). Perhaps most significantly, Neville becomes a teacher at Hogwarts, where, we can imagine, he will encourage and support the next generation of students who, like him, struggled with magic.

REFERENCES

Rowling, J.K. 2007. US Book Tour. (http://bibliophilists.wordpress.com/2007/10/22/highlights-of-jk-rowlings-us-book-tour/).
—. 2011. "Hatstall." Pottermore.com (screen shot available here: http://lady-slytherin-forever.tumblr.com/post/8982434761/hatstall-very-interesting-post-if-you-take-more).

Filthy Half-breeds, Mudbloods, and Disgusting Little Squibs

SOCIAL STIGMA IN WIZARDING BRITAIN

TY HAYES

Status symbols are a familiar concept to most people – from the latest expensive gadget or invisibility cloak to a degree from Harvard or Order of Merlin. We acknowledge that there are things that elevate an individual's social standing. The flipside of this is objects or attributes that have the capacity to lower someone's place in society. These are stigma symbols and someone possessing one can be said to be stigmatised. The most influential study of stigma was published in 1959 by the Muggle symbolic interactionist[1] Erving Goffman. His book, which takes examples of the mentally ill, the physically disabled and homosexuals among others, sets up a framework for thinking about the lives of stigmatised individuals. This framework covers aspects of living with stigma from the treatment one can expect to receive if stigmatised; encounters between the stigmatised and "Normals" (i.e., someone without a stigma who is in the majority and therefore socially acceptable); strategies for the management of a spoiled identity (which indeed is the subtitle of Goffman's book) such as the ways individuals deal with their stigma; and particular types of people that arise in a society with stigmatising practices.

This chapter will introduce Goffman's concepts as they apply in the wizarding world, a world which, as our own, includes prejudices and stigmatised identities. Muggle-borns, werewolves, house-elves, goblins, blood traitors, Squibs, and even Harry himself are often on the receiving end of attitudes and practices that discriminate against them for their nature or behaviour, ranging from verbal insults all the way to systematic incarceration for little more than being from the "wrong" background. This chapter will look at some of the prejudicial attitudes and behaviours of the wizarding world, what effects this stigmatisation has on those so stigmatised, and how they cope with widespread, and in some cases institutionalised, discrimination.

---

1   Symbolic Interactionism, as discussed in chapter 2, is a school of sociology whereby the researchers are concerned with how people relate to each other and interact as mediated by signs and symbols and symbolic rituals and practices.

Filthy Mudbloods

Perhaps the class of people who suffer the most pervasive stigmatisation at the hands of the ruling class in wizarding Britain are Muggle-borns. Throughout the whole of her time at Hogwarts, Hermione is subjected to taunts from much less intelligent students who consider her Muggle heritage to make her ritually unclean. Indeed the offensive slang that is most often aimed at Hermione and other Muggle-born witches and wizards is "Mudblood" – literally calling her blood dirty for having come from Muggles. The stigma of being Muggle-born seems quite pervasive throughout the wizarding world. Even generally mild and gracious potions teacher Horace Slughorn expresses his surprise that some of his favourite and most talented students over his years of teaching have come from non-magical households. It is as if he expects talent and power to come hand in hand with pureblood – Slughorn tells Harry of the latter's mother that he "Thought she must have been pure-blood, she was so good" (HBP 70). In this encounter Slughorn (who has been in hiding because he doesn't want to help the Death Eaters and ultimately joins the fight against Voldemort, his followers and his highly prejudicial regime) is quick to deny charges of prejudice against Muggle-borns, but his words and attitude betrays him. Slughorn's good nature and concerted efforts to avoid discriminating against Muggle-borns cannot be doubted, but this exchange is exemplary of the prevalence of stigmatising attitudes against Muggle-borns throughout the wizarding world.

The behaviour towards Muggle-borns is worst from the traditionalist, blood supremacist pureblood families. The Black family (including those married out to other pureblood families such as Bellatrix and Narcissa) provide a particularly good example. The painting of Walburga in the entrance hall of 12 Grimmauld Place is constantly horrified that there are "Mudbloods, [blood-]traitors, [and] filth" in her family home. Although already dead, she cannot bear to think that there are Muggle-borns or even purebloods that associate with them in the house. The Black family house-elf, Kreacher, also regurgitates the stigmatising opinions of his mistress, and behaves very offensively to Hermione despite the low status that house-elves have in the wizarding world – little more than slaves or pets. That the Blacks permitted (or quite probably encouraged) the most lowly and poorly treated part of their household to espouse such views on Muggle-borns, suggests that Kreacher was afforded more symbolic value than a Muggle-born witch or wizard – Mudbloods are more reviled in some circles than the shrivelled elf that cleans the toilets.

It is significant and telling that the Blacks value house-elves above Muggle-borns as it points to a trend in most stigmatising attitudes in both the magical and Muggle worlds. The idea that a stigmatised person is not fully human is attested by Goffman and put forward as a (usually subconscious) reason that stigmatised people are treated as lesser beings than Normals. In the case of Muggle-borns it is a metaphorical "not fully human" (or indeed "not fully wizard"), but where half-breeds and werewolves are concerned this attitude is actually grounded in fact, obviously accompanied by the suppressed premise that this implies they are not as worthy of equal opportunities, civility or other behaviour that puts them in the same class as respectable purebloods. Returning to Slughorn's conversation with Harry about Muggle-borns, upon hearing Harry's assertion that a Muggle-born (Hermione) is the best witch in his year, the potions teacher says he finds it "Funny how that sometimes happens" (HBP 70). Without too great a leap, we could quite easily imagine him continuing this sentence "it's almost as if they're real wizards, isn't it." The patronising attitude Slughorn displays, although lacking malice, shows that the expectations that wizards of magical descent have of Muggle-borns are low and puts them in a separate category to themselves. It "others" the Muggle-born population and doesn't expect them to have similar capabilities to "proper wizards."

TRANSMISSION OF STIGMA

The stigma that Muggle-borns carry can even be transmitted to purebloods, at which point they become known (to those that stigmatise them) as blood traitors. Andromeda Tonks, one of the more sympathetic Black family members, is disinherited and estranged from her family for marrying the Muggle-born Ted Tonks. It is a reasonable assumption that Ted Tonks is not seen as good enough for Andromeda. Since she insisted on marrying him, however, and it is a disgrace to have a Muggle-born in the family, she had to be removed from the family tree so that he would not appear in it either. The notion that the family name would be tainted by Muggle blood is more abhorrent to the Black family than maintaining familial relations with their children – the purity of their blood acting as a status symbol (and reflected in the family motto Toujours Pur – Forever Pure) incompatible with the stigma of Muggle(born) blood. However, the stigma-by-proxy that Andromeda suffered is not as potent as that of her husband. After the fall of the ministry into Voldemort's hands, Ted Tonks goes on the run from the authorities for being Muggle-born and refusing to register with the Muggle-born Registration Commission; but he believes Andromeda "should be okay, [because] she's pureblood" (DH 295).

Voluntarily consorting with stigmatised individuals is not the only way to "catch" a stigma, in the Muggle or wizarding worlds. Lupin displays a strong paternal protectiveness towards his unborn son when he offers to accompany Harry on his quest, an offer that, it is later revealed, is motivated by wanting to distance himself from his offspring. He is concerned that his stigmatised status will be inherited by Teddy either by infecting him with lycanthropy and so giving Teddy his own primary stigma or just by association, resulting in stigmatization by virtue of being the son of a werewolf. We know from Lupin's relationship with Harry during the former's time at Hogwarts that he would be an excellent father and is not afraid of responsibility or taking care of children. This desire to distance himself from his child then is not a wilful abandonment as Harry seems to think but a difficult decision with the child's best intentions at heart.

Transmission of stigma can also apply from child to parent. The Weasleys' Aunt Muriel and Rita Skeeter's gossiping about Kendra Dumbledore's treatment of her daughter, Ariana, provides an illustrative, if misunderstood, example. Muriel and Skeeter are under the impression that Kendra was ashamed at producing a non-magical child and fearful of the stigma it would place upon her – on top of being married to a convicted criminal, for which she would already know what it was like to live a stigmatised life. They assumed that she sequestered her youngest child away in a basement lest the world find out she existed and her stigma transferred to Kendra. Most parents of stigmatised individuals protect their children, sheltering them from the stigma that the outside world would impute on them (Goffman 1959). However, rather than concluding that Kendra was a concerned parent protecting her child, people assumed she took Ariana's lack of magic to be an indictment of her motherhood that would cause her to be seen by the world as "the mother of a Squib" and "the wife of a criminal" rather than a magnificent witch in her own right and the mother of a brilliant wizard (Albus). Despite knowing that Ariana was not, in fact, a Squib, we can conclude from the reception of this supposition when it is published in *The Life and Lies of Albus Dumbledore* and accompanying *Daily Prophet* articles, that such sequestering practices, even if uncommon and newsworthy, are not unheard of within the wizarding world.

THE WISE

Almost all blood traitors are what Goffman would term "the Wise." According to Goffman, the Wise are those people (often with a close personal relationship to a stigmatised individual, such as the wife of a psychiatric patient) who do not subscribe to the prejudicial and stigmatising behaviours prevalent throughout society and do not let the stigmatisable status of an individual cloud their judgment on such persons. They are often afforded honorary status as "one of us" within communities of stigmatised people, and in return help the stigmatised people pass for Normals (as such they can often spot an otherwise passing individual because they are familiar with techniques which are employed to this end).

Ron's offer to "tell everyone Hermione's [his] cousin" (DH 209) as a way of evading the problems that the new ministry policy against Muggle-borns would cause for her is a typical behaviour for a wise individual. Perceiving the Ministry of Magic's stigmatisation and persecution of Muggle-borns to be unfounded and unjust, he contrives a way to protect his love interest from the consequences of her ancestry. He does this without concern for his own safety (displaying his Gryffindor traits) – effectively offering to perjure himself and compromise his own pureblood privilege, which should protect him in this instance. His plan further extends to preparing Hermione for an inquisition by teaching her the Weasley family tree – which would further enable her to pass.

The Order of the Phoenix (and Dumbledore in particular) is not only Wise with regard to Muggle-borns. They are also exceptionally accepting of stigmatised groups such as werewolves and half-breeds, as demonstrated by the general good will of the group towards Lupin and Hagrid respectively. Dumbledore insists on their value to society and places his trust in them repeatedly. However, both Lupin and Hagrid evoke a level of fear in most in the wizarding world, including first the Board of Governors and later the Hogwarts High Inquisitor, mainly due to prejudices about their kind. Lupin himself speaks of this treatment as normal to the trio: "You have only seen me amongst the Order, or under Dumbledore's protection at Hogwarts! You don't know how most of the wizarding world sees creatures like me! When they know of my affliction, they can barely talk to me!" (DH 213)[2].

The Wise not only accept the stigmatised, but often offer them personal help. Snape and Dumbledore, for example, are responsible for helping Lupin to cope with his stigma, the former preparing Wolfsbane potion for him which ameliorates the effects of his condition during full moon and the latter providing the Whomping Willow and Shrieking Shack arrangement to allow Lupin to attend Hogwarts like a normal wizarding child. The Order (and blood traitors more generally) as Wise not only disavow the prejudice that these stigmas engender but actively contribute to helping stigmatised individuals live as normal a life as possible. Unsurprisingly, it would appear that Dumbledore is the "wisest" wizard in Britain.

---

2   Ron's initial reaction in the Shrieking Shack four years prior is exemplary: Despite knowing and respecting Lupin all year, he instantly tried to move far away from him and shouted "Get away from me, werewolf!" after Hermione revealed the truth about his condition (POA 345).

Strategies for the Management of Stigma

Contrary to our Muggle world, where some stigmas (for example, certain physical disabilities) are patently visible from the initial meeting with the subject of that stigma, the majority of the stigmas in the wizarding world are not as apparent, more similar to stigmas such as sexual deviancy and mental illness in our world (certain half-breeds being the exception). The scholarly term for those who cannot help that their stigma is apparent, either due to its visibility or a prior outing event, is "discredited." This reflects the discredited status of the unconscious assumption of Normals that everyone is like them. The discredited individual cannot maintain a presentation that that does not include the attribute which stigmatises him or her because it would be at odds with the other person's perception of them. Discredit*able* individuals, conversely, are those whose stigma is hitherto invisible and unknown by others. The discreditable individual can blend in as a virtual Normal, albeit one with a secret to be kept which, if it came out, would expose their stigma.

Returning to Goffman provides us with a framework for understanding the level to which the stigmatised individual needs to go in order to hide their stigma considering the factors of visibility, obtrusiveness, "known-about-ness" and perceived focus. With regard to managing stigmatised identities, we can see how different strategies must be used by, for example, Hagrid, Filch and Lupin, in the management of their stigmas. Hagrid the half-giant has an expansively visible stigma – at ten or so feet tall he cannot reasonably expect people to believe he just had an overactive growth spurt. Rather than attempt to hide his stigma, Hagrid as a discredited individual has to deal with it out in the open. He does this through means of a (metaphorical and actual) thick skin and living a secluded life in his hut surrounded predominantly by beasts rather than people. The only people we see him socialise with regularly are Harry, Ron, Hermione, Dumbledore and certain other Order members – in other words, only Wise individuals.

Filch, by contrast, has a fairly unobtrusive stigma in most everyday encounters – his status as a Squib is not something that presents itself in social encounters or appreciably affects his abilities to perform his caretaker duties, at least not insofar as anyone can notice. As a discreditable individual, Filch is most worried about people finding out about his stigma – that he cannot perform magic – which is why he reacts so badly when Harry find his Kwikspell letters.

Of Harry's closest friends, Lupin is the one who seems to struggle most with his stigma, perhaps due to the intrusiveness of it – seriously affecting his daily routine for considerable periods of time – or an internalized prejudice reflecting the particular voracity of public opinion against werewolves.

Consequently, we can examine his various attempts to deal with his stigma as an indicative case study of some strategies that stigmatised wizards employ.

Lupin is a shabby and ill-looking man, which we (now) know is due to his condition. However, it is the sickly appearance that constitutes the premise for Lupin's first attempt at managing his apparent social identity and avoiding stigmatisation for being a werewolf. Lupin's physical appearance and noticeable extended absences mean that he cannot completely disattend his stigma and pretend to be a full and healthy Normal. However, there is nothing that obviously identifies his illness as lycanthropy, so he makes use of this and covers for his absences by claiming merely to be chronically ill. This is not strictly a lie (from his perspective, though other werewolves of a different ideology might very much contest that), but is clearly him trying to avoid explaining the actual problem. (Note here that a Wise person may be able to see through this cover by noticing periods of absence coinciding with the full moon, as Hermione does.) This strategy works quite effectively for the majority of the academic year he teaches at Hogwarts, until he unfortunately exposes himself and discredits this story and his identity as a Normal by transforming on school grounds with witnesses. It seems reasonable to assume that such a story (a werewolf employed at Hogwarts) would make front page of the *Daily Prophet* and completely out Lupin as a werewolf to the whole of wizarding Britain. He immediately resigns in anticipation of being sacked by the very traditionalist and prejudiced Board of Governors.

For two years following his resignation from Hogwarts, Lupin has very little luck in securing employment due to his status as a discredited individual. On the other hand, he is free of the psychological torment, which plagued him up until his disgrace – the constant fear of being revealed as a werewolf. This marks a significant moment in his stigmatised "career" – the shift from *information* management (i.e., projecting the appearance of a Normal so that his status as stigmatised is not known) to *stigma* management. Unfortunately, Lupin does not fare too well at this. Judging from his general self-deprecation, he seems to get stuck at the intermediary stage of identity dissonance. Unable to reconcile his werewolf side with a normal role in society due to prejudice, he feels unable to carry on personal relationships and withdraws into self-imposed emotional isolation.

Lupin's isolationism and withdrawal is profound by the beginning of the Second Wizarding War. He reveals that he has spent months living "underground... Almost literally" (HBP 334) with his "fellow" werewolves. The fact that he identifies himself with werewolves, claiming them to be his equals (although clearly a bad thing, in his opinion they are lesser beings than humans and wizards), shows that he is on his way to forming a functional identity that manages his stigma. The werewolves he has been with "have shunned normal society and live on the margins" (ibid). The way that Lupin talks, it seems that the werewolves are living in a pack of sorts, a ghettoised existence of stigmatised individuals that have grouped together to form communities of similarly stigmatised individuals. This stage of a stigmatised individual's career is documented in our world as well for people coming to terms with a stigmatised identity.

A strong correlate of this ghettoised existence of werewolves can be drawn with those living in the Muggle world with HIV. The stigmatised status of HIV positive individuals leads to their ostracision from general society and profound difficulties in securing gainful employment, leading to existence in squalid low-rent areas (which in addition to marginalising HIV positive individuals, leads to the further proliferation of infection by concentrating populations into small areas) (Haile et al. 2011). Ghettoization does however have its upsides. Bringing together people that face similar problems stemming from stigma constructs a space that can be supportive by providing groups of stigmatised people to work through their problems together[1]. When individuals come together in this way they can construct new ways of looking at and living in the world – new subjectivities and ethical tenets – that place more value on their deviation from the Normals rather than seeing it as a failing (Troiden 1989). While we might well revile these other werewolves (and in particular, this ideology's strongest exponent, Fenrir Greyback), their strategy for coping with the identity dissonance seems quite effective. The werewolf pack/ghetto shelters its members from the stigma they would face trying to exist in Normal society through an ideology that justifies their thirst for blood and flesh. From what we see of Greyback, he is fulfilled by his life and finds it thoroughly enjoyable which compared with Lupin's perpetual melancholy and continual self-loathing is a somewhat better method for dealing with the psychological burden of stigmatisation.

PROFESSIONALS

Fenrir Greyback is, effectively, a professional werewolf. Although we do not really know anything about his daily life, whether for rewards, status or sheer bloodlust, Greyback is the quintessential violent werewolf mercenary and is, from Lupin's description of the werewolves' response to his rallying call, well respected within the werewolf community. He is fighting for the rights of werewolves with his actions, thinking that "under [Voldemort's] rule they will have a better life" (HBP 334), and he is representing his kind to the

---

1   Nash (2006:3) captures this eloquently: "It is possible for subjects to read resistive meaning in space… in this way, subjects can appropriate spaces to allow for new or alternative subjectivities and identities to operate."

Normals in charge (who by the height of the Second Wizarding War are You-know-who and his cronies).

The existence of professionals among stigmatised groups is commonplace. Professionals are highly regarded in communities of their kind, champion the cause of stigmatised groups and negotiate with Normals for increased tolerance and acceptance of their kind (Goffman 1959). They provide a community ethic for living as stigmatised to their fellows, which is based on their interactions with Normals and usually aimed at securing the most favourable negotiation through awkward social encounters for both the stigmatised and the Normals. Goffman (1959: 133) tells us that professionals usually advise against a stigmatised person "fully accepting as his [sic] own, the negative attitudes of others towards him," and instead encourage them to challenge prejudices and discrimination where they are encountered – a piece of advice that Lupin needed to heed if he were to have overcome his self-loathing. Curiously though, Greyback embraces all the negative qualities associated with werewolves and encourages his brothers to do the same – a form of minstrelization which most stigmatised individuals in the Muggle world who take on the role of professional would advise against. Greyback is clearly advocating a militant secessionism among the werewolves – that they are special and superior to full-human wizards and as such should not kowtow to their mundane social order.

Hermione can also be considered a militant professional, battling against the stigma carried by Muggle-borns. Unlike Greyback however, she advocates integration over segregation and is never found arguing that Muggle-borns are in any way special or better than purebloods- merely that they should be treated as equals. Unlike some of her Muggle-born counterparts who try to pass as half-bloods or purebloods while the ministry was under Voldemort's control, Hermione never shirks her Muggle-born heritage. She even embraces and attempts to reclaim derogatory names, proclaiming herself "Mudblood, and proud of it!" (DH 489)

SUMMARY

In this chapter we have seen a wide gamut of stigma within the wizarding world. We have seen how witches and wizards can be stigmatised for the way they were born; diseases they contract at a later point in life, often through no fault of their own; through choices of behaviour and through association – accidental or intentional with other stigmatised groups or individuals. We have also looked at how these stigmas affect the stigmatised peoples' everyday lives, from verbal abuse to unemployment. Stigmas in the wizarding world, just as in the Muggle world, strain family and social relationships and have been known to estrange families both because of the stigma itself, or the negative effect that the stigmatised person fears his family's association with him may result in for them.

The roles that the Wise – as (provisionally) unstigmatised people who are often complicit in stigmatised peoples covering and passing, or at least do not subscribe to the stigmatising behaviours of other Normals – and Professionals – who aim to champion the rights of stigmatised individuals – have also been considered. The Order of the Phoenix in particular, provided a useful example of the Wise whilst Greyback and Hermione both provided good examples of professionals.

The strategies that stigmatised individuals use to navigate their way through life have also been introduced. Lupin's (temporarily successful) attempt at passing as Normal by covering his lycanthropy with more mundane illness represents one of the most common tactics for negotiating mixed social settings, even in the Muggle world. His later attempts to withdraw from social life lead to a period of depression, which unfortunately does not properly resolve itself before his untimely death. Greyback's modification of his ethic to a new set of values which glorify the qualities more usually reviled about werewolves – one where his behaviour is not only acceptable, but superior to that of Normals – is a more sustainable method for coping with stigma, especially when combined with living in a secluded community that shares this ideology. Finally, Hermione's embracing and staunch defence of her Muggle-born heritage shows how one need not accept one's stigma by isolating oneself and that stigmas can and should be challenged. Stigma is endemic in both the wizarding and Muggle worlds, and value systems that condemn some people based on innate or acquired traits or behaviours need thorough examination lest we succumb to the monstrosities of the second wizarding war's treatment of half-breeds, Muggle-borns, and Squibs.

REFERENCES

Goffman, Erving. 1959. *Stigma: Notes on the Management of Spoiled Identity.* London: Penguin

Haile, Rahwa, Mark B. Padilla and Edith A. Parker. 2011. "Stuck in the quagmire of an HIV ghetto: The meaning of stigma in the lives of older black gay and bisexual men living with HIV in New York City." *Culture, Health & Sexuality*, 13(4): 429-442.

Nash, Cathrine Jean. 2006. "Toronto's Gay Village (1969-1982): Plotting the politics of a gay identity." *Canadian Geographer*, 50(1): 1-16.

Plummer, Ken. 1989. "Lesbian and Gay Youth in England." Pp. 195-224 in *Gay and Lesbian Youth*. Edited by G. Herdt. Abingdon, UK: Routledge.

Plummer, Ken. 1975. *Sexual Stigma*. Abingdon, UK: International Library of Sociology.

Troiden, R. 1989. "The Formation of Homosexual Identities. Pp. 43-74 in *Gay and Lesbian Youth*. Edited by G. Herdt. London: Harrington Park Press.

"Let the Sorting Now Begin"

HOGWARTS HOUSES, CLUBS, SECRET SOCIETIES, AND THEIR MUGGLE WORLD REFLECTIONS

DREW CHAPPELL

The wizarding world offers a range of opportunities for group membership, from Quidditch teams to House affiliations to secret societies. In this chapter, I will analyze these groups across a number of different trajectories, including the traits required to join particular groups, the missions or focuses of the groups, and the status of the groups within the wizarding world, and suggest parallels in social and cultural groups in outside (Muggle) society. It is my hope that through this study, the connection between wizards, witches, and Muggles might be further illuminated; our common need for group membership goes beyond our differences as users of magic and those who live in (blissful?) ignorance of its impact on our world.

Group membership is a long-standing research interest in the social sciences; in fact, this concept might be considered the basis of sociology. Although the study began with macro-level investigations of societies as a whole, the rise of the Chicago School in the late 1800's led to a more micro-level investigation of how small groups function. Their introduction of symbolic interactionism pointed toward the importance of group function as indicator of societal life as a whole, even and especially when social groups resisted conformity or even societal law (Blumer 1986). Although not officially connected with formal structures, these social groups might be seen as ideological state apparatuses, defined by Louis Althusser as institutions that establish power through ideological control of thought (Althusser 1971). The groups create certain norms and expectations which their members "buy into" in order to navigate life in the group.

What groups exist in given societies, the level of difficulty of joining groups, and the "member benefits" of group belonging are all important considerations as researchers consider the impact of socialization on individuals. Groups have an impact on their members in myriad ways, contributing to those members' ontological and epistemological lenses on the world. Thus, it seems appropriate to apply such study to the groups that exist in the wizarding world, and suggest some ways in which they might guide young people's development and/or understanding of their societies.

The wizarding world offers a blueprint for making successful life choices. Elsewhere, I have argued that its example is particularly useful to Muggle young people navigating a complex and ambiguous postmodern society (Chappell 2008). Others have analyzed its views of authority (Mendlesohn 2002), and its commentary on contemporary Muggle media representations of war and terror (Strimel 2004). These studies point toward the relevance of Hogwarts students' philosophies and actions in contemporary Muggle society – we learn, theorists submit, about ourselves through learning about Harry and his friends.

The wizarding world includes multiple student (and adult) groups, including Houses, clubs, teams, and secret societies. Each constitutes its own "mini society" with rules of engagement, entrance requirements, and member benefits. Whether grouped together by the Sorting Hat (Hogwarts Houses), physical ability (Quidditch teams), or common cause/interest (Dumbledore's Army), these groups serve a number of important functions at Hogwarts. They protect and support their members, push them to excel, and grant knowledge and abilities beyond what those students possess as individuals.

Theorist Nick Lee (following Deleuze and Guattari) argues that human beings – including children – create *assemblages*: "open ended swirl[s] of extensions and characteristics, changing their powers and characteristics," (Lee 2001: 115). These assemblages extend the knowledge, power, and/or influence of their users. In social group structures, assemblages allow members of a group to become more than the sum of their parts, to function as a stronger, more knowledge/able unit. In the case of Hogwarts, assemblages include not only peer groups, but also *relationships* of students to teachers, spells, creatures, and items. These groups and relationships open up worlds for the students beyond their dormitories, classrooms, or even Hogwarts itself.

COMMON TRAITS: HOUSES

At Hogwarts, students are sorted into one of four Houses in their first year of attendance. A student's House becomes a large part of his or her identity, an identity in relation (and sometimes in contrast to) the other Houses. As the Sorting Hat itself said: "Though condemned I am to split you/Still I worry that it's wrong" (OOTP 206). The Hogwarts Houses parallel membership in boarding school, or in college dormitories, where young people share a closeness because they live in close proximity. The Sorting Hat is perhaps analogous to Muggle residential life questionnaires that attempt to develop a picture of the interests and beliefs of incoming students in order to place them with appropriate roommates. Fortunately, the Sorting Hat sees into the students' minds, and so may have a better picture of where the student "ought to be" (SS 117).

Each House is associated with a specific trait, and this trait helps to define the thoughts and actions of the students assigned to the Houses. House traits are values: bravery (Gryffindor), intelligence and wit (Ravenclaw), hard work and loyalty (Hufflepuff) and ambition (Slytherin). These traits reflect the beliefs of the Houses' founders. Although many students embody their traits from the time they are sorted or we meet them (Harry was clearly a brave Gryffindor, Draco an ambitious Slytherin, for example), many students "grow into" their Houses, taking their time in the adoption of the associated values. As discussed in Chapter 11, Neville Longbottom, who in his first year seemed like the least likely person to be sorted into Gryffindor due to his many fears, but by his seventh year is serving as the leader of Dumbledore's Army at Hogwarts, is a good example of growing into one's House. This House association parallels many group memberships that take time to grow into; conversely, they mirror clubs or societies whose missions and moral outlooks might become defining characteristics for those who join.

House membership grants Hogwarts students many advantages. Through discussion in dormitory rooms and common rooms, young people gain "insider information" through peer networks (an example of assemblages). Hermione Granger often helped her fellow Gryffindors – especially Neville Longbottom and Ron Wesley – with schoolwork. Fred and George Weasley tested their borderline ethical items on Gryffindor students, and later used the common room as a first "distribution center" for these items. In Slytherin, Draco Malfoy continually selected Crabbe, Goyle, and Pansy Parkinson as collaborators in his schemes (as lookouts, or carriers of false information) because of those students' House affiliation. This House network crossed the age barrier; older students were willing to help their younger Housemates because they felt a kinship with them, as with Oliver Wood's training of Harry in his first year and Hermione's relationship advice to Ginny.

PHYSICAL APTITUDE: QUIDDITCH TEAMS

Quidditch, the most popular wizard sport in Europe, is a large part of life at Hogwarts. Quidditch teams draw in not only students, but professors as well. Whether players expect to go on to play professionally (some students, like Victor Krum already do so) or enjoy the game as a school activity without plans to continue, the sport is its own culture within the school and without. Playing Quidditch carries a "cool factor" that builds players' self-esteem and popularity in the school. It is similar to being a member of a school sports team in the Muggle world; however, because Quidditch is the only sport played at Hogwarts, it captures more focus from the students than the multiple sports in Muggle schools. *Everyone* follows Quidditch!

To play on a Quidditch team, a student must meet certain physical requirements. His or her body must be in good health, and he or she must be a good flyer. In addition, each position on a team favors a different type of bodily ability; Beaters are typically tough in order to smack the heavy Bludgers, Chasers and Keepers strong and coordinated to handle the Quaffle, and Seekers light and agile in order to speed to the Golden Snitch. These physical demands mean that only a select number of students are chosen for the teams, and they must keep up with such activity as well as completing their class assignments.

The benefits of playing on a Quidditch team are both bodily and social. Playing Quidditch keeps one's body in excellent shape, and this conditioning has an impact on one's mental clarity and functioning. It also teaches tenacity, sportsmanship, and teamwork. In addition, Quidditch players can count on their teammates for support and guidance. Professional Quidditch players often become quite famous, and even well past their playing days they are still remembered for their feats on the pitch. One example of this continuing fame is Ludo Bagman, the former Beater for the English Quidditch team and later Head of the Department of Magical Gaming and Sports.

Harry Potter's best friend Ron Weasley is perhaps the clearest example of how Quidditch can transform a student's sense of self and social identity. Prior to winning the role of Keeper on the Gryffindor team in his fifth year, Ron was very much "one of the Weasleys," a boy defined by his family and his relationship to Harry Potter. Despite his position in the Gryffindor social circle, Ron's sense of self suffered from comparisons to his older family members and his famous best friend. When he began playing Quidditch, Ron struggled as Keeper, leading Slytherin to taunt him by chanting "Weasley is our King" (OOTP 407). But as his playing improved, Ron's popularity rose; playing well and winning were important to his fellow students. Eventually he became a player-hero on the Gryffindor team, admired by the entire school. This was an important step for Ron toward defining himself as an individual, and allowed him to face his great trial as he destroyed Salazar Slytherin's locket in the Forest of Dean. In this trial, Ron was able to put aside his self-doubt and affirm his worth both as Harry and Hermione's friend and his own person; perhaps this feat was in some small way related to his time spent on the Quidditch team.

EXCLUSIVITY: THE SLUG CLUB AND THE DEATH EATERS

While House membership and Quidditch include and exclude certain students based on internal motivations and values or athletic ability, another type of wizarding group uses exclusivity as its primary focus and goal. Selection is based on the perceived importance of family: students' families' place in a perceived wizarding society hierarchy, or family heritage as indicator of a magical bloodline. "Good" families have long histories of success in the wizarding world, and are made up of members who have worked for the Ministry of Magic or made great discoveries, or other significant contributions. This ontological framework parallels the class system in the Muggle world, where one's job, education, and/or family history of wealth and influence can determine one's cultural capital and ability to join certain groups.

Professor Slughorn's Slug Club is one example of this type of group. Slughorn (a member of the ambitious Slytherin House) "collected" students who he thought would be of benefit for him to know, based on their family histories and/or magical ability or perceived potential. Students invited into the club during Harry Potter's tenure at Hogwarts included Harry Potter, Hermione Granger, Ginny Weasley, and Blaise Zabini. For the most part, these students found the Slug Club rather dull and confusing; but they participated, perhaps in hopes that there might be some assemblage-style gains to be made. Clubs based on exclusivity seek to further the fortunes of their members through connections. Zabini, a Slytherin member of the Slug Club, states that Slughorn himself is "Just trying to make up to well-connected people" (HBP 149). This strategy parallels those of clubs and societies such as fraternities and sororities on older Muggle university campuses, which aim to create friendships and connections for select groups of students.

Some wizard groups exist on the more troubling end of this exclusivity spectrum, like the Death Eaters, Voldemort's select group of followers. The Death Eaters dedicated themselves to the elimination of all non-magical blood from magical training and society, and use violence to obtain this aim. They had no democratic process, but submitted to the orders of their leader (usually) without question. This submission extended to sacrifices such as branding with the Dark Mark and sometimes giving up status and freedom. Interestingly, within the Death Eaters, there was a hierarchy based on degrees of magical heritage and manifested through inclusion and exclusion. For example, although the werewolf Fenrir Greyback worked for the Death Eaters (some might even consider him a member of the group), he was not given the "honor" of being branded with the Dark Mark (DH 453). The Death Eaters resemble groups in the Muggle world such as the Ku Klux Klan, who hope to achieve the dominance of one racial group through the subjugation or eradication of others.

Community and Common Causes:
Dumbledore's Army, S.P.E.W., and the Order of the Phoenix

In contrast to the clubs focusing on exclusivity are those that emphasize common cause: Dumbledore's Army, The Society for the Protection of Elfish

Welfare (S.P.E.W.), and the Order of the Phoenix. This is not to suggest that The Slug Club and the Death Eaters do not have a common cause – they do – but to look at such a cause as *central* to the club or society's mission. These clubs do not exclude members, but rather seek out those wizards and witches dedicated to their cause. In this way, they resemble service organizations in the Muggle world that look outside themselves for their purpose, trying to create positive change in society.

These groups believe that commonalities were more important than differences, especially in the face of a threat. Dumbledore's Army in particular focused on the strengths of its members and formed a support system to help those who were struggling with expectations. Through this training, the group as a whole was made stronger and relationships were forged across the borders of House affiliation. In the case of S.P.E.W., at first Hermione had trouble convincing anyone to join or take an interest in the lives of house-elves. Yet through her efforts, Harry built a relationship with Kreacher, Regulus Black's former house-elf, which led Kreacher to divulge the history of Black's locket, one of the Horcruxes the group sought. During the Battle of Hogwarts, Ron championed freeing the house-elves from the kitchen so they would not get harmed, a sentiment that prompted Hermione finally to express her love for him.

Leadership in these groups is not made by one person, but rather a democratic process. This generates a feeling of ownership by all members, no matter their role in the group. As in the Muggle world, at times this democratic process gets rocky, with multiple ideas of what the group should do next. In the case of the Order of the Phoenix, for example, Molly Weasley questioned whether Harry Potter should be exposed to the secrets and plans of the Order: "What's wrong, Harry, is that you are *not* your father, however much you might look like him…. You are still at school and adults responsible for you should not forget it!" (OOTP 89, emphasis in original). While Mrs. Weasley's concern is ultimately overruled, her caution shows the deliberative processes at work in the group.

Although these groups were open to all who believe in their mission and values, two of the groups, Dumbledore's Army and the Order of the Phoenix, relied on secrecy to protect their members. This secrecy was paramount in situations where the health of the group (e.g., in the face of disbanding by Dolores Umbridge) or of wizards and witches more broadly was at stake. In this way, the Order of the Phoenix parallels certain Muggle military or investigative units that function through collecting, guarding, and acting on secret information. The wizarding world did not have knowledge of the day to day operations of the Order, but such recognition was not important to the members of the group.

IMPLICATIONS

There are multiple implications of an analysis of the groups extant in the wizarding world. Through looking at membership requirements, expectations, and benefits, we can derive some general ideas about how similar groups function in Muggle society. We can also suggest how young people might use wizarding society and its groups as a blueprint for how to successfully navigate their own Muggle group memberships: which groups to join, the expectations of such groups, and their member benefits.

First, the importance of students acting together in Harry's adventures shows that group membership is vital to success, both academically and socially. Without his friends, Harry would not have succeeded in his adventures. Hermione and Dumbledore usually had greater knowledge of wizarding lore, while Ron knew a great deal about wizarding society, having grown up immersed in it. Neville and Luna taught Harry to value all people, regardless of whether their abilities were readily apparent. Through these networks and the assemblages they constructed, Harry was able to defeat Voldemort and fulfill the prophecy surrounding his birth.

Second, Harry's tenure at Hogwarts shows that groups with different focuses help young people develop holistically. Harry was a member of multiple groups: Gryffindor House, the Gryffindor Quidditch team, Dumbledore's Army, the Order of the Phoenix, and the Slug Club. Each of these groups allowed him a window on a certain type of society with its attendant ideas and value systems. The groups allowed him to develop physically, intellectually, socially, personally, and morally/ethically. No one group on its own was responsible for his development; it took all of them in combination – as well as his unique personality – to build the person of Harry Potter.

Lastly, the groups that succeeded in wizarding society avoided exclusivity and worked toward the common good. The Slug Club, while it brought Harry closer to Professor Slughorn, had little impact on the Battle of Hogwarts. The Death Eaters, of course, were defeated during the battle. By contrast, Dumbledore's Army and the Order of the Phoenix were able to survive persecution and defeat Voldemort's forces. It could be argued that S.P.E.W. defies this trend, because it never accumulated the type of membership Dumbledore's Army enjoyed, despite its focus on the social good. Yet, S.P.E.W.'s mission was readily apparent in the actions of Harry and his friends at the end of their tenure at Hogwarts. S.P.E.W. was not needed as a club because its values had been internalized by Hermione's friends.

These implications relate to Muggle young people's participation in clubs in schools, universities, and communities. The groups Harry encounters, joins, and rejects promote certain types of group membership and illuminate such memberships' functions in a postmodern society. In this way, paying attention to Harry's actions demonstrates the usefulness of sociological analysis not only in the wizarding world but in the Muggle world as well. To quote Dumbledore, "It is our choices, Harry, that show what we truly are, far more than our abilities" (COS 333) – and these choices include the choice of which groups to join and how to navigate within them.

References

Althusser, Louis. 1971. "Ideology and Ideological State Apparatuses (Notes Towards an Investigation)." Pp. 127-186 in *Lenin and Philosophy and Other Essays*, edited by L. Althusser. New York, NY: Monthly Review Press.

Blumer, Herbert. 1986 [1969]. *Symbolic Interactionism: Perspective and Method*. Berkeley, CA: University of California Press.

Chappell, Drew. 2008. "Sneaking Out After Dark: Resistance, Authority, and the Postmodern Child in J.K. Rowling's Harry Potter Series." *Children's Literature in Education* 39(4): 281-293.

Lee, Nick. 2001. *Childhood and Society: Growing Up in an Age of Uncertainty*. Maidenhead: Open University Press.

Mendlesohn, Farah. 2002. "Crowning the King: Harry Potter and the Construction of Authority." Pp.159-181 in *The Ivory Tower and Harry Potter: Perspectives on a Literary Phenomenon*, edited by A. Whited. Columbia and London: University of Missouri Press.

Strimel, Courtney. 2004. "The Politics of Terror: Rereading Harry Potter." *Children's Literature in Education* 35(1): 35-52.

"The whole point of the tournament is international magical cooperation"

RESISTING A UNIFIED WIZARDING COLLECTIVE IDENTITY

MYA FISHER

INTRODUCTION

Since the events of September 11th in the Muggle world, international cooperation among Muggle nations and peoples has been critical to continuing peacekeeping efforts, economic development, and public policy. Globalization has led to increased integration of world systems, defying traditional barriers such as nation-state borders, language and cultural differences; making cooperation necessary among nations and between its citizens. This complexity and interdependence require individuals to be knowledgeable, understanding and familiar with cultures, practices, and customs of other nations. International sporting events like the Olympic Games and the World Cup have been one means of fostering interpersonal connections between citizens of different nations. In recent years, international student exchanges and study abroad programs have also been a way of facilitating and promoting positive international relations, by encouraging grassroots appreciation and friendships between students from different countries.

Until the age of 14, Harry Potter's view and understanding of the magical world is limited to the context of Great Britain. He is faced with the fact that the magical world extends beyond the borders of Great Britain when he attends the 422nd Quidditch World Cup and when Hogwarts School of Witchcraft and Wizardry hosts the Triwizard Tournament later that same year. The goal of the two events is to bring inhabitants of the magical world together through friendly contests with an eye towards cooperation and cross-cultural understanding. Increased interdependence of economies and the emerging threat of Voldemort's return make cross-cultural understanding, cooperation and positive relations spanning national boundaries and species categories all the more necessary. The logic behind such ideas is that those who have friends or personal connections with foreign peoples or foreign cultures will be less likely to engage in war, seeking instead positive and peaceful relations. However, establishing positive relations and connections between people is not always simple or easy.

Bringing groups together does not instantaneously result in friendship and positive relations as proposed by the intergroup contact hypothesis. The intergroup contact hypothesis states that "increasing contact and communication between members of opposing groups will reduce intergroup conflict" (Delamater and Myers 2007: 425). In the case of student exchanges, it makes sense that over time students on both sides of an international exchange will share the information they have gained about the other group and culture when they return home. In international sporting competitions like the Olympics or World Cup, bringing citizens together to participate in sports with excellence is the mechanism that will facilitate and increase positive relations between nations.

But intergroup contact does not work immediately, and sometimes it results in intensifying group boundaries and associated identities such that there are significant obstacles to cooperation and integration, particularly in instances of competition. Further consequences of the conflict are antagonistic behaviors toward out-groups as explained by social identity theory of intergroup behavior. Tajfel and Turner's (1979) theory says that individuals identify as members of a social category or group, and affiliate themselves with positive attributes in order to maintain a positive self-concept. In order to maintain this positive self-concept, in situations where groups are vying for a limited resource or in competition, group identity may become salient. Therefore the individual will act in ways to reinforce their positive self-concept by framing the out-group negatively, often employing stereotypes. Many of these processes are clearly visible during Harry's fourth year at Hogwarts.

The Quidditch World Cup:
Inter-Group Connections and Narrowing Identities

The 422nd Quidditch World Cup reveals both the challenges and merits of international sports competitions in facilitating positive relations across national and cultural boundaries. In some ways, international sports competitions like the Muggle Olympics and Quidditch World Cup exemplify a simplified idea of the contact hypothesis for both spectators and participants. The contact hypothesis emerged as a theoretical approach for reducing prejudice and negative attitudes between groups experiencing conflict. When taken at its most basic, some will suggest that simple contact between groups is enough to improve intergroup relations. In the case of international sports competitions, the contact of interest is between spectators. In spite of language barriers, the Ministry of Magic is able to organize detailed arrivals of Portkeys from around the magical world, accommodate 100,000 magical spectators and erect a stadium, all without notice of Muggles.

Spectators in the venues and around the host areas mix and mingle with one another, and can cheer for their own athletes. And when their own are not competing, spectators can support and cheer for favorites from other countries. Even though a British team is not competing in the Championship match, Harry and the Weasleys are cheering their neighboring team, the Irish. Although it is unclear as to why they are cheering for Ireland rather than Bulgaria, perhaps their affinity for the Irish team via Britain's shared history with Ireland, and personal friendship with Seamus Finnegan, has something to do with it.

In the same way that spectators may cheer for teams other than their own (particularly when their own are not represented) in international competitions, individuals are likely to cheer for those teams with whom they share some common feature, idea or personal connection. When walking to get water, Harry finds himself in a sea of green surrounding an area of tents clearly inhabited by fans of Ireland. When happening upon Seamus Finnegan and his mother, they make clear their support of Ireland among the tents stating, "Why shouldn't we show our colors?" (GOF 82). She goes on to further inquire as to whom Harry and his friends are rooting for with, "You'll be supporting Ireland, of course?" To which they nod in agreement. As Harry continues walking through the campground he sees areas marked out by fans of both teams. Both groups of fans have bedecked their tent areas with flags, posters, and other materials that make their affiliations crystal clear. This is the first time Harry realizes the immense size and diversity of wizards within the magical world.

While the world known to Harry Potter centers on life and events at Hogwarts and in Great Britain, the wizarding world stretches far beyond the boundaries of the small nation. Since his entry to the magical world at the age of eleven Harry has learned of the numerous distinctions between Muggle and wizards, and among wizards (pureblood, half-blood, Muggle-born). But it is at 14 that he realizes there are other various nationalities and ethnicities from around the wizarding world. Walking through the tent grounds on the way back from getting water, he notices a group of young people he's never seen before. Ron surmises they "go to some foreign school" then tells Harry and Hermione about his brother Bill's Brazilian pen pal. Coming face to face with these *foreigners* of roughly the same age, force a narrowing of Harry's existing social identity as a wizard. It's perhaps the first time that he might consciously and specifically classify or identify himself as a wizard from Great Britain, rather than simply a wizard. As social identity theory (Tajfel and Billig 1974; Tajfel and Turner 1979) posits, everyone claims membership in social categories, and that membership provides a definition of who one is. Moreover, these identity claims become salient and meaningful in particular contexts.

In Harry's case, he consciously begins to identify not only with the broad social category of wizard, but specifically from Great Britain while walking amongst the tents at the World Cup, and as a student at Hogwarts School of Witchcraft and Wizardry when he comes across these school-age wizards. Social identity theory continues by asserting that this conscious social identity shapes interactions between groups and its members. Moreover, negative interactions between groups (intergroup conflict) is understood in terms of opposing groups struggling to reaffirm their group and membership in the positive, and as a zero sum game, the opposing group in the negative (Tajfel and Turner 1979; Hogg 2006). These struggles and dynamics are illustrated in the interactions between students of the three schools participating in the Triwizard Tournament that takes place at Hogwarts.

The Triwizard Tournament: Intergroup Contact

The Triwizard Tournament is a 700 year old "friendly" competition between the three largest wizarding schools in Europe – Beauxbatons, Durmstrang and Hogwarts. The goal of the Tournament is to establish and maintain ties between young witches and wizards of different nationalities. International exchanges between academic institutions, like the Triwizard Tournament, have the potential to increase knowledge and understanding between those who share membership in the magical world, but whose local cultural practices, values and orientations toward the world may create obstacles to cross-cultural cooperation, communication or friendship. It is an opportunity to learn about others who inhabit the magical world and to extend social networks beyond the boundaries of their school and nation.

In the realm of international exchanges, simple contact or exposure to members of others cultures (groups) does not necessarily mean that students will get along or become friends. Unlike the Quidditch World Cup, where there is no direct interaction off the field between competing teams, in the Triwizard Tournament Harry and his fellow Hogwarts schoolmates are directly investing in the outcome of the contest. Dumbledore and the faculty seem to be concerned with presenting a positive image of Hogwarts to the visitors, indicating the strength of their identification as Hogwarts' teachers. As host, the Hogwarts castle is cleaned, scrubbed and decorated in ways not only to shine in presentation, but also to instill pride among its students. The suits of armor are freshly polished, portraits have been de-grimed, and giant banners of the Hogwarts Houses and bearing the school's coat of arms hang in the Great Hall.

The tension Henry senses in the castle on the day the visitors are set to arrive shows that they really want to make a good impression. But upon arriving at Hogwarts some of the visitors' comments indicate not all of them are impressed by Hogwarts. Tensions increase when visiting students disparage the name and image of Hogwarts because this results in an injury to a source of Hogwarts students' pride, necessitating a corrective response in order to repair the damage to their self-concept. For example, when a student laughs derisively during Dumbledore's welcome speech when he invites all to be comfortable and enjoy their stay, Hermione bristles and retorts, "No one's making you stay!" (GOF 251). Although the Beauxbatons student doesn't hear her, it is possible that Hermione's comment itself is a corrective response in the face of Hogwarts castle's magnificence. Later in the school year, at the Yule Ball, Fleur Delacour openly criticizes the Hogwarts decorations to Roger Davies:

> Zis is nothing…. At ze Palace of Beauxbatons, we 'ave ice sculptures all around ze dining chamber at Chreestmas. Zey do not melt, of course… they are like 'uge statues of diamond, glittering around ze place. And ze food is seemply superb. And we 'ave choirs of wood nymphs, 'oo serenade us as we eat. We 'ave none of zis ugly armor in ze 'alls, and eef a poltergeist ever entaired into Beauxbatons, 'e would be expelled like *zat*. (GOF 418, emphasis in original)

Fleur's comments about the Beauxbatons Palace may be seen as a strategy to repair an injury to her own identity as a Beauxbatons' student. In order to repair her positive sense of belonging to Beauxbatons Academy, she must expound on the positive dimensions of her own school, primarily the beauty of the palace. This process of dismissing Hogwarts' castle as unimpressive and basically plain, illustrates an effort to recalibrate her self-concept back in the direction of the positive.

An additional dimension of the interactions between students during the tournament is a phenomenon that also occurs within the context of Muggle international exchanges, the exoticizing of the foreign other, both in body and in language. Prior to the arrival of the representatives from Beauxbatons and Durmstrang at Hogwarts, rumors run rampant about the tournament, the tasks, but also how the students from the visiting school might be *different* from themselves. These visitors are unknown to Harry and his schoolmates; they are foreign, exotic and clearly a group of *others*. The category "other" refers to people who are distinguished from one's own group or culture, in this case school and nation. The visiting students come from far off places, with clothes, accents and modes of transportation that are foreign and mysterious to Harry and his fellow classmates.

One example of this exotification is the male Hogwarts students' fascination and attraction to the Beauxbatons female students. Ron sums up the attitude in his exclamation, "I'm telling you, that's not a normal girl!… They don't make them like that at Hogwarts!" (GOF 252-253). Although

Harry retorts by saying, "They make them okay at Hogwarts" (GOF 253) the implication that these girls are fundamentally different has already been expressed. During the opening feast Ron's and other Hogwarts boys' eyes can be seen following the bouncing bottoms of the Beauxbatons girls as they flutter into the Great Hall. One explanation for their difference is that some of the female students are part *Veela*. However, such a conclusion is in and of itself exotification. Native to Bulgaria, Harry and his friends see them for the first time at the Quidditch World Cup where they are the mascot for the Bulgarian national team. Veela are extraordinarily beautiful semi-human women who have the power to entrance men with their beauty; so it is not surprising that Ron explains his attraction to the Beauxbatons female students by labeling them as Veela. His attraction to these unique women positions the Hogwarts women as ordinary and not as desirable.

It is this air of mystery and foreignness the tournament aims to lessen. In some ways, the goal is to make difference less stark and distinct, and more just shades along a spectrum of normality. At the year's opening feast, Dumbledore instructs Hogwarts students to "extend every courtesy to our foreign guests while they are with us" (GOF 188). He sets the stage for the theme of the tournament, which is for students to not only encounter, but meaningfully engage with the visiting students in a way that reflects well upon the school. Meaningful engagement, rather than simple contact, is the prescription for successful intergroup contact (Henry and Hardin 2006). Bringing students of the three schools together in a meaningful way is a year-long project full of interesting encounters that show the strength of students' identification with their respective schools because, despite the efforts of Dumbledore, the Hogwarts teachers, and the Ministry of Magic, the fact that the exchange is centered on a *competition* reinforces school affiliations and, in some instances, creates divisions between students of the three schools and among the students of Hogwarts.

A Hogwarts Divided: Intergroup Conflict

Upon first hearing about the competition, Hogwarts students want to support their school champion, whoever he or she might be, against the rival schools. However as the champion selection process gets under way, and students begin to submit their names for consideration, House divisions within Hogwarts become primary. The Goblet of Fire serves as the impartial selector of the tournament champions. As outlined in social identity theory, each individual has a number of identities that function in daily life – status characteristics like gender, class, race, and group affiliation. In the case of the Triwizard Tournament, the champion selection process highlights the salience of student affiliation with their Houses.

Although the champion represents the entire school, students from each House would prefer a champion from their own House. A week before the champion selection, the names of students who may be submitting their name for consideration – Warrington, Diggory, Johnson – begin to fly around Hogwarts. "We can't have a Slytherin champion!" (GOF 261) Harry exclaims regarding Warrington. "That idiot, Hogwarts champion?" (GOF 236) Ron remarks about Diggory. "I wouldn't have thought he'd have wanted to risk his good looks" (GOF 261) Seamus says of him later. Harry, Ron and Hermione are excited, however, to hear that fellow Gryffindor Angelina Johnson put her name in the Goblet for consideration. "Well I'm glad someone from Gryffindor's entering... I really hope you get it, Angelina!" Hermione said (GOF 261). "Yeah, better you than Pretty-Boy Diggory" Seamus added (ibid). It is clear that Harry and his classmates are viewing the champion selection through the narrow identity category of their respective Houses, rather than of the broader category of Hogwarts' student. However, when Cedric is named as the Hogwarts' champion Ron's singular objection is drowned out by the thunderous applause of all the Hogwarts students. In the face of the other schools' champions, the students became singularly unified in their support of Cedric as the Hogwarts champion and the common goal of winning the tournament for the honor of their school.

Unfortunately, the Goblet of Fire names a second champion from Hogwarts and the division amongst students along House lines (and historic allegiances) is again brought to the forefront of Hogwarts' student minds in the competition. The mysterious selection of two champions for Hogwarts – Cedric Diggory and Harry Potter – divides the school, reinforcing social identities among House lines. The Gryffindors are behind Harry, throwing him an impromptu celebration in the Common Room following the selection ceremony. Angelina exclaims, "Oh if it couldn't be me, at least it's a Gryffindor" (GOF 285). Although none of them believe Harry didn't put his name in the Goblet, that doesn't seem to matter in light of the fact that he is from their House. If Harry were to win, the glory would belong to not only Hogwarts, but the Gryffindor House as well. It is this that makes students so invested in wanting the champion to be from their House.

In addition to the process of enacting social identities based on House membership, non-Gryffindor students engage in antagonistic actions toward Harry and his fellow Gryffindors, exhibiting features of intergroup conflict. Such antagonistic behavior is characteristic of intergroup conflict when groups are competing for some outcome that each believes important – in this case the Triwizard Cup (Delamater and Myers 2007). A central characteristic of intergroup conflict is that members of each group strongly identify with their own group, applying positive attributes to their own group and negative attributes to the group with whom they are competing. In the days following the champion selection Hogwarts is divided. The Hufflepuffs rally behind Cedric, exhibiting quite cold behavior towards Harry and the Gryffindors. Harry interprets their coldness to feeling that Harry's selection as co-champion somehow stole their champion's thunder. Yet he is perplexed by the attitudes of the Ravenclaws, who also turn a cold shoulder toward Harry as a school champion. They justify this behavior with the belief that he intentionally disobeyed the rules by putting his name in the Goblet in order to garner more fame and notoriety. And while he did not expect anything but negativity on the part of the Slytherins because of his history with Malfoy, he is not prepared for the badges that read – *Support Cedric Diggory – The* REAL *Hogwarts Champion!* – in bright red letters; and – *POTTER STINKS* – in glowing green letters.

But these divisions do not last the duration of the tournament. Following Harry and Cedric's success in the first task against the dragons, these internal divisions within Hogwarts seem to lessen as students begin to understand that if either Harry or Cedric win, in the end, it is a win for Hogwarts. Harry sees fewer *POTTER STINKS* badges and does not sense as much open hostility from his schoolmates. The danger and success of the two champions in the first task seems to have facilitated the creation of a superordinate group identity, they are all once again Hogwarts students vying for a school win in the tournament. According to Hogg (2006) the resolution of intergroup conflict is achieved precisely in this manner. Although the Slytherins are somewhat resistant to this redefinition, the division and negative interactions between the school Houses are virtually eliminated once students have accepted this common in-group identity. But, the tournament is not only about the competition, but the day-to-day interactions of the students.

Intergroup Contact Hypothesis Revisited: The Yule Ball

A simultaneous goal of the tournament is student exchange; having students interact socially to begin building connections and relationships. From Harry's perspective, it does not appear as though there is much mixing of the three schools on a social or day-to-day level. Students do not study together, and although Viktor is often seen in the Hogwarts' library, it's only to see Hermione. They share meals together, but sit apart. Most importantly they do not room together, instead staying on the Durmstrang ship moored on the Black Lake and in the giant Beauxbatons carriage in a paddock adjacent to Hagrid's hut on the grounds. The exchange is unidirectional in that students only ever come to Hogwarts; there is no knowledge of any Hogwarts students setting foot in either of the visitor's dwellings. When the visitor's arrive, Ron has a fleeting idea of offering Krum space in the Gryffindor Tower. However fleeting, it does suggest some expectation or desire of a more integrated visit. Yet this does not happen. In the Muggle world of study abroad, exchanges of this type are problematic in facilitating interactions between visiting students and students of the host institution. Visiting student dorms and classes are sometimes separate from domestic students, so they very rarely interact socially. Visiting students do not really meaningfully interact with the locals in an everyday context, which is considered the ideal way of reaping the full benefits of the exchange experience. It's not really until the Yule Ball that we are able to see some of the relationships that have been able to form despite limited contact.

Students from the three schools mix freely at the Ball; and these inter-school pairings indicate that even though they are not formally exchanging in terms of academics, students from the three schools are interacting socially. The two biggest inter-school pairings at the Yule Ball are Viktor Krum with Hermione and Roger Davies with Fleur Delacour. During the evening, Parvati is asked to dance by a Beauxbatons student and soon her sister Padma goes to join them. Even Hagrid's crush on Madam Maxime crosses school boundaries. There were also intra-school, inter House pairings like Cedric and Cho. In the end, as with most parties, the students seem to enjoy themselves. However, Ron's response to Hermione attending with Viktor illustrates some classic inter-group conflict behavior.

During the Yule Ball, Ron and Hermione have a conversation where Ron clearly articulates his resistance to the ideals of the exchange part of the tournament. At first his argument centers on his identification as a Hogwarts' student in opposition to Krum's Durmstrang:

> He's from Durmstrang!... He's competing against Harry! Against Hogwarts! You – you're – ... *fraternizing with the enemy*, that's what you're doing! (GOF 421, emphasis in original)

Krum's otherness is summed up in Ron's declaration that he is an enemy. There is clearly a competition between Hogwarts' champions and particular others. Ron's organizing the schools in this oppositional framework does not facilitate crossing any lines for friendship or connections of any kind. If lines are crossed, then allegiances are questioned. Ron implies inter-school connections like Hermione and Krum's is not genuine, but serve some sinister or ulterior purpose for the non-Hogwarts individuals. According to Ron, Krum is "just trying to get closer to Harry – get inside information on him – or get near enough to jinx him" (GOF 422). Having a mindset of mistrust creates barriers for Ron to accepting or interacting with the visiting students. For him, befriending these others has a cost – losing the tournament. In his current state of mind, he refuses to accept the benefits of the exchanges. Even

Hermione's explanation of the aims of the tournament ("getting to know foreign wizards and making friends with them") falls on deaf ears as he retorts "No it isn't!... It's about winning!" (GOF 423).

For Ron, the tournament and exchanges with the visiting students is a zero-sum game, and trust or engagement will somehow cost them in the tournament. He can see nothing to gain from social interactions. Hermione argues for him to look beyond the immediate goal of winning the competition and think about the long-term value of engaging with the foreign wizards and witches. This engagement is expected to lead to greater international cooperation across the magical community. At its most basic cooperation is about shared responsibility and to some degree reciprocity, but motivated from a place of fairness.

PARTING OF THE WAYS: WILL THE TIES BIND?

The magical world is as diverse as the Muggle world, facing phenomena like globalization and rumors of a reemerging enemy. The Muggle Olympics that began more than 3000 years ago has been a long-standing project that is part of a larger movement to facilitate a better world through sports competition with an eye toward excellence, peace, friendship, and respect. Bringing peoples of the world together under a banner of friendly competition gives fans an opportunity to support athletes representing their nation and taking pride in their successes. People come together as individuals of different nations. Although peaceful relations is one goal of such events, recognizing global community membership and interdependence does not replace identifying as a citizen of one's own nation. Putting people in the same space does not guarantee they will interact or, if they do, that those interactions will necessarily be positive.

It is evident that when encountering citizens of other nations one's own citizenship and identity categories are made salient and perhaps brought to bear on their experience at the event. This is what happens when Harry attends the Quidditch World Cup. Any antagonism toward the competing team does not necessarily extend to interactions with other fans or beyond the actual game. But Harry does see that fans of either team do their best to make sure others know whom they are supporting. So their identity as a fan emerges in contrast to the presence of rival fans. There does not appear to be any antagonism directed toward the opposing team's fans or national divisions within the groups of fans; unlike the inter-group distinctions and intra-group divisions that emerge during the Triwizard Tournament.

One's social identity is sharpened in the context of international travel, particularly student exchanges. Traveling to a foreign country as a student makes dimensions of identity salient in the face of foreign others. School affiliation, citizenship and other social characteristics that are personally meaningful shape patterns of engagement and interactions toward out-groups and its members. When compared to out-groups, if one's self-concept is deficient by comparison, then students engage in corrective behaviors, often in antagonistic ways. The Triwizard Tournament acts as a mechanism for both unity and for division. School membership is made salient by the arrival and existence of visiting students. Divisions and allegiances within Hogwarts are hardened when two champions are selected. Student actions reinforce and support these social identities and fuel their antagonistic attitudes and actions toward the other students. However, despite these divisions, there are some positive interactions and bonds that emerge from the tournament.

Finally, the integration and budding friendly relations that tournament supporters like Dumbledore want are clearly exhibited in the pairings and mingling of students at the Yule Ball. Despite sporadic objections to exchange and cultural understanding both initially and throughout the Quidditch World Cup and Triwizard Tournament, the unity and the willingness of people in the magical world to unite to fight Voldemort and his supporters in the Second Wizarding War indicate that the seeds of cooperation perhaps may have been planted during these events. In later years, Fleur marries into the Weasley family. Viktor and Hermione remain in touch, and he even attends Bill and Fleur's wedding. Internal House divisions within Hogwarts become inconsequential in the final battle against Voldemort, with Gryffindors, Ravenclaws, Hufflepuffs, and even some Slytherins (Rowling 2008) uniting to defend the school. Such undertakings may not have been possible without the opportunities and lessons of the Tournament.

International sports competitions and international student exchanges are long-term projects, predicated on the notion that repeated interactions between groups will break down barriers of difference and conflict, replacing them with bridges of understanding and cooperation. The Quidditch World Cup and Triwizard Tournament make clear that such undertakings are not always smooth, and results are not always immediately visible. However, the long-term benefits and goals of positive inter-group relations are clearly worth the effort because, in the end, one man alone could not destroy Voldemort. The talents, perspectives, knowledge and cooperation from diverse groups of magical individuals aid Harry in his defeat of the Dark Lord. Overcoming the obstacles of division and difference he encountered during his fourth year at Hogwarts set Harry on a course that brought all manner of beings from across the magical world together to fight Voldemort. His legacy is one of unity and cooperation; in other words creating ties that bind.

REFERENCES

Delamater, John and Daniel J. Myers. 2007. *Social Psychology*, Sixth Edition. Belmont, CA: Thomson-Wadsworth.

Henry, P.J. and Curtis D. Hardin. 2006. "The Contact Hypothesis Revisited: Status Bias in the Reduction of Implicit Prejudice in the United States and Lebanon." *Psychological Science* 17(10): 862-868.

Hogg, Michael. 2006. "Social Identity Theory." Pp. 111-136 in *Contemporary Social Psychological Theories*. Edited by P.J. Burke. Stanford, CA: Stanford University Press

Rowling, J. K. 2008. Interview with Pottercast.

Tajfel, Henry and John Turner. 1979. "An Integrative Theory of Intergroup Conflict." Pp. 33-47 in *The Social Psychology of Intergroup Relations*. Edited by W. G. Austin and S. Worchel. Monterey, CA: Brooks/Cole.

Tajfel, Henry and Michael Billig. 1974. "Familiarity and Categorization in Intergroup Behavior." *Journal of Experimental Social Psychology* 10: 159-170.

Using A Magical Lens to Study Collective Memory and Cultural Trauma Among Muggles

Shruti Devgan

Introduction

The devices, creatures and techniques in the wizarding world can be located within the theoretical framework of collective memory and cultural trauma that has been written about in the Muggle world. This chapter presents an analysis of four such signifiers in the magical world: dementors, the Dark Mark, Pensieve, and Occlumency. I argue that the presence of such magical creatures and equipment concretizes and clarifies experiences of cultural trauma and collective memory in the Muggle world. The signifiers in the magical world are evoked vis-à-vis the dark memories of Lord Voldemort and the first wizarding war. When the wizarding community acknowledges Lord Voldemort's resurgence, past traumas begin to repeat themselves.

In this chapter, I will concentrate on ways in which the collective identity and collective memory of witches and wizards is formed in relationship to Lord Voldemort. The collective identity of witches and wizards at Hogwarts is constructed around the memories of mass murders or genocide carried out by Lord Voldemort. The genocide that Lord Voldemort planned and executed with the help of his supporters during the First Wizarding War is evoked thereafter to bring forth the continued relevance of these memories. Lord Voldemort's motivations in unleashing a reign of terror are ascribed to his preoccupation with creating a race of witches and wizards that have pure magical blood instead of what is labeled as half-blood or Mudblood. It is in opposition to the remembrance of violence and terror associated with Lord Voldemort that Harry Potter is the benevolent and brave protagonist for the community of witches and wizards. The collective memory of Lord Voldemort as a perpetrator of violence against innocent witches and wizards leads a substantial section of the wizarding community to ascribe qualities of heroism and victory to Harry Potter. Potter embodies victory against the atrocities and injustices associated with Lord Voldemort in the past as well as the present. When Voldemort re-emerges in the magical world, many of the witches and wizards condemning violence and genocide gravitate towards Potter again. I argue that the lexicon associated with memory and trauma in the wizarding world is symptomatic of the presence of objects, creatures and practices that are experienced only in tangential, indirect, and imaginary ways among Muggles.

THEORETICAL FRAMEWORK

Collective memory is constructed in the specific context of society and shared by groups as an important basis along which identity is imagined and formed (Connerton 1995; Halbwachs 1992). Memories do not exist only at the individual level. Instead, the fact that individuals can recall certain events in similar ways is a consequence of the contemporary social framework that exhumes memories of some events just as it keeps others suppressed. Paul Ricouer brought out the importance of the current social framework in providing an impetus to recollect certain events that may have some basis in objective reality. However, memories of these events may be distorted or reinterpreted in a different light given the present social conditions. As Ricouer (2004: 21) wrote, "We have nothing better than memory to signify that something has taken place, has occurred, has happened before we declare we remember it." To this extent, collective memory is always partial and incomplete. There are mnemonic divisions between groups depending on their interpretations that in turn impinge on their collective identity (Lindo-Fuentes et al. 2007).

Cultural trauma mediates in the creation of certain memories and identities. Cultural trauma comes about when an entire group of people is affected by a painful, disturbing event as direct victims or indirectly as descendants of victims (Alexander 2004). Cultural trauma is not inherent, given or taken-for-granted. Rather, it is the meaning ascribed to an event or series of events by a larger group or collective that imparts it a "traumatic status" (ibid). Trauma hinges around pain and suffering at the level of the collective, just as it does at the level of individuals. To the extent that it is the 'remembrance' of trauma for a larger group, it becomes a resource for identity and a collective conscience. As Ron Eyerman (2004: 60) writes with reference to the memory of slavery among African Americans as a cultural trauma, "The trauma in question is slavery, not as institution or even experience, but as collective memory, a form of remembrance that grounded the identity formation of a people... as a cultural process, trauma is linked to the formation of a collective identity and the construction of collective memory."

The meaning ascribed to an event is culturally determined by individuals at a given historical stage. However, to the extent that these meanings are transmitted across generations, cultural trauma has an element of indirect, mediated transition. This is in keeping with Marianne Hirsch's (2002: 74) idea of "post memories" or generational distance from the event and identity formation through "indirect and multiple mediation." Eyerman (2004) also writes about the importance of time-delayed mediation and representation of trauma. Trauma must first be established as trauma by a cohort of individuals by means of interpretation and agency. It is not merely sufficient that a group undergoes pain and suffering for it to be established as a cultural trauma. Thus, some elements of an event are selected as more important than others in establishing an event as traumatic and these form the basis for collective or group identity and memory. To borrow from Eyerman again, he writes, "As opposed to psychological or physical trauma, which invokes a wound and the experience of great emotional anguish by an individual, cultural trauma refers to a dramatic loss of identity and meaning, a tear in the social fabric, affecting a group of people that has achieved some degree of cohesion. In this sense, trauma need not necessarily be experienced by everyone in a community or experienced directly by any or all..." (2004: 61).

Finally, Avery Gordon has written about haunting and its sociological relevance. Sociologically speaking, haunting means the selective ways in which scars or ghosts of the past possess continued social salience. Ghosts of the past or difficult memories affect current social circumstances, decisions, and life choices in ways that warrant recognition and acknowledgement in the present, so that a different future can be visualized and brought about. Individuals and groups are haunted by past events that reemerge from the nooks and crevices of memories, ideally, to bring about a shift from trauma to creating a space for reconciliation and healing. Haunting is then qualitatively different from trauma to the extent that it warrants the need to change status quo. "...[H]aunting, unlike trauma, is distinctive for producing a something-to-be-done. Indeed, it seemed to me that haunting was precisely the domain of turmoil and trouble, that moment...when things are not in their assigned places... when disturbed feelings cannot be put away, when something else, something different from before, seems like it must be done" (Gordon 2008: xvi).

It is within this theoretical framework of collective memory, cultural trauma and haunting that I will analyze the following objects, creatures, and practices: dementors, the Dark Mark, Pensieve, and Occlumency.

SOCIOLOGICAL ANALYSIS OF MAGICAL DEVICES, CREATURES & TECHNIQUES

Dementors

Dementors are guards of the wizard prison, Azkaban. They are cloaked and hooded in a way that their faces are completely hidden but their hands are an indication of what lies beneath, "glistening, grayish, slimy-looking, and scabbed, like something dead that has decayed in water" (POA 83). Professor Lupin describes them as among:

...the foulest creatures that walk this earth. They infest the darkest, filthiest places, they glory in decay and despair, they drain peace, hope, and happiness out of the air around them. Even Muggles feel their presences, though they can't see them. Get too near a dementor and every good feeling, every happy memory will be sucked out of you. If it can, the dementor will feed on you long enough to reduce you to something like itself... soulless and evil. You'll be left with nothing but the worst experiences of your life... (POA 187)

Harry Potter is once confronted with dementors during a game of Quidditch, and the experience illustrates the feelings of utter desolation that Professor Lupin describes. Lord Voldemort killed Harry Potter's parents and his mother sacrificed her life to save Harry's. The appearance of dementors on the Quidditch field make Harry lose his focus and instead his mind is flooded with memories of the past. He felt "as though freezing water were rising in his chest, cutting at his insides" and he heard a woman (his mother) screaming "Not Harry, please no, take me, kill me instead" (POA 179).

In the wizarding world, dementors are associated not simply with surveillance but also evoke extreme reactions of dread and losing touch with oneself because of this surveillance and memories of Lord Voldemort. Muggles in contemporary world are subject to monitoring by visible people such as guards or devices such as surveillance cameras but they are also subject to the power of the invisible gaze even when they are unaware of it (Foucault 1979). One of the most glaring and blatant examples of the latter is the constant monitoring over the Internet or the presence of hidden cameras or phone tapping devices. Dementors serve as a physical, albeit shadowy manifestation of the nature of dread and resultant trauma that individuals and collectivities – both Muggles and witches and wizards – experience because of this invisible gaze. Even though most witches and wizards have not been inmates of Azkaban, they are cognizant of the feelings that dementors engender because of prior interpretations and representations to which they have access. It is not simply the psychological consequences of hollowness that are at stake here but the threat of being physically imprisoned or the fear of being imprisoned in the wizard prison that the dementors evoke. Muggles might experience this same fear and paranoia because they inhabit a world of constant surveillance. Dementors provide a description of the subjective feelings that cultural trauma brings out within a community tied together by memories of horrific events.

The Dark Mark

The Dark Mark is a symbol that portends hauntings and traumatic memories. "[I]t was a colossal skull, comprised of what looked like emerald stars, with a serpent protruding from its mouth like a tongue" (GOF 128). At the Quidditch World Cup the Dark Mark appeared on the horizon and an older wizard, Arthur Weasley explained the gravity of the symbol, "The terror it inspired…you have no idea, you're too young. Just picture coming home and finding the Dark Mark hovering over your house, and knowing what you're about to find inside….Everyone's worst fear…the very worst…" (GOF 142).

In the Muggle world, the Dark Mark finds parallels in the Nazi swastika and the terror it evoked for Holocaust victims or hooded figures or the noose for African Americans subjected to racial violence of the worst kind. The perpetrator and victims of cultural trauma attach feelings of revulsion and fear to such symbols to such an extent that even when members of a community know of certain events like the Holocaust, slavery, or Lord Voldemort's killings indirectly, they nonetheless experience emotions of foreboding and anticipation of terror. For some of Lord Voldemort's supporters, the Dark Mark represents renewed hope; but for the wizarding community at large its meaning centers around violence and death. Thus, mnemonic divisions are present in the responses to the appearance of the Dark Mark. A sense of collective identity is forged vis-à-vis the Dark Mark – either as followers of Lord Voldemort who rejoice in the reappearance of the Dark Mark and bear its physical evidence on their arms; or as the larger collective that is terrorized and threatened by it.

Pensieve

The Pensive is a stone basin containing a swirling foggy substance or the physical form that memories take. Witches and wizards can use their wands to extract selective memories from their minds and place them in the basin to revisit them at will. The idea of the Pensieve alludes to the element of selectivity inherent in memory work along with a concrete manifestation of "time-delayed negotiation" (Eyerman 2004: 71) with memories, especially painful and difficult experiences. As Albus Dumbledore explains to Harry Potter:

> I sometimes find, and I am sure you know the feeling, that I simply have too many thoughts and memories crammed into my mind… At these times,…I use the Pensieve. One simply siphons the excess thoughts from one's mind, pours them into the basin, and examines them at one's leisure. It becomes easier to spot patterns and links, you understand, when they are in this form. (GOF 597)

The Pensieve is a literal manifestation of postmemories among Muggles, or the process through which memories get transmitted intergenerationally in a community in that it enables actual physical transportation of an individual to the memories of "others." Even though the Pensieve allows for individuals to gain access to objective facts, to the extent that they are filtered through another's memories, the element of indirect mediation, representation and interpretation that Muggles experience is also found in the wizard world. The ability to extract memories and place them in a tangible object is the basis for a common ground between the owner of certain memories and the consumer or audience member. This in turn becomes the basis of identification between the one evoking the memories and the other who literally witnesses them.

An example of how the Pensieve becomes a means of identification between individuals is when Harry Potter enters Professor Severus Snape's mind and discovers that the hatred and disregard that Snape expressed for Harry's deceased father is, in fact, justified. Harry discovers one of Snape's worst memories in which his father is bullying Snape and identifies with the latter whom he otherwise thoroughly despises. When he tumbles out of Snape's memories, Harry feels a sense of horror because "he knew how it felt to be humiliated in the middle of a circle of onlookers, knew exactly how Snape had felt as his father had taunted him, and that judging from what he had just seen, his father had been every bit as arrogant as Snape had always told him" (OOTP 650). By means of the Pensieve, Harry mnemonically identifies with Snape and begins to understand the latter's social location and consequent temperament.

Occlumency

Occlumency can be defined as the specialized skill to stop another individual from accessing one's memories and thoughts associated with the past. Once mastered, it is also a way to block out traumatic memories. In the Muggle world, perpetrators of violence or painful trauma take over their victims' cognitive processes and resulting feelings (Caruth 1995). In other words, perpetrators cause not just physical harm but also invade their victims' thoughts and memories pervasively, persistently and across generations. Similarly, in the wizarding world, Lord Voldemort is skilled at penetrating thought processes and memories or the "art of Legilimency" (OOTP 530). Harry Potter is the mediating link between Lord Voldemort's power to access memories and feelings and grave consequences for the larger community of witches and wizards. Dumbledore contends that as long as Harry Potter can block out these disturbing visions, the community of witches and wizards can stay protected from the violence that Lord Voldemort perpetrates. Dumbledore recommends Occlumency for Harry Potter to maintain a sense of solidarity with the other witches and wizards and to ensure that Harry Potter does not lose his self-identity.

Among Muggles, Occlumency can be performed by the mass media.[1] To the extent that the mass media is largely responsible for disseminating past images of violence and report on future possibilities and patterns, they can block out certain depictions of violence made available to the public at large. The mass media[1] censors gruesome images and selectively circulates others, thereby initiating an "official denial" (Cohen 2001). So, for instance in the aftermath of the terror attacks of September 11, 2001 in the United States, the mass media has been instrumental in racial profiling by circulating biased and narrow images of Arab and Muslim-Americans. These images are a practice in harmful Occlumency and Islamophobia, reducing a broad and diverse religious group and falsely labeling all Muslims as "others" synonymous with terrorism and fanaticism. Another example from a different context is in the Indian nation-state where there are several atrocities against religious-ethnic minorities like the Muslims and Sikhs that are depicted in narrow, sanitized ways by the mass media to create a political discourse of a healthy, secular democracy. So, while Occlumency is practiced at the individual level in the wizarding world and advocated as a technique to negate dangerous mnemonic connections, such as between Lord Voldemort and Harry Potter, in the Muggle world, Occlumency is performed in tacit ways. Occlumency in the Muggle world, such as that practiced by the mass media, becomes a way to create a collective identity that takes into cognizance certain events and images while ignoring or denying others.

CONCLUSION

The peculiar devices, creatures and techniques in the magical world that this chapter discussed allow Muggles to find a language to convey ideas of collective memory and cultural trauma. In this chapter, I have analyzed four signifiers within a sociological theoretical framework and drawn parallels between the wizarding and Muggle world. The experiences of cultural trauma, collective memory, and haunting are similar between the magical and non-magical world, but the former has access to greater, more exaggerated devices and techniques that allow them to revisit the past and reconcile with the present and future in ways that can only be imagined in the Muggle world.

---

1 The mass media is not the only agency that creates this kind of discourse but it is one of the most important arms of the state thus acts as an agent of Occlumency.

REFERENCES

Alexander, Jeffrey C. 2004. "Toward a Theory of Cultural Trauma." Pp.1-30 in *Cultural Trauma and Collective Identity*. Edited by J. Alexander et al. Berkeley, CA: University of California Press.

Caruth, Cathy, ed. 1995. *Trauma Exploration in Memory*. Baltimore, MD: Johns Hopkins University Press.

Cohen, Stanley. 2001. *States of Denial: Knowing About Atrocities and Suffering*. Cambridge: Polity Press.

Connerton, Paul. 1995. *How Societies Remember*. Cambridge: Cambridge University Press.

Eyerman, Ron. 2004 "Cultural Trauma: Slavery and the Formation of African American Identity." Pp.60-111 in *Cultural Trauma and Collective Identity*. Edited by J. Alexander et al. Berkeley, CA: University of California Press.

Foucault, Michel. 1979. *Discipline and Punish: The Birth of the Prison*. New York, NY: Vintage Books.

Gordon, Avery. 2008. *Ghostly Matters: Haunting and the Sociological Imagination*. Minneapolis, MN: University of Minnesota Press.

Halbwachs, Maurice. 1992. *On Collective Memory*. Translated by Lewis A. Coser. Chicago, Ill.: University of Chicago Press.

Hirsch, Marianne. 1997. *Family Frames: Photography, Narrative and Post-memory*. Cambridge, MA: Harvard University Press.

Lindo-Fuentes, Hector, Erik Ching and Rafael A. Lara-Martinez, eds. 2007. *Remembering a Massacre in El-Salvador: The Insurrection of 1932, Roque Dalton, and the Politics of Historical Memory*. Albuquerque, NM: University of New Mexico Press.

Ricoeur, Paul. 2004. *Memory, History, Forgetting*. Chicago, IL: University of Chicago Press.

PART IV

STRATIFICATION

"Or She"

GENDER (IN)EQUALITY IN WIZARDING SOCIAL INSTITUTIONS

MEREDITH RAILTON

"Everything about you is horrifying: your voice, body, hair, inability to be witty and panicky desires for approval and companionship."

Humans are born into a sex category, either biologically a male or female (most of the time). But out gender is a social category ascribed (while based on sex) by society; and society makes it tough for those lacking a Y-chromosome to achieve social equality. The opening quotation sums up Curtis Sittenfeld's (2001:3) personal experience and general social commentary of what it's like for a girl growing up in Muggle society. We struggle with pressure forced upon us – to be pretty, thin, popular, etc. – and growing up we may see those problems as insurmountable.

Starting at an early age and continuing throughout our lives, Muggle society teaches girls and women to be feminine, submissive to men, weak, agreeable, and dependent. From infancy parents attach pink bows on their baby girls' bald heads to make sure everyone knows what gender they are. As toddlers, some of girls' first toys are baby dolls that we're told to nurture. We learn our genders from every possible source: television, books, news programming, schools, music, families, peers, and social institutions.

In the wizarding world, witches receive gendered and gendering messages from their society as well. However, I would argue that the social construction of gender is not as rigid as it is in our Muggle world. To illustrate this point, this chapter will examine four social institutions in the wizarding world: Education, Government, Sports, and Hate Groups.

As explained in chapter two, social institutions are social organizations in which the majority of members of a given society participate. Social institutions in Muggle society often bear the marks of gender inequality. For example, women's soccer in England is only semi-professional. At this level, women's soccer teams are usually affiliates of men's professional soccer teams, have smaller stadiums than men's professional soccer teams, and make significantly less money than men's professional soccer teams. The United States also has no professional women's soccer league. The progress that has been made – such as the institution of the Women's World Cup – is recent and can be compared to the state of men's professional soccer in the 19th century.

In other words, women's professional soccer is about a century behind men's professional soccer in terms of development ("History of Women's Soccer").

Gender rigidity in social institutions and society in general is harmful to men as well as women. A popular trend has been for men to claim that they are being victimized by the growth of feminism and women's progress in society because it is a threat to their masculinity. As Hugo Schwyzer (2011) explains, however, it is the "straitjacket" of traditional stereotypes of masculinity that men are expected to live up to that harms them. Says Schwyzer (2011: 1):

> Men are suffering because their emotional, psychological, intellectual, and sexual potential is stunted by their own efforts to live up to an impossible masculine ideal… Being a man, in other words, is defined by divesting oneself of anything remotely associated with femininity (like kindness, sensitivity, intuition, empathy).

In the Muggle world, these constraints on masculinity make it difficult for non-hyper masculine men to be accepted as "real" men. Gender rigidity in the wizarding world, in contrast, appears to be much less prevalent in social institutions. In this chapter, I will show how witches and non-hyper masculine wizards have equal representation and participation in social institutions in the wizarding world. More importantly, I will demonstrate that the quality of involvement is a standard to which the Muggle world should aspire.

EDUCATION

Hogwarts School of Witchcraft and Wizardry was founded "a thousand years or more ago" (GOF 176) and serves as the educational institution for most of wizarding Britain. If one studies the faculty members, administrators, and curriculum of the school, it becomes apparent that Hogwarts represents a social institution that is more gender equal than in the Muggle world.

In addition, what appears to be a staff with a good balance of male and female teachers, there is an equal number of men and women Heads of House. Also, women instructors aren't relegated to "soft" subjects. In the Muggle world, male teachers dominate the "tough" subjects such as math and science while female teachers usually dominate the "soft" subjects such as English and art. While we have Severus Snape, a male, teaching the scientific subject of Potions, we also have Minerva McGonagall, a female, teaching the difficult subject of Transfiguration. In McGonagall's own words, "Transfiguration is some of the most complex and dangerous magic you will learn at Hogwarts" (SS 134). Arithmancy, a subject akin to theory of mathematics, is taught by Septima Vector while Astronomy is taught by Aurora Sinistra – both females. The subjects that could be deemed "soft" also seem to be balanced; Sybill Trelawney instructs the "lofty" Divination while Rubeus Hagrid instructs

Care of Magical Creatures. Unlike Muggle schools, the gender representation among the teachers of Hogwarts doesn't stick the male or female instructors into a niche based on gender.

Also, narrow Muggle proscriptions about "male" and "female" jobs are likewise irrelevant among the Hogwarts staff. For example, a male, Argus Filch, holds the post of caretaker, a job that entails housekeeping duties such as cleaning. The connotations of the word "caretaker" are usually ascribed to traditional notions of femininity, meaning the traditional view of mothers as caretakers of house and children (to read an analysis of why Filch doesn't live up to his post's title, see chapter 11). Before and after becoming the Care of Magical Creatures professor, Hagrid fills another role that Muggle usually prescribe to women. In addition to being the Keeper of Keys and Grounds, Hagrid consistently goes out of his way to care for animals. When he hatches a dragon egg, Hagrid exclaims with pleasure that the baby dragon "knows his mommy!" (SS 235). Despite his hyper-masculine appearance, the character traits of compassion and care demonstrated by Hagrid offer an image to the students of Hogwarts that defies Muggle constraints on masculinity.

While women still lag behind men in top-level administrative positions at schools in the Muggle world, it appears the glass ceiling in the wizarding world was cracked centuries ago. Although the Headmaster is a male up to the end of Harry's sixth year and during what would have been his seventh, we know via portraits that there have been a number of Headmistresses of Hogwarts. The first Headmistress of Hogwarts was Phyllida Spore, who held the position sometimes before her death in 1408 (Rowling 2007; HP4). Eoessa Sakndenberg (HP2), Dilys Derwent (OOTP 468-469), Dolores Umbridge, and Minerva McGonagall also held the position of Headmistress of Hogwarts.

During Harry's school years, Professor McGonagall, Dumbledore's Deputy Headmistress, frequently takes over during the sitting Headmaster's absences and serves as the permanent Headmistress after the end of the Second Wizarding War. Not only does McGonagall serve as Headmistress, she steps up and takes charge of the Battle of Hogwarts. During the preparations for the fight, McGonagall essentially becomes the General of the forces opposing Voldemort and her leadership went unquestioned. McGonagall is not criticized for being a powerful woman – she receives a significant amount of respect from her students, colleagues, and the magical community in general (though maybe not from the Death Eaters).

The other Heads of magical schools in Europe are Madame Maxime of Beauxbatons and Igor Karkaroff of Durmstrang. The post of Headmaster/ Headmistress of magical institutions of higher learning commands a certain respect and influence in the magical community and receives it regardless of the gender of the current post holder.

It is important to note that gender equality in social institutions does not just apply to women. The Muggle world, as stated before, holds men to a certain standard of masculinity that many fail to live up to, earning them scorn for not being "real" men. One of the greatest illustrations of how the wizarding world rejects these constraints can be found in the example of "the most inspirational and best loved of all Hogwarts headmasters" (DH 20), Albus Dumbledore. While Karkaroff seems to be a stereotypically masculine male holding a top-level administrative position, Dumbledore is anything but a stereotypical masculine male. Dumbledore holds many traits normally prescribed to women, such as being gentle and non-aggressive. Also, Dumbledore is a celibate gay man (Rowling 2007), completely transcending the Muggle masculine ideal of active heterosexuality. In sum, in the wizarding world's social institution of education, witches and wizards are free to be themselves without fear of condemnation or negative career repercussions for failing to adhere to a restrictive patriarchal system.

GOVERNMENT

In the Muggle world, there are currently only four female heads of state. In addition to the rampant gender inequality of governments in terms of representation, women who do hold government positions are sharply criticized for being un-feminine. Hillary Clinton, for example, was hounded during her primary bid for the U.S. presidency for not being feminine enough. When she did show her feminine side – wearing a shirt that showed a hint of cleavage and tearing up during a press conference – she was just as sharply criticized for not being tough enough. Sarah Palin was also painted in a very negative light by the U.S. and international media, repeatedly being sexualized as well as being portrayed as incompetent. In addition to the unfair treatment of women politicians in the Muggle world, Muggle government has historically been oppressive to women in terms of laws. Women weren't able to vote until the early 20th century, marital rape wasn't criminalized until the 1970s (Clay-Warner et al. 2009), and sex discrimination in the workplace is still prevalent.

The Ministry of Magic, by contrast, appears to be much more equal, though admittedly not 100% so. It is fairly balanced in terms of employment, top-level administrators, as well as policies. Both males and females work at the Ministry. Two top-level male employees who work at the Ministry are Cornelius Fudge (Minister for Magic) and Kingsley Shacklebolt (Auror Department, eventual Minister of Magic) while two top-level female employees are Amelia Bones (Head of the Department of Magical Law Enforcement) and Dolores Umbridge (Senior Undersecretary to the Minister for Magic). At the Ministry of Magic, merit, not gender, appears to dictate government careers.

Despite Hermione's Ministry position being "very high up" in magical law enforcement, the top seat – Minister for Magic – is, like its Muggle counterpart, still male dominated. The list of known Ministers for Magic reveals that, like in the Muggle world, the overwhelming majority of these appointees are male. However, there are two known female Ministers for Magic, Artemisia Lufkin and Millicent Bagnold. More impressively, the first female Minister for Magic was appointed in 1754 (Rowling 2006). Magical Britain's counterpart has only had one female Prime Minister, Margaret Thatcher. In the Muggle world, the first female to achieve an elected head of state, of Sri Lanka, wasn't until the mid-20th century; and Thatcher wasn't elected in Britain until 1979 ("Women heads of state"). Progress for women in the political realm, it seems, occurred much quicker in the wizarding world than in the Muggle world. If a female could become Minister for Magic in the 18th century, it's clear that women were participating in politics in the wizarding world long before women in the Muggle world.

SPORT

In the world of magical sports, Quidditch is the game. Regardless of gender, almost everyone in the wizarding world appears to love Quidditch, sometimes – as with the Muggle world and soccer – fanatically. Ron Weasley's enthusiasm for the Chudley Cannons is displayed both by his room decorations and interactions, such as when he interrupted a conversation between Cho Chang and Harry to express outrage over her favorite professional team. Oliver Wood cared so much about his team winning matches that he even said he didn't care if the Firebolt threw Harry off so long as he caught the Snitch first. Additionally, girls show as much enthusiasm for the sport as boys: Luna Lovegood made an animated lion hat while Dean Thomas painted an animated banner to show their support for the Gryffindor House team one match; witches like Cho passionately defend the professional team they support as do wizards like Ron; and Angelina Johnson shows the same intensity as Wood during her tenure as Captain of the Gryffindor House team. Moreover, regarding Angelina's position as Captain, the fact that the players, male and female, recognized and respected her authority, rather than challenging it or claiming her outbursts at Harry were due to being "emotional," shows the normality of women occupying structural positions of power.

Furthermore, Quidditch is a coed sport. It is almost unfathomable to imagine soccer being coed above the age of 10 or so in the Muggle world. Though a few female players have been extended invitations to join men's professional soccer squads (such as Brigit Prinz of Germany), there is no co-ed soccer at the professional level in Europe ("History of Women's Soccer").

And yet in the wizarding world, Quidditch is coed at both the school and professional levels. Ginny Weasley, Katie Bell, Cho, and Angelina all play on House teams alongside Fred and George Weasley, Ron, Cedric Diggory, and Harry. Whereas the Muggle world has separate leagues for men and women, there is no such division in the wizarding sport of Quidditch. While there are no professional teams that exclude women that we know of, there is one professional team that is exclusively female, the Holyhead Harpies.

Being a woman participant in the sport of Quidditch doesn't relegate one to second-class involvement in the institution at the school or professional level. For example, both Ginny and Cho played at the most crucial position on the team, the Seeker, alongside Harry, Draco Malfoy, and Cedric Diggory. Also, both Ginny and Oliver Wood go professional after school. Ginny follows what in the Muggle world is a traditional male athlete career path, becoming a sports correspondent after she retires from playing. This illustrates further how, unlike in the Muggle world, Quidditch is watched, played, and enjoyed by everyone regardless of gender.

Hate Groups

Despite the gender inclusiveness of Quidditch as an institution, one nevertheless notices that here are no girls on the Slytherin House team. It is interesting to note that the Slytherin House, a House known for Dark wizards and corruption, is the only House team that has no female players.

The Slytherin House is closely affiliated the Death Eaters. Voldemort's charming society appears to be very traditional in terms of patriarchy. There are only two female members of the Death Eaters: Bellatrix Lestrange and Alecto Carrow. After Voldemort's initial downfall, it was Bellatrix who led the group responsible for torturing Neville Longbottom's parents while looking for information on Voldemort. In the Second Wizarding War, Bellatrix was present during every battle. Bellatrix was so high-up in the ranks of the Death Eaters that Voldemort trusted her to guard a Horcrux and the sword of Gryffindor (which could be used to destroy Horcruxes) in her Gringotts' vault; and during a Death Eater meeting at Malfoy Manor, Voldemort comments that her opinion "means a great deal" (DH 9). However, despite her position of leadership among the Death Eaters, Bellatrix is blindly devoted to her male master, Voldemort, and dedicated her entire existence to his service. When Narcissa tries to help Draco in the task designated to him by Voldemort (to kill Dumbledore), Bellatrix shows scorn and comments, "If I had sons, I would be glad to give them up to the service of the Dark Lord!" (HBP 35). This complete subservience falls in line with the overtly patriarchal aspect of the Death Eaters.

Although Bellatrix Lestrange is considered Voldemort's most powerful follower, his "best Lieutenant" (DH 737), her female presence seems to be the exception to the rule within the Death Eaters. Aside from Bellatrix, the only other female Death Eater is the considerably less powerful Alecto Carrow. Alecto was appointed to teach at Hogwarts as opposed to a more involved position in the war, and she was always joined with her brother, Amycus. Outside of Alecto and Bellatrix, we see a strictly male group of Death Eaters. Their gender ideology and practice, it appears, is for Death Eaters to be male and to have pureblood housewives who are quite passive a la Narcissa Malfoy.

Patriarchy in the wizarding world appears to be associated with corruption and evil. This organization has many parallels to hate groups in the Muggle world, like the Ku Klux Klan and the Nazis. Both of these groups were overwhelmingly patriarchal and excluded women from high level participation and seats of leadership. When women were involved, they were relegated to "traditional" roles (i.e., being the mother or wife of a member). And yet even when it comes to hate groups the wizarding world shows more equality than the Muggle world, for neither the KKK nor the Nazis ever had a significant female member like Bellatrix.

Conclusion

The wizarding world isn't a perfect world of gender equality; but the social construction of gender in that society appears to be more progressive and accommodating of gender diversity than the Muggle world. Their social institutions are strikingly more gender egalitarian than ours. Females and non-traditionally masculine men have had significant roles in magical society for ages, with women working, competing, and politicking alongside men for centuries. The institutions of the wizarding world – particularly educational and sport – appear to be non-discriminatory and fully egalitarian in regards to gender; and other institutions, such as the government and even hate groups, are moving closer to structural gender equality faster than their Muggle counterparts.

REFERENCES

Clay-Warner, Jody, Jennifer McMahon-Howard and Linda Renzulli. 2009. "Criminalizing Spousal Rape: The Diffusion of Legal Reforms." *Sociological Perspectives.* 52:505-531.

"History of Women's Soccer." Retrieved 6 Aug. 2011. (http://www.soccer-fans-info.com/history-of-women-soccer.html).

Rowling, J.K. 2007. Interview at Carnegie Hall

Rowling, J.K. 2006. Official Website (http://www.jkrowling.com)

Schwyzer, Hugo. 2011. "How Men's Rights Activists Get Feminism Wrong." Retrieved 6 Aug. 2011.(http://goodmenproject.com/ethics-values/how-the-mens-rights-activists-get-feminism-wrong/).

Sittenfeld, Curtis. 2001. "Your Life as a Girl." Pp. 3-10 in *Listen Up: Voices From the Next Feminist Generation.* Edited by B. Findlen. Emeryville, CA: Seal Press.

"Women Heads of State." Center for Asia-Pacific Women in Politics. 4 March 2009. Retrieved 2 Jan. 2011. (http://www.capwip.org/participation/womenheadofstate.html).

"Wanagoballwitme?"

INTER 'RACIAL' DATING AT HOGWARTS

JENN SIMS

Whether encouraged as it is in Brazil or outlawed as it was in South Africa and the United States, race mixing occurs all over the world. But the notion of races "mixing" rests on the assumption that pure and separate races exist. According to evolutionary biologists, however, there is no biological basis for the division of humans into racial groups (Graves 2001). Genetics research agrees (Fujimura et al. 2008). Racial groups, therefore, are created by humans based on perceived ancestry and/or phenotype; and the mantra that race is socially constructed is a keystone in sociological discourse. By "socially constructed" sociologists mean that racial categories are not reflective of natural divisions among humans but instead are products of sociohistorical processes and projects of differentiation (Omi and Winant 1994).

"Race" can be defined as "a concept which signifies and symbolizes social conflicts and interests by referring to different types of human bodies" (Omi and Winant 1994: 55). In the United Kingdom there are six major "races": white, black, Asian (e.g., Indian, Pakistani), Chinese, mixed race, and "other." And despite there being no laws prohibiting it, most Muggles here and elsewhere date and marry someone from their own race. According to the 2001 UK Census, only about two per cent of marriages are between people of different races, with white/black and white/mixed couples being the most prevalent (Office of National Statistics 2005). These mixed race couples are important to sociologists because it is theorized that increased intermarriage indicates increased structural integration of racial minorities into the mainstream and is evidence of declining prejudicial attitudes toward those of a different race (Gordon 1964).

While only a tiny portion of Muggle Britain engages in exogamy, i.e., dating and marriage outside one's group, interracial dating and marriage is extremely common in the British wizarding world. For example, at the Yule Ball held the year Hogwarts hosted the Triwizard Tournament there was a plethora of mixed race couples. Among the four Champions, two crossed racial borders in selecting dates. Cedric Diggory, a white wizard, attended with Cho Chang, a Chinese witch. Harry Potter, a white wizard, secured a last minute date with Parvati Patil, an Indian witch. Parvati's twin sister Padma's (reluctant) attendance with Ron Weasley marked a third white/Asian Yule Ball couple. Glancing around the Great Hall, one could see other mixed race couples as well. There was a black wizard with an Asian witch and another black wizard with a white witch (HP4). Finally, while black/white couple Angelina Johnson and Fred Weasley at first "were dancing so exuberantly that people around them were backing away in fear of injury" (GOF 420), they could later be seen sweetly slow dancing late into the night (HP4).

The Yule Ball was a special occasion, but that doesn't mean that Hogwarts students need an extraordinary event to bring people of different races together romantically. Ginny and Dean, white and black respectively, dated throughout most of her 5th/his 6th school year. After Cedric's tragic death, Cho interracially dated Harry and then Michael Corner. And years after their Quidditch playing days, Angelina and George Weasley (no doubt bonded over mutual grieving at the loss of Fred during the Battle of Hogwarts) married across racial lines.

RACE AND RACIALIZATION

With so many witches and wizards ignoring race in matters of the heart, do we conclude that the wizarding world is a color blind utopia in which everyone is judged, not by the color of their skin, but by the content of their character? Not quite. While the differences among people that Muggles consider indicative of race is not a means of demarcation among witches and wizards, magic is. In other words, magic in the wizarding world is *racialized*. Races are formed when sociohistorical processes divide humans into groups based on some particular feature that is assumed to signify an intrinsic essence that makes people different, and some considered better, than others (Omi and Winant 1994). In the British Muggle world, the human features used for racial grouping are geography-based biology/genetics (i.e., birth place of one's parents, grandparents, etc.) and phenotype (i.e., skin color, hair texture, etc.). However, these are not failproof criteria for assigning racial group membership. For example, according to the racial logic in Muggle Britain, a person with one white and one black parent is racially mixed. However, if this person is dark skinned and another person does not know her/his parents, s/he is considered and, more importantly, treated as racially black instead. In other words, social factors such as others' *knowledge* of one's family, often more so than appearance or some biological or genetic "essence" from that family, are important in determining race.

The construction of magical race does not utilize phenotype like Muggle race, but it does (purport to) utilize biology/genetics. Wizarding categorization is based on "amount" of magical blood, i.e., a particular human feature that is assumed to signify an intrinsic essence that makes people different, and some considered better, than others. This indicates that magic has been racialized. In the wizarding world, there are three major magical "races." As Ron and Hagrid explained to Harry and Hermione following an incident in which Draco called her "Mudblood," there are "purebloods," i.e., witches and wizards with no Muggle heritage; "half-bloods," i.e., witches and wizards with a mix of Muggle and magical heritage; and "Muggle-borns," i.e., witches and wizards like Hermione who come from non-magical families. If one includes Squibs and Muggles, there are five magical "races." However, as with the Muggle construction of race, the use of "intrinsic" characteristics for racial grouping is illogical because the construction of race is actually contingent upon widespread knowledge of one's biological *and* social background.

Dean Thomas is a perfect example of the social, not biological, nature of racial classification. His mother and step-father are both Muggles. His biological father left when he was small, and the family does not know if he was a wizard or not. Dean, therefore, is racially ambiguous. By the racial criteria of the wizarding world, he is either half-blood (if his father was a wizard) or Muggle-born (if his father was not). It is not known. Nevertheless, Dean is considered and treated as a Muggle-born because both of his "parents," even though he is only biologically related to one, are Muggles. Dean's case shows that non-blood relationships and public knowledge (or lack thereof) of a person's family figure prominently into the construction of race.

Lord Voldemort is another example of the social nature of racial classification. Tom Riddle, Jr. has one magical and one Muggle parent. By wizarding logic this ought to make him racially half-blood. Yet as a powerful wizard, descended from the famous Salazar Slytherin, and one who "pruned" his family tree by killing his Muggle relatives, he is accorded all of the privileges and status of a pureblood. When Harry said his name to a group of Death Eaters while in the Department of Mysteries, Bellatrix yelled, "You dare speak his name?! You filthy half-blood!" (HP5). Yet, as Harry reminded them, "Did you know he's a half-blood too?.... Yeah, his mother was a witch but his dad was a Muggle" (OOTP 784). The fact that the Death Eaters, pureblood fanatics like Bella, and most in the wizarding world chose to ignore this fact and accorded Voldemort pureblood status is evidence that social, often more so than strictly biological, factors lay at the heart of constructions of race. Blood in the wizarding world, like skin color in the Muggle world, does not indicate natural biological/genetic divisions but is used as a justification for social divisions and hierarchies.

Before continuing, it is important to mention that there is a difference in acceptance of racial *classifications*, however (il)logical, and acceptance of a racial *hierarchy* based on them. While the latter may be limited to pureblood extremists, racists and Death Eaters, the former – acceptance of the idea of there being different races – is not. Ron says that calling a Muggle-born witch or wizard "dirty blood" and considering them less than purebloods is ridiculous; and many others agree. But no one says that the idea of the existence of distinctive magic races in the first place is ridiculous. The Longbottoms and Weasleys consider themselves purebloods and consider others to be members of different races, even though they reject the Death Eater ideology of pureblood supremacy. For example, during the Second Wizarding War when he learned from Lupin that Muggle-borns were being rounded up and imprisoned, Ron asked "What if purebloods and half-bloods swear a Muggle-born's part of their family? I'll tell everyone Hermione's my cousin" (DH 209). While a sweet gesture that conveyed his strong feelings of protectiveness of Hermione, his offer nonetheless indicates that he too believes that he and Hermione (and for that case Harry as a half-blood) are members of different races. Hermione buys into the wizarding world's construction of race as well, identifying herself as Muggle-born (e.g., HBP 185) and even attempting to re-claim the racial slur "Mudblood" (DH 489). Likewise, many half-blood witches and wizards accept the social construction of magical race and identify with their ascribed status. Remember that Harry told the Death Eaters that Voldemort was "a half-blood *too*" (OOTP 784, emphasis added), demonstrating that he, Harry, considers *himself* a half-blood. Others, such as Seamus Finnigan who identifies as "half and half" (HP1) and Severus Snape who daubed himself the "Half-Blood Prince" (HBP 604), also accept the wizarding world's racial categories, even if not always the hierarchical ordering.

MIXING RACE

In the Muggle world, reactionary responses to mixed race couples have ranged from curious stares to verbal intimidation and abuse to familial rejection and disownment (Root 1999). These same responses occur in the wizarding world, not towards black/white or white/Asian couples, but towards couples that mix by the above discussed magical races. Returning to the Yule Ball, during the Champions' procession into the Great Hall people were shocked to see Hermione Grainger with Viktor Krum, a white couple, while paying no negative attention to Cedric with Cho or Harry with Parvati, both mixed race couples. This is because in the wizarding world Hermione and Krum *are* what is considered a mixed race couple. She is Muggle-born and he is pureblood. Students stared and gaped "in unflattering disbelief" at Hermione with Krum; and his female admirers gave her "looks of deepest loathing" (GOF 414). In addition to being surprised that a popular athlete would date a bookworm, and at how different Hermione looked with hair and makeup and no heavy bag of school supplies, students focused on this particular couple no doubt due to amazement that someone of a high status race like Victor would select a date who is a member of a lower status race.

Viktor's Durmstrang high-master Igor Karkaroff was especially displeased with his star pupil's choice of a date. Interrupting Krum and Hermione's dinner conversation, Karkaroff joked "with a laugh that didn't reach his eyes" for Krum to not go "giving away" information about the school lest Hermione "know exactly where to find us" (GOF 417). Dumbledore commented upon this "secrecy" saying, "one would almost think you didn't want visitors" (ibid). Yet the fact is that Dumbledore's assessment was correct; Muggle-borns like Hermione were exactly who Karkaroff did not want at Durmstrang (GOF 165).

While Hermione and Krum attended the Yule Ball together and remained friends thereafter, other students had longer term relationships. Ginny and Dean, as mentioned earlier, would be considered a mixed race couple in the Muggle world; however, to the wizarding world the fact that he is black and she is white never drew negative attention or prejudice. Unlike some Muggle black men who date white women, Dean was not subjected to threats of violence from white students or charges of racial disloyalty from black students for dating Ginny. To the contrary, Ginny's brother Ron answered Harry's query as to what Ginny saw in Dean with "He's brilliant" (HP6) while having instantly declared he didn't like her previous, white boyfriend Michael at first sight of him (OOTP 348). Ginny, for her part, was not called derogatory names like "Ni---r lover" or shunned by friends and family like white Muggle women who date black men in the UK and elsewhere sometimes experience.

Yet while Muggle notions of race were irrelevant to their relationship, like with Krum and Hermione, the fact that a pureblood (Ginny) was dating a Muggle-born (Dean) *was* relevant. As a magically interracial couple, they drew both the attention and criticism that they might have received in the Muggle world for being a black/white couple. For example, discussing Ginny's inclusion in the Slug Club with Draco and Blaze Zabini, Pansy Parkinson noted that "a lot of boys like her" and that even difficult-to-please Blaze "think[s] she's good looking," (HBP 150). Zabini, a pureblood black wizard, responded – not that he wouldn't date a white woman – but that he "wouldn't touch a filthy little blood traitor like her whatever she looked like" (ibid). These sentiments suggest that Ginny's history of associating with and dating those outside her magic race has "spoiled" her previous purity. Just like Muggle white women who date outside their race are sometimes socially "demoted and became untouchable in the eyes of other whites" (Root 1999: 49), Ginny suffered a similar defamation of character by others of her magical race for interracially dating.

The unenthusiastic response of some to mixed race relationships reaches an apex of intensity when marriage occurs. Even the *idea* of interracial marriage can be considered outrageous. Professor Dumbledore revealed in his notes on Beetle the Bard's tale *The Fountain of Fair Fortune* that *"more than one parent has demanded the removal of this particular tale from the Hogwarts library"* because it "depicts interbreeding between wizards and Muggles" (TBB 39-40, emphasis added). Some parents, exemplified by Lucius Malfoy's letter to the late Hogwarts headmaster, do not want their children "to be influenced into sullying the purity of [their] bloodline by reading stories that promote wizard-Muggle marriage" (TBB 40). Mr. Malfoy and the other parents who wanted *The Fountain of Fair Fortune* censored were, unfortunately, not asking for anything too farfetched. In the Muggle world, organized bodies such as the USA's Motion Picture Association banned depictions of interracial romantic relationships until well after World War II (Gaines and Leaver 2002).

Yet, if children do nonetheless "sully the purity of their bloodline" by marrying outside their race, parental and familial care and concern could sometimes vanish. In the Muggle world, cases of children being disowned for marrying outside their race are sadly common place. Maria P. P. Root's (1999) book *Love's Revolution* draws on research with 175 Muggle families and documents the heartache and rejection that people (disproportionately white women) sometimes face from their families for crossing the color line. George Weasley did not suffer any such consequences for marrying Angelina. But Andromeda Black Tonks can relate to these Muggles all too well.

Born into the aristocratic pureblood Black family, Andromeda nonetheless chose to marry a Muggle-born man, Ted Tonks, rather than making a "lovely respectable pureblood marriage" like her sisters Bellatrix and Narcissa (OOTP 113). For this transgression, Andromeda was disowned by her parents and cut off by her sisters, who "never set eyes on [her] since she married the Mudblood" (DH 10). Root (1999: 57) explains that in the Muggle world, white parents sometimes see a son or daughter's marriage to a non-white person "as a significant breach of their identity and possibility also their status as 'white people.'" Disowning those who interracially marry makes the family "able to maintain its racial authenticity." In Andromeda's case, her Aunt's burning her off of the Black family tree and Bellatrix's murder of her half-blood niece can be seen as physical manifestations of the Black's attempt to remain "Toujours Pur."

CONCLUSION

Looking at who is considered to be racially "mixing" can expose the major social divisions in a given society. With regard to the wizarding world, juxtaposing the complete normality of black/white and white/Asian couples with the excessive attention and sometimes violence that is directed at pureblood/Muggle-born couples demonstrates that the manner in which British Muggles and British witches and wizards construct race differs. Most importantly, however, it reiterates sociologists' assertion that race is not biological or genetic, but socially constructed.

REFERENCES

Fujimura, Joan, Troy Duster, and Ramya Rajagopalan. 2008. "Race, Genetics, and Disease: Questions of Evidence, Matters of Consequence." *Social Studies of Science, 38*, 643-656.

Gaines, Stanley O., Jr. and Jennifer Leaver. 2002. "Interracial Relationships." Pp. 65-78 in *Inappropriate Relationships: The Unconventional, the Disapproved, and the Forbidden*. Edited by R. Goodwin and D. Cramer. Mahway, NJ: Lawrence Erlabaum Associations.

Gordon, Milton. 1964. *Assimilation in American life: The Role of Race, Religion, and National Origins*. Oxford: Oxford University Press.

Graves, Joseph L., Jr. 2001. *The Emperor's New Clothes: Biological Theories of Race at the Millennium*. New Brunswick, NJ: Rutgers University Press.

Office of National Statistics. 2005. "Focus on Ethnicity and Identity."

Omi, Michael and Howard Winant. 1994. *Racial Formation in the United States from the 1960s to the 1990s*. New York, NY: Routledge.

Root, Maria P. P. 1999. *Love's Revolution: Interracial Marriage*. Philadelphia, PA: Temple University Press.

"An owl OR a cat OR a toad"

ANIMALS AS SUBSTITUTIONS IN THE WIZARDING WORLD

ANNA CHILEWSKA

C. Wright Mills in his book *The Sociological Imagination* asks us to look at a structure of a society as a whole and to consider its components as well as the relationship between components in order to understand it. One of the main components of the wizarding world is the various animals that interact with wizards and witches. Where do those animals belong, what are their functions, and does a wizard's choice of an animal companion reflect the wizard's positioning within his or her own society? To answer these questions, in this chapter I explore the position of non-human animals, both magical and non-magical in the wizarding society. I argue that animals hold a fixed place that is imposed by members of the wizarding world and that their primary purpose is their servitude as food, ingredients, clothing, ornaments, study aids and entertainment. I also argue that relationships between human and non-human animals are formed mostly out of human necessity to create bonds and substitute absent humans with those animals that are best suited to fill the gaps of individuals who are outsiders within their own wizarding society.

Moreover, wizard society is highly stratified, where the hierarchical rankings of individuals are based on certain characteristics that are closely connected to one's ancestry, parentage, abilities and physical qualities. I will examine the social stratification in terms of how individuals fit into set positions in wizarding hierarchies and whether their positioning (willed or imposed) plays a role in their human-animal interfacing. Within the same society, the ideology displayed by most wizards towards animals is that of anthropocentrism and speciesism, meaning that wizards hold the power over most non-human beings.

ANIMALS AS INGREDIENTS

The position that most animals occupy in the wizarding society is that of commodity. The wizarding world uses animals mainly as food, clothing and ingredients. When Harry first arrives at the Hogwarts School of Witchcraft and Wizardry, he partakes in a welcoming feast, which consists of "roast beef, roast chicken, pork chops and lamb chops, sausages, bacon and steak" (SS 123). For the annual Christmas Feast the school offers "a hundred fat, roast turkeys" (SS 203). The slaughtering and consuming of animal flesh is an everyday occurrence that is not questioned by anyone. And the presentation of animal foods is in chops, parts and slabs. The entire animal is rarely displayed because displaying only parts distances the consumer from it and does not prompt a reflection on one life sacrificed for the sake of another. Furthermore, the anthropocentric attitude allows the wizarding society to use other species for their own purposes and value other species in terms of their usefulness.

In addition to consuming the flesh, the wizarding society uses animal parts for objects of everyday use. Dragons serve as an example of such practices. Before beginning the first year at Hogwarts, Harry must purchase gloves that are made of "dragon hide" or something similar to it (SS 66). Dragon blood, as the Hogwarts headmaster Albus Dumbledore discovers, has twelve human uses, one of which is an oven cleaner. Dragon meat is used by Hagrid as a healing agent to reduce swelling. Dragon heartstring is used as the core of a wand, and both Hermione Granger and Lucius Malfoy have dragon heartstring in theirs.

And even though the utilization of animal parts is so widespread in the wizarding society, Harry does not seem to make a connection between a dead animal and its parts he has been using in his potion class. For example, in addition to Dragon heartstring, magic wands are filled with other animal parts such as unicorn hair or phoenix feathers. Yet when a unicorn is slain and one of the centaurs asks Harry if he knows what unicorn blood is used for, Harry, in his ignorance, is startled by "the odd question" and answers that he has used only "the horn and tail-hair" (SS 258). It is interesting that Harry finds the question about blood "odd" but does not find the practice of using horn and tail-hair peculiar. Because Harry's contact is reduced to horns, hairs, or other parts, the entire animal does not appear to hold any meaning to the boy. The anthropocentric community, to which he belongs, readily dismisses or ignores the life that lies beneath the useful parts.

Animal Experimentation

One of the skills that students learn at the School of Witchcraft and Wizardry is transfiguration. This class, more so than the others, resembles an animal experimentation laboratory. For example, the students are asked to transfigure a live hedgehog into a pincushion. The troubling fact here is not that only Hermione Granger is able to do this satisfactory, but rather that other students' pincushions curl up "in fright if anyone approaches [them] with a pin" (GOF 233). The fear and potential pain of the hedgehog is never questioned and students move on to other assignments. In the first year Transfiguration exams, students have to transfigure a mouse into a snuffbox. If the box is pretty, marks are awarded. If the box still has whiskers, marks are deducted. In the second year of schooling, students must transfigure a beetle into a button and two white rabbits into a pair of slippers. In the sixth year syllabus, an owl is to be changed into a pair of opera glasses. In addition to transfiguring animals, students also learn to "vanish" them. Part of the fifth year curriculum is to vanish snails and mice; and again, the troubling fact is not that Hermione is the only one able to perform the magic (and advance to vanishing kittens), but rather that no one pauses to consider the ontological fate of the animals. Other classes also are unkind to non-human animals. For example, during potions lessons students behead and slice dead caterpillars or watch their teacher – professor Snape – test out a potentially poisonous potion on a toad belonging to Neville Longbottom (POA 126-127).

The lack of empathy and the clear positioning of non-human animals at the level of test objects and study aids are further illustrated when the imposter professor Moody demonstrates a *Cruciatus* Curse on a live black spider. Harry recalls:

> At once, the spider's legs bent in upon its body; it rolled over and began to twitch horribly, rocking from side to side. No sound came from it, but [he] was sure that if it could have given voice, it would have been screaming. Moody did not remove his wand, and the spider started to shudder and jerk more violently. (GOF 214)

As Moody tortures the spider, Hermione Granger yells "Stop it!" (GOF 214). However, she does this not because she is looking at the struggling spider but at the horrified Neville Longbottom and wants his fear to cease. Hermione's aim is clearly to protect the life and well being of her classmate even though it is a spider who suffers the most for no reason that can be justified. During the same lesson professor Moody kills a spider to show a killing curse known as *Avada Kedavra*. As he concludes the presentation, Moody sweeps the spider's lifeless body onto the floor as if it were a mere speck of dust. Again, no one questions the events, and no one mourns the creature's passing. It appears to be taken for granted within the school walls that animals' lives do not belong to them but to the teachers, students and lessons and may be used in any fashion.

ANIMALS AS ENTERTAINMENT

In a world where animals occupy the lowest level of social hierarchy, it is not surprising that they are treated as entertainment. When Hogwarts hosts a Triwizard Tournament, one of the tasks that each champion must complete is to retrieve a golden egg from a dragon. In order for the task to be as challenging as possible, the school requests nesting dragon mothers and puts them in an enclosure. During the tournament, Harry tries to lure the mother away from her nest so he may capture the golden egg, but he needs all his persuasive techniques to do so as she remains "too protective of her eggs" and is "afraid to move too far away from them" (GOF 355). If one were to strip away the scales and the fiery breath, one would understand that this is a mother – like any other mother – whose purpose is to protect those lives she created. But because the dragon is not a human-animal, she is seen by all participants and spectators as an obstacle that needs to be conquered. The wizarding society seems to be practicing an old belief that "Nature is a piece of property, an inheritance, owned and operated by mankind, a sort of combination park, zoo and kitchen garden" (Wischnitzer 1985: 165). Therefore, the entire tournament becomes a gaze and the dragon an actress that is expected to perform a task; but she is also expected to fail her task so that the superior being – Harry – may succeed at his.

THE SUBSTANDARD SOCIETY AND NON-HUMAN ANIMALS

The wizarding world is divided into social classes, although the boundaries between each are not always clearly defined. As Lucius Malfoy and his son Draco would want many to believe, at the top of the social ladder stand those wizards who come from pure wizarding families (where both parents are wizards). Second in status are half-blood wizards, those who have one magical and one Muggle (non-magical) parent. Finally, Muggle-born wizards, offspring of two parents with no magical abilities, rank at the bottom of the hierarchy. The Malfoys, the Blacks, and other elitists families view Muggle-born wizards as being "just not the same" as purebloods and point out as often as they can that wizards from Muggle families have not been "brought up to know our ways" and should not be allowed to attend Hogwarts (SS 78).

In addition to pureblood and mixed-blood wizards, Harry's magical world hosts a number of individuals who exist somewhere on the periphery. They form a "substandard society" because they are rarities who do not fit in with the rest of the wizards and witches. These are individuals who are born to wizard families but possess no magical abilities, known as Squibs, and individuals who come from families where either one or both parents are non-humans, known as half-breeds. The substandard society can also be viewed as individuals whose characteristics often do not allow them to be fully realized beings in their own world or whose needs must be satisfied elsewhere.

Filch's Cat

In Harry's world, the type of interaction that one has with animals is largely dependent on the social class to which one belongs as well as to the social marker by which one is defined. Squibs have a strong connection with animals and treat them as friends and companions. Argus Filch, who is a caretaker of Hogwarts, is a product of a rare incidence of someone being born in a wizard family who does not have any magical powers. In his own society, Filch is a person whose existence is constantly marked by his difference. Because he is part of the wizard society he would not be comfortable in the Muggle world; on the other hand, as a failed wizard, he cannot be fully integrated into the wizard society either. Filch is an unattractive man whose sole purpose in life is to catch students in the act of doing something wrong. He has no friends and his only companion is a female cat called Mrs. Norris, described as "a scrawny, dust-coloured creature" (SS 132). Filch is not a caring, compassionate person; he misses the days when corporal punishment was inflicted on students and he reminisces of the time when a student could be hung by his "wrists from the ceiling for a few days" (SS 248). And, the only occasion when students are exposed to Filch's softer side is when he interacts with Mrs. Norris. He calls her "my sweet" and is inconsolable after Mrs. Norris is petrified by a Basilisk.

The relationship that Filch has with his cat is multilayered. She might be his only friend but she is also a reflection of Filch and everything that makes him a part of the substandard society. She shares his characteristics: they are both unattractive and scrawny "with bulging, lamplike eyes" and are both hated by all students (SS 132). Moreover, both Filch and Mrs. Norris are inconsequential to students' lives. Their interaction with them is limited to catching students wandering the halls after hours and breaking school rules. Just as his cat, Filch lives and lurks in the shadows to emerge unexpectedly out of the dark, his face often "loom[s] suddenly" (SS 241) only to hide again and remain in the shadows. Everything that makes him an outsider is contained within Mrs. Norris's characteristics. She is not only his friend and his reflection, but also a substitution for a human friend or a human companion. Sir Keith Thomas, a Welsh historian, described pets in relation to the social predicament of their owners: "The pet is a creature of its owner's way of life" and suggested that "people feel it necessary to maintain a dependent animal for the sake of emotional completeness" (Thomas 1983: 119). Given that Filch's social status of a Squib makes it difficult for him to form relationships, the cat's title *Mrs* suggests that Filch has created a metaphorical marriage between himself and the only female who would have him, and who willingly runs to him every time he calls.

Hagrid and his Beasts

Formation of bonds within the substandard society involves much more than a preference for certain animal species. The American scholar John Eisenberg (1971: 132) suggests that "in order for bonding to take place, it would appear that the organism must be able to perform some satisfying act of a self-reinforcing nature with the bonded object." In short, a person will seek out some sort of "reward" that will result out of the bonding experience. Whereas Filch creates a metaphorical marriage in order to fill the void created by the absence of a human companion, Rubeus Hagrid becomes a "collector" of non-human animals who are outsiders in their societies in the same way that he is in his.

Hagrid is the school's groundskeeper and gamekeeper. He lives away from the castle in a run-down shack. He is a giant man, with a "face almost completely hidden by a long, shaggy mane of hair and wild, tangled beard" (SS 46). Furthermore, Hagrid is prone to drink, speaks in an ungrammatical way and his writing is "a very untidy scrawl" (SS 135). Juxtaposed to the elite institution of magical higher learning next to which he lives, everything about Hagrid suggests outsider. He is uncomfortable with most people, in large part because of size. And like Filch, he lives alone, with only animals for company. Also like Filch, the company he keeps is a reflection of his belonging to a substandard society.

Hagrid lives with "an enormous black boarhound" called Fang of whom he is very fond (SS 140). Others animals to which he is mostly drawn are creatures whose very shape and form make them outsiders within their own species. In the six years that Harry attends Hogwarts School of Witchcraft and Wizardry, Hagrid is associated with animals that produce fear or are generally disliked. First, he buys a giant three-headed dog, whom he names Fluffy; and then he hatches a dragon to whom he sings lullabies. Next, Harry and Ron learn that Hagrid has been taking care of a giant spider, Aragog, ever since the spider was an egg. When the spider gets accused of a crime, it is Hagrid who protects the arachnid and his family. When Harry and Ron meet Aragog, the spider speaks of Hagrid's goodness and of how much respect he has for his caretaker (COS 277-278). As the new Professor of Care of Magical Creatures, the first creature Hagrid introduces to students is a giant beast known as a Hippogriff, which you must take care not to insult because "it just might be the last thing you ever do" (HP3).

While Hagrid seems accustomed to stand out in every crowd because of his enormous size, he appears the happiest when he is surrounded by giant creatures. Furthermore, the Hogwarts' groundskeeper clearly favours animals that are met generally with fear, repugnance or disdain. In fact, most of his animal friends are classified as XXXXX, i.e., "known wizard killer / impossible to train or domesticate" by the Ministry of Magic's Department for the Regulation and Control of Magical Creatures (FB xxii). The result is that while others are terrified of fire-breathing dragons and angry Hippogriffs, Hagrid considers them "Beau'iful" (POA 114). Because he is half-giant, and because giants are reputed to be savages from whom wizards and witches need to be protected, he chooses to interact with and protect those who are regarded with the same attitude. The personal network Hagrid creates with his chosen non-human animals is a marker of his self-identity that has been, in part, imposed by the wizarding society. It has been suggested in the late twentieth century that "dog owners come to resemble their pets" because there is a desire to choose a breed that is "consistent with [the owner's] social identity" (Franklin 1999: 99). The same can be said about Hagrid. His social and personal identity, as I already mentioned, is that of an awkward giant man called a savage or an oaf who comes from a race of vicious, bloodthirsty brutes. And yet, like most of the animals that he befriends, he is a gentle giant who can be dangerous only when provoked.

Hermione Granger and Crookshanks

Randy Malamud, in his study *A Cultural History of Animals in the Modern Age*, says that "animals are thickly enmeshed in human culture simply because people are so interested in them. We use them in a range of ways – some benevolent, some silly, some violent – in the service of our own cultural drives, desires, fantasies and obsessions" (Malamud 2007: 3). Wizarding culture shares this interest in animals and allows students to bring them to school. When Harry Potter first receives a letter from Hogwarts about being accepted, he is informed that he may "bring an owl OR a cat OR a toad" (SS 67). While Harry brings a snowy owl and Ron an old rat, Hermione does not acquire a non-human companion until their third year.

Although Hermione occasionally lacks self-esteem as a young girl and is subjugated to offensive remarks because of her Muggle parents, she is a good friend to many students and a good advisor. Hermione is intelligent, has sound judgment and clarity of perception. She is the one who, during the search for the sorcerer's stone, frees herself from Devil's Snare and saves Harry and Ron from its deadly grasp. She is the one who, two years later, helps Harry save Sirius Black and Buckbeak the hippogriff from certain death. And in the sixth year, in her true academic fashion, Hermione deduces that the word Prince in "Half-Blood Prince" might be a woman's last name and not a man's title. No other student at Hogwarts equals Hermione's intellect and clarity of mind, and no other student possesses her impeccable work ethics and thirst for academic knowledge. Therefore she finds an equal in her cat companion Crookshanks, whom she purchases from the Magical Menagerie in the Leaky Cauldron. On many levels, Crookshanks complements Hermione's drive to succeed at everything she does and her superior moral judgment.

Crookshanks is a large orange half-kneazle feline with thick fur and "oddly squashed face" (POA 60). Unlike the relationship that Filch and Hagrid have with their animal companions, where the connection is based on emotional needs, Hermione's companion fulfills her intellectual needs that humans are unable to provide. Whereas Harry and Ron often act in a foolish manner and on impulse, Crookshanks has the ability to solve problems on his own and recognize potentially dangerous persons and situations. He immediately takes a dislike to Ron's pet rat Scabbers, who is later revealed to be Peter Pettigrew, and independently seeks out the rat in order to destroy him. Like Hermione, who does not yield when she knows she is right, Crookshanks goes after Scabbers whom he senses is a fraud despite protests from Ron and pleading from Hermione. When Harry is threatening to kill Sirius Black because he is convinced that Black was responsible for the death of his parents, Crookshanks first tries to take Harry's wand away and when that fails, he leaps "onto Black's chest" and forms a shield over "Black's heart" (POA 342). Being able to perceive right from wrong, Crookshanks takes charge and saves an innocent man from a certain injury, if not death.

Like Hermione, who is praised for being clever and frequently referred to as the brightest witch her age or the best student in her year (HP3, HBP 70), Crookshanks also is recognized for his intellect, being described by Sirius Black as the "most intelligent of his kind that I've ever met" (POA 364). Hermione is the first student to guess that professor Lupin is a werewolf, while Crookshanks recognizes that a large black dog is, in actuality, Sirius Black. Moreover, he shares Hermione's need for adhering to rules and academic honesty. When Harry and Ron make up answers for the Divination homework, the cat makes his disapproval known. Harry recalls: "Crookshanks wandered over to them, leapt lightly into an empty chair, and stared inscrutably at [him], rather as Hermione might look if she knew they weren't doing their homework properly" (GOF 222).

CONCLUSION

Most animals in the wizarding world do not fare well. Some lose their lives, some are given away, others are set loose when their usefulness reaches its end. The wizarding society lives with animals and interacts with them, but does not always consider them to be more than body parts, study aids or sources of food. Those who have the strongest connections to non-humans are those whose characteristics of whatever sort prevent them from forming certain types of bonds with their own kind. But despite the lack of compassion that witches and wizards often show to them, the animals persevere, urging us to look more critically at our own relationships with those around us.

REFERENCES

Eisenberg, John. 1971. "Introduction." Pp. 131-139 in *Man and Beast: Comparative Social Behavior.* Edited by J. Eisenberg and W. S. Dillon. Washington, D.C.: Smithsonian Institute Press.

Franklin, Adrian. 1999. *Animals and Modern Cultures: A Sociology of Human-Animal Relations in Modernity.* London: Sage Publications.

Malamud, Randy. 2001. "Introduction." Pp. 1-26 in *A History of Animals in the Modern Age.* Edited by R. Malamud. Oxford: Berg.

Mills, Charles Wright. 2000 [1959]. *The Sociological Imagination.* Oxford: Oxford University Press.

Thomas, Keith. 1983. *Man and the Natural World: Changing Attitudes in England 1500-1800.* London: Allen Lane.

Wischnitzer, Rachel. 1985. "Picasso's Guernica: A Matter of Metaphor." *Artibus et Historiae* 6: 153-172.

"You'll never know love or friendship, and I feel sorry for you"

VOLDEMORT AS A QUEER CHILD

GRÁINNE O'BRIEN

According to Freud, to understand adult desires, one must examine childhood experience (Freud 1920). This chapter will examine latent homosexual desire in Tom Riddle, the forced suppression of which, I maintain, may have been partly responsible for the creation of Lord Voldemort. Voldemort's sublimation would have begun during his childhood when he was in an orphanage, unable to express himself, magically or sexually, because of the repressive nature of the environment. Once established, the sublimation continued into his adulthood.

In past work regarding Lord Voldemort, I have expressed the view that the wizarding world is the perfect, microcosmic, queer world (O'Brien 2010). I subscribe to the belief that "queer" not only can refer to sexuality but also can refer to anything that goes against the dominant society (Halperin 1995). Queer implies anything that is deviant, i.e., a refusal to conform to societal norms. It includes, but is not limited to, behaviours that go against the heteronormative expectations of society. "Heteronormativity" refers to the "institution of heterosexuality" and the idea that heterosexuality is the only normal, socially acceptable way to live (Giffney 2009).

This chapter will trace the life of Tom Riddle, Jr. who became Voldemort, The Dark Lord, discuss his queerness as a child in terms of psychoanalytic theory and then examine the possibility that his "queerness" was the root of his darkness.

THE PUREBLOOD MOTHER AND THE MUGGLE FATHER

From his conception, Tom Riddle, Jr. was destined to live an abnormal existence. His mother, Merope, was mistreated and abused by her family. She experienced both verbal and physical abuse at the hands of her father and brother. "Pick it up!" her father once bellowed at her. "That's it, grub on the floor like some filthy Muggle, what's your wand for, you useless sack of muck?" (HBP 205). The abuse she experienced affected her ability to perform magic, and though she was a very capable witch, her repeated abuse made her feel terrified and incapable of performing magic properly. Once she was free of her abusive father and brother, she found just how capable of performing magic she was.

Tom's father was local Muggle man, Tom Riddle, Sr. Merope magically seduced him (likely via love potion) into marrying her. Riddle, Jr. was conceived, therefore, under unusual circumstance in terms of sexual consent. Likely consumed with guilt at her actions, Merope stopped giving Tom, Sr. the love potion, hoping that he would love her without the magic or at least stay for the sake of their unborn child. However, she was wrong on both accounts. The Muggle abandoned Merope and she – left impoverished, heartbroken, and alone – died almost immediately after Tom, Jr. was born.

Riddle was raised in a Muggle orphanage until he was eleven years old, at which time Dumbledore, who was given the responsibility to tell him about Hogwarts, arrived. The child Dumbledore met had clearly evident psychological issues. He demonstrated serious paranoia, kleptomania, and was a "quazi pathological child" (Stockton 2009). Tom Riddle, Jr. was "growing sideways" as his circumstances had resulted in abnormal growth and left him unable to "grow up straight" (ibid). He had suffered a traumatic conception and birth and loveless early upbringing. As a result he was practically incapable of growing up "normal" in accordance with the societal view of what "normal" is.

Tom had a very aggressive personality, even at the young age of eleven. To me, the aggression that Dumbledore witnessed in the orphanage was a glimpse of the desire for power that would eventually consume Riddle and evidence that he had been forced to repress himself growing up in the institution. I believe that his desire for power was sublimation, resulting from his need to constantly supress himself, due to an unaccepting, and hostile environment. The Muggle orphanage was not an ideal environment for him to be free, magically or sexually. He could not understand either urge, and the constant need to repress them damaged him.

KNOWING YOU ARE SPECIAL

Dumbledore encountered a very disturbed child when he first met Tom. During his conversation with Mrs. Cole, who ran the establishment, she said he, "was a funny baby...when he got older he was.... 'odd'" (HBP 267). He demonstrated his power over the other children in the orphanage by stealing their possessions and traumatizing them. Mrs. Cole told Dumbledore of two examples: the death of Billy Stubbs' rabbit, found hanging off the rafters of the orphanage; and the apparent mental anguish he caused two other children in a cave[1]. Dumbledore claimed Riddle had "obvious instincts for cruelty,

---

1   Here I wish to pose a difficult but interesting question. Given the terror and trauma that had rendered the children incapable of discussing what happened, would

secrecy and domination" and could use his powers "against other people, to frighten, to punish, to control" (HBP 276). Already at the age of eleven, Tom has demonstrated that his desire for power was much stronger than any human attachment he may have made. Dumbledore believed that Riddle regretted revealing so much of himself during their first encounter, in the excitement of finding out he was a wizard that he let his guard down. I disagree. In regards to his sexuality and "queerness," I believe he let his guard down around Dumbledore because Riddle saw something familiar in Dumbledore, and felt the need to reveal more of himself. He confided: "I knew I was different.... I knew I was special. Always, I knew there was something" (HBP 271). In research on queerness and homosexuality, it has often been shown that children "knew" there was something different about them from a very young age (Stockton 2009). Could Riddle be alluding to something here? Was his magical ability not the only thing that made him a queer and different child?

Once Riddle arrived at Hogwarts he learned the value of using his good looks and unassuming manner to charm his fellow students and teachers and was able to manipulate them to get what he wanted. It is interesting to note that Dumbledore was the only person to recognise there was something off about him. The sixteen-year-old Riddle, who came out of his diary in the form of a memory, told Harry that Dumbledore was the only one who did not fall for his charms, who mistrusted him. This, I believe, is evidence that Dumbledore saw something in Riddle that others did not: Recognition of the queer nature, that was Dumbledore's also, combined with Tom's inclination towards evil.

Dumbledore continued to "ke[ep] an annoyingly close watch" on him (COS 312), I believe, seeing more than just a growing desire for power but also a reflection of his own desires and queerness. Dumbledore himself had the same desire for power when he was younger. He had fallen in love with Gellert Grindelwald, and the two "flirted with the idea of exactly what Voldemort goes on to do" (Rowling, quoted in Granger 2008: 181-182); however Grindelwald soon became consumed with power, desire, and darkness. After Dumbledore's heartbreak at the death of his sister Arianna, he chose to live a safe, celibate life, devoting his time to his students and Hogwarts. He chose to suppress his love for Grindelwald and lust for power and not allow either to consume him. In contrast, Riddle successfully rid himself of not only sexual desire, but any desire for human contact whatsoever; his repression was absolute. The asexual

---

it be hard to believe that some kind of sexual experimentation may have occurred? Silence in children can indicate abuse or trauma in their past. Something important happened there; Riddle clearly saw the encounter with the children in the cave as a pivotal moment in his life, evidenced by the fact that he later chose the location to hide a Horcrux, part of his soul.

nature of both Dumbledore and Lord Voldemort is also a powerful reflection on the treatment of homosexuality in the wizarding world, and highlights that even when one is not sexually active, abstaining completely, he or she is still queer.

I maintain that Dumbledore recognized in Riddle the desire to pursue that same darkness that he himself had turned away from and a young man struggling with his queerness as he had been. And yet, he did not spend much time on, nor give much attention to Riddle, beyond observing him from afar. Dumbledore was the member of staff who was adamant the children of Hogwarts not have access to knowledge in books like *Secrets of the Darkest Arts*, which describes how to create a Horcrux (DH 102), perhaps evidence of Dumbledore's attempts to suppress the darkness he sensed was growing within Riddle, without taking the time to try to uncover why Riddle was the way he was or offer him guidance.

HOW TO ACQUIRE THE BLOOD OF THE ENEMY

By the time Harry Potter is born, Tom Riddle, Jr.'s transformation into Lord Voldemort was complete. He had created six Horcruxes and probably intended to have his seventh be created as a result of the murder of Harry Potter. His fixation about the child Harry came from his belief in a prophesy about Voldemort's death. Voldemort became evil beyond repair and because of his Horcruxes was as close to immortality as he could be. When trying to kill baby Potter, however, he accidentally transferred part of his soul to the child and Potter survived. Having failed to kill him, we now see Voldemort's desire for something in addition to and more than power: He transferred his need for power, to a desire to *acquire* Harry. The two desires became entwined.

Without a doubt, his infatuation with Harry Potter should be examined within this Muggle notion that Voldemort was a queer wizard. Voldemort killed Harry Potter's parents and marked but failed to kill Harry the infant. In Harry's first year at Hogwarts, Voldemort came face to face with Harry for the first time since he attempted to kill him as a baby. Instead of trying to kill him now, he tried to recruit him to "save your own life and join me" (SS 294), perhaps inviting Harry to become at Hogwarts what he had been as Tom Riddle, Jr.

Voldemort further demonstrated his desire to acquire Harry when he missed the opportunity to finally defeat him in the graveyard where Voldemort's father, Tom Riddle Sr. is buried, after the Triwizard Tournament. Voldemort used Harry's blood to regenerate his human form. He claimed it was because Harry's blood, which contained the magical protection from his mother's sacrifice, would make him even more powerful than before. His need to have Harry's blood run through his own veins, to complete the connection of their souls that already exists, is evocative of a desire to keep Harry close. It also provided him with an opportunity to penetrate Harry both metaphorically and physically. Harry was taken prisoner, and forced to take part in the magical ritual that provided Voldemort with the human body he needed to return to power. The ritual included fourteen-year-old Harry, bound and gagged to the grave stone of Voldemort's father, penetrated by a phallic object, a dagger, to provide the life giving liquid, his own blood, to regenerate Voldemort, against his will (HP4). Harry's life force has provided Voldemort with the body he needed, and he has, in this way, successfully penetrated Harry, and gotten what he needed from him, a human shape. He has, in essence, satisfied himself, using Harry as a means to acquire what he needs.

Having regained his human shape, instead of simply killing the helpless Harry, he demonstrated his vain, egotistical, narcissistic traits by freeing him and duelling him in a show for his followers, the Death Eaters. This act was about humiliating Harry, taunting, mentally abusing him before finally killing him. He was also stroking his own ego, and catering to his narcissistic, high opinion of himself and his power. However, he failed to kill Potter because their wands connected as the two battled. Their wands, the representations of their phallus, will not allow them to destroy one another. The wands recognise each other: They are one; they have the same core, just as Harry and Voldemort share the same soul.

The fact that Voldemort failed to kill Harry three times up to this point, is telling. Does he really want to kill him? Was he on some subconscious level trying to protect Harry, keep him alive? If Harry was dead after all, who will be his equal enemy, who will he fixate his desire on? Who will he fantasize about? Only when it became clear that Harry will not relent and join Voldemort, does he seriously begin to attack him.

Once Voldemort failed to kill Harry in the Little Hangleton Graveyard his behaviour changed. His craving for power becomes more intense, but was shown in different ways. Even after regaining a new body, and revealing himself to be "back" to Harry and his followers, Voldemort continues to hide. (However, this was to his advantage, as fear of the unknown created a panic through the wizarding world.) He was still hiding, still repressing. Finally, with the Ministry, *Daily Prophet*, and Hogwarts under his control he broke the society that had supressed him for so long and created a new regime that was forced to accept him.

But he was still not satisfied; he was not free of his need for more power. It was at this point that Voldemort became more obsessed with the phallus, or rather, the ultimate phallus: the unbeatable Elder Wand. According to Lacan, the symbol phallus is representative of being the ultimate man (Mc Afee 2004). His desire to acquire this wand appears to surpass his desire to acquire Harry, something that may have seemed impossible up until this point. Voldemort was convinced that Harry would eventually come to find him, that his "seduction" of Harry was absolute; so he shifted his focus from Harry to the Elder wand. This change of focus was wasted, however, as through a set of seemingly coincidental circumstances Harry became the master of the Elder Wand.

This was not the last time Voldemort's infatuation with the phallus clouded his judgement. The last Horcrux, the last piece of Voldemort's soul, Dumbledore informed Harry, was in his snake Nagini. Dumbledore believed he was as fond of her as he could be of anything in his life. Nagini, along with the Basilisk that was the beast of Slytherin which attacked Muggle-borns at Tom Riddle, Jr.'s orders, are examples of the importance of representations of the phallic in Voldemort's life. Nagini was literally sliced in half by another, more powerful phallus: the sword of Gryffindor, a manifestation of Harry's phallus since Harry was a "true" Gryffindor. After this defeat, Voldemort fell, relatively easily, killed by his own rebounding curse. It could be said that he was the victim of a symbolic castration which left him impotent and easily defeated (Minsky 1996). Lacan would conclude that his obsession with the phallic would imply that Voldemort had an endless longing and yearning for completion, though it has no status in reality (Minsky 1996), further demonstrating how unhinged Voldemort became towards the end of his life.

Above I have mentioned Voldemort's love of his snake, and that this can be interpreted as a phallic metaphor. What should be mentioned here is the relation that Voldemort had to the snake, not only in connecting their souls, but also physically. Harry and Dumbledore believed that Voldemort became more snake like physically as he ripped himself apart, becoming less whole, less "normal." Freud theorizes that boys' over evaluation of their penis, rooted in a castration fear, is narcissistic (Freud 1920). As Voldemort, who above all other wizards, could talk to and control this fierce representation of the phallic, became less human, he became more snake like, thereby adhering to Freud's stereotype of homosexuality as narcissistic self love rather than love of another (Dean and Lowe 1999). Voldemort's love of his snake in particular, and the phallus more generally, manifested physically in his appearance.

CONCLUSION: THE FLAW IN THE WIZARDING WORLD

The importance of patriarchy, heteronormativity, and "straightness" in the wizarding world (from wand lore, to the repression of "lesser" beings such as werewolves, house-elves and goblins) cannot be denied. Stockton's notion that a "queer" child is received by society as an "evil" child is evocative of how Tom Riddle, Jr./Lord Voldemort was perceived. Many in the wizarding world believe the most interesting relationship during the Second Wizarding War was either the "hatred" between Lord Voldemort and Harry Potter, or the "love" that Albus Dumbledore had for Harry. I argue a different opinion. The relationship between Albus Dumbledore and Tom Riddle, Jr., the neglect Riddle experienced at the hands of a wary and suspicious teacher, ensured the completion of Riddle's repression of his queerness, and led to manifestation of the evil Lord Voldemort.

Dumbledore was championed by the wizarding world as being "the only one he ever feared," the only wizard that Lord Voldemort was afraid to face. I believe it to be more than that. Dumbledore failed Riddle. He never showed any of the support and tutoring that he generously bestowed in later years on Harry Potter. Much of what Dumbledore did for Potter, I believe, was overcompensation for his guilt feelings for failing to mentor young Tom Riddle, Jr. In many ways, Dumbledore helped to create Lord Voldemort, and his guilt about this may have been why he raised Harry to defeat him.

REFERENCES

Dean, Tim 1999. "Homosexuality and the Problem with Otherness." Pp. 120-146 in *Homosexuality and Psychoanalysis*. Edited by T. Dean and C. Lowe. Chicago, IL: Blackhall.

Freud, Sigmund. 1920. "The Psychogenesis of a Case of Female Homosexuality" Pp. 145-175 in *The Standard Edition of the Complete Psychological Works of Sigmund Freud (Vol. 18)*. Edited by J. Strachey. London: Vintage.

Giffney, Noreen. 2009. "The New Queer Cartoon." Pp. 365-378 in *The Ashgate Research Companion to Queer Theory*. Edited by N. Giffney and M. O'Rourke. London: Ashgate.

Granger, John. 2008. *The Deathly Hallows Lectures: The Hogwarts Professor Explains Harry's Final Adventure*. Allentown, PA: Zossima Press.

Halperin, David. 1995. *Saint Foucault: Towards a Gay Hagiography*. Oxford: Oxford Press.

McAfee, Noëlle. 2004. *Julia Kristeva*, London: Routledge.

Minsky, Rosalind. 1996. *Psychoanalysis and Gender*, London: Routledge.

O'Brien, Grainne. 2010. "Queering the Half Blood Prince." Presented at the Age of Sex Event, 6 May 2010. Prato, Italy.

Piippo, Taija. 2009. "Is Desire Beneficial or Harmful in the Harry Potter Series." Pp. 65-82 in *Critical Perspectives in Harry Potter* Edited by E. Heilman. New York: Routledge.

Stockton, Katheryn Bond. 2009. *The Queer Child: Or Growing Sideways in the Twentieth Century*. North Carolina: Duke University Press.

PART V

BEYOND THE VEIL

"Differences of habit and language are nothing at all if our aims are identical and our hearts are open"

FAN FICTION AS A FORUM FOR THE SOCIOLOGICAL IMAGINATION OF THE NEW MILLENNIUM

JUSTYNA DESZCZ-TRYHUBCZAK

INTRODUCTION

In one of her numerous public appearances, the 2008 Harvard University Commencement, J.K. Rowling discussed her understanding of the role of imagination in words that could be taken as a quasi definition of social imagination: "I have learned to value imagination in a much broader sense. Imagination is not only the uniquely human capacity to envision that which is not, and therefore the fount of all invention and innovation. In it's arguably most transformative and revelatory capacity, it is the power that enables us to empathize with humans whose experiences we have never shared."

Rowling's comments are indeed redolent of C. Wright Mills' (1959) account of sociological imagination as "the capacity to shift from one perspective to another," a capacity which, Mills stresses, requires both systematic cultivation and "a playfulness of mind" in combining ideas that would not be expected to come together. Most of the young participants of the Harvard ceremony, as well as young fans of Harry Potter series, belong to "digital natives" or millennials, i.e., young people whose adolescence and maturation are taking place at a time when "digital media are part of the taken-for-granted social and cultural fabric of learning, play, and social communication" (Ito et al. 2008: vii) and when people "immersed in new digital tools and networks are engaged in an unprecedented exploration of language, games, social interaction, problem solving, and self-directed activity that leads to diverse forms of learning" (vii). These diverse forms of learning and communication are in turn reflected in "how individuals express independence and creativity, and in their ability to learn, exercise judgments, and think systematically" (vii). Such an "alchemy between youth and digital media" is revolutionary as it suspends adult normativity, opening up a space for youth activism within the social group which has always been systematically controlled in relation to its access to information, self-expression, and means of social communication. To some extent, the subversiveness of the current empowerment of young people is attributable to their creative interactions with popular culture, which in turn often occur within the supra-national communal spaces of fandom. As Henry Jenkins (2006: 288-289) succinctly puts it, "[y]oung people are finding their voice through their [creative] play with popular culture and then deploying it through their participation in public services or various political movements."[2]

Writing fan fiction, and the concomitant participation in fandom communities, may also be one of the activities providing young people opportunities to create and test new social visions. More specifically, it can be regarded as a connecting stage in the informal and playful cultivation of social imagination skills, which later may result in young people's civic engagement. Some of such visions may become widely shared as texts circulate within a fan community and become an agenda in youth activist movements. Fan fiction related to Harry Potter books is a particularly graphic example of this process, as proved by Heather Lawver's projects of setting up an imaginary Hogwarts online and running its own Web-based newspaper, the *Daily Prophet*; by massive international protests against the efforts of Warner Brothers to curtail Harry Potter fandom; and by the formation and campaigns of Harry Potter Alliance. This chapter discusses the potential of fan fiction to encourage the development of youth social imagination on the examples of young people's texts redefining oppressive aspects of the Ministry of Magic and Hogwarts, which are often regarded by critics as prime examples of conservatism and oppression in Potterverse.

THE PHENOMENON OF FAN FICTION:
THE INTERSECTION OF POPULAR CULTURE, CONVERGENCE CULTURE, AND PARTICIPATORY CULTURE

Fan fiction ("fanfic" or "fic" for short) are narratives deploying characters and settings from literature and other media, created and published by fan readers of given pre-existing texts. Contrary to traditional literature, fan fiction is distributed informally, usually on-line, and not for profit.[3] As Catherine

---

2   Proposing such an optimistic model of youthful engagement means the acknowledgement *"the engaged youth paradigm"* (W. Lance Bennet 2008), which foregrounds the importance and potential of civic actions carried out online and which sees young people's media engagement as empowering. Nevertheless, one has to bear in mind an alternative position on this issue, and in particular, the misgivings of some critics concerning dispersal, personalization and privatization of the political sphere, which marginalize the importance of the civic. (See David Buckingham, qtd. in Bennett 2008). Still, individualization of online activities does not necessarily mean the lack of open debates on public issues.

3   For the history of fan fiction, see Francesca Coppa (2006) "A Brief History of Media Fandom" Pp. 41-59 in *Fan Fiction and Fan Communities in the Age of Internet: New Essays*, ed. by K. Hellekson and K. Busse. Jefferson, NC and London: McFarland.

Tosenberg (2008: 185) points out, "[f]an writers are often characterized as refusing merely to consume media, but rather to engage actively with texts." This is so as fan fiction often involves aesthetic and thematic experimentation, pushing original texts in new directions, thereby ensuring their ongoing circulation and semantic transformation. These new developments may concern not only changes in plots or configurations of characters, but also, and particularly importantly, the emergence of reformative viewpoints on politics and society. Moreover, fan texts are often "a work in progress" or "serial" as they result from the author's on-going revisions in response to collaboration with and comments from other members of a given fannish community (Busse and Hellekson 2006). In this sense, fan fiction may be seen as "philosophically opposed to hierarchy, property, and the dominance of one variant of a series over another variant" (Derecho 2006: 77). Fantasy, "a default cultural vernacular" of books, films and a variety of digital forms, is particularly congenial to such activity (Miéville 2002). As Ethan Gilsdorf (2009: 141) remarks, "[w]ith no elaborate backstory or creation myth, baseball and football don't have the imaginative narrative possibilities that Harry Potter does…. some universes, like Tolkien's and Rowling's, offer entry-level toolboxes to build stuff with." This possibility to engage in creative activities is particularly appealing, as Gilsdorf notes, to those bored "with knowing their worlds too well," or one might add, those wishing to change them. Indeed, in the case of young readers it was the Harry Potter series that "has generated an unprecedented number of voluntary literary responses by adolescent readers" (Bond and Michelson 2003: 111).

The phenomenon of fan fiction in general has been thoroughly studied from literary, psychological, and pedagogical perspectives.[4] Nevertheless, to give justice to the potential of fan fiction to shape adolescent social imagination, it is worthwhile discussing it in a broader context of current cultural transformations, as a form of young people's participation in the public sphere through unmediated "experience of online publishing, discourse, debate, cocreation of culture, and collective action" (Rheingold 2008: 102). In particular, writing fan fiction can be regarded as a "communal online

---

4   An extended study of fan fiction and its history as a literary phenomenon can be found in Sheenagh Pugh's *The Democratic Genre: Fan Fiction in a Literary Context* (2005). Fan fiction can also be approached from a psychological perspective, as a space for fans to engage in affective play of destabilizing boundaries between internal and external realities by playing out fantasies and desires about their own identities. Finally, fan fiction has been analyzed in light of its potential for increasing both expertise at writing and media literacy. For a detailed bibliography of critical studies of fan fiction see *Fan Fiction and Fan Communities in the Age of Internet: New Essays (Busse 2008)*

sandpit" (Pugh 2005) on the informal "civic playground" (Van Someren 2009) of popular culture, in which, contrary to common stereotypes, fans are not passive consumers "merely responding to a media or celebrity system" (Urbanski 2010: 16). Instead, as Henry Jenkins comments, fans identify with texts "as fans and as citizens simultaneously" and thus "more readily blur the boundaries between fiction and fact and entertainment and politics." This in turn may actually facilitate, to use Jenkins's phrase, the transformation of "personal reaction into social interaction" (qtd. in Urbanski 2010: 16), as well as into specific solutions to civic issues. Moreover, as fans focus their critical activities on one cultural product, they tolerate disagreements and alternative views, which in turn, Jenkins (2011) argues, prevents "social fragmentation and isolation some contemporary critics have lamented."

It is also to be noted that the creation and dissemination of fan fiction occur within the culture of convergence, that is, the environment generating new platforms within which more and more people are able to participate and collaborate, not through formal political and social institutions, but through communal media and social software enabling unprecedented volumes of production and scopes of dissemination. As W. Lance Bennet (2008: 1-2) notes, these developments have been accompanied by "a notable turning away from public life into online friendship networks, gaming and entertainment environments, and consumer pursuits. Where political activity occurs, it is often related to lifestyle concerns that seem outside the realm of government." In this context, fan fiction can be an example of grass root activity that may effectively prompt more formation and exchange of diverse social visions than traditional political debates in dominant media.

Finally, fan fiction is an element of participatory culture, a phenomenon closely related to convergence culture and enabled by the growing dominance of interactive media, "peer-to-peer forms of communication, and many-to-many forms of distribution" (Ito et al. 2008: viii). It is also marked by "relatively low barriers to artistic expression and civic engagement," "strong support for creating and sharing one's creations with others," "some type of informal mentorship whereby what is known by the most experienced is passed along to novices," the conviction of all members that their contributions matter, and the sense of "some degree of social connection with one another" (Van Someren 2009). This sense of connectivity is particularly significant in the case of youth activism, for, as danah boyd argues, "[i]n order to engage in political life, people have to have access to public life at first . . . Politics starts first with the school, with your friends . . . then they grow to being about civics . . . . You need to start with the dramas that make sense to you" (qtd. in Rheingold 2008: 102-103). In this context writing fan fiction entails both involvement in new modes of production and participation in new social structures characterized by profound co-dependency and peer support.

CRITICS ON THE MINISTRY OF MAGIC AND HOGWARTS

Critics analyzing the social order and politics of J.K. Rowling's books have repeatedly accused her of ambiguity and inconsistency in presenting the social and political structure of Potterverse. Suffice it to mention Farah Mendlesohn's 2002 critique of "the consolatory rhetoric" of Harry Potter series, stemming from the immutable status quo based on heredity and patronage in the guise of friendship as prerequisites for peace and social justice, which turn results in a "muddled morality that cheats the reader." As Mendlesohn argues with reference to such motifs as Hermione's isolation due to her intellectual aspirations, Harry's dependence on protective adults, or the prejudice against Muggles that marks both Voldemort's followers and his opponents, the series only superficially promotes tolerance, social mobility, and equality, whereas in fact it is heredity and elitism that matter as factors guaranteeing social justice and peace. In a more recent critique of social and political structures in the wizarding world, Daragh Downes (2010) stresses the dissolution of the utopian potential for transformation of Hogwarts and the wizarding community in general that did emerge during the struggle against Voldemort only to be forfeited by the return to the old world order and its hierarchies.[5] In this sense Hogwarts may be seen as "the stagnant little world" in which any destabilization of hierarchies and norms is temporary or as an institution controlling the pupils' minds and bodies (Chappell 2008). Downes also criticizes Rowling for failing to develop the possibility of a "friendly cooperation" between magicals and Muggles, signaled by the Potterwatch broadcast mentioning how wizards and witches risk their lives to protect Muggle friends and neighbors.

More generous readings have been proposed by Henry Jenkins (2006: 171), who argues that the Potter saga asserts "children's rights over institutional constraints," which, coupled with the popularity of the texts among reluctant readers, encourages a critical reflection on limitations and constraints imposed on young people's reading preferences and artistic expression. In the same vein Drew Chappell (2007: 281) appreciates Rowling's imagining "culture in which… child agency is possible, where young people become builders of context, awakening to the network of relationships and institutions that frame

---

5   To counter this argument, Travis Prinzi (2009: 257) contends that Rowling purposefully "left us in a world in which much injustice still exists" as "to eliminate all prejudice and slavery, and create peace and harmony in the world in that one final year would be an utter insult to the depth of the problem of racism." Instead Rowling wishes to indicate that change has to occur gradually, as a consequence of emotional and mental transformations of individuals. Therefore, in the final novel she presents hopeful beginnings of such inner transformations in the main characters so as to initiate a debate "for our own world, which alas is so much like the Wizarding one."

their lives." In this sense, Harry and his friends' attempts at questioning and resisting injustice and oppression through the understanding of and negotiating with institutions and adults shaping their lives correspond to children's actual experiences in a postmodern world offering "multiple opportunities and layered identity constructions" (Chappell 2007: 292). In an equally positive interpretation of Hogwarts, Roni Natov (2002: 133) notes that although Hogwarts epitomizes the deficiencies in the social organization of both the Magical and the Muggle world, "it is also a wondrous and humorous world" in itself and through the unruly playfulness of its students.

"IF HARRY AND HIS FRIENDS CAN COME TOGETHER WITH LOVE IN THEIR HEARTS, A SENSE OF PLAYFULNESS AND A VISION FOR A BETTER WORLD . . . WHY CAN'T HIS FANS?" - SLACK[6]

The following analysis of three pieces of fan fiction by young authors is to illustrate the intuitive workings of sociological imagination of young readers of the series in their thinking about systems of governance and social constructions of race. As will be shown, the selected fics testify to the young readers' constructive approach to the series that goes beyond sheer consumption of the texts towards a critical and creative reworking of the given contexts, including the implementation of alternative ideas of governance and social justice. This activity in turn may be seen as a sign of young people's ability to engage in actual political and social projects.

Envisaging New Politics

In "A Bad Week at Wizengamot," the young poster by the name DisobedienceWriter speculates what would happen if Harry was found guilty of inappropriate usage of magic against dementors and decided to leave Britain for good. Whereas the fic is focused on Harry's exploits abroad, especially in France, where he sets up his own winery and produces poisonous wine that kills Voldemort, the author also includes complex and intriguing ideas about the foundations and functioning of the British Ministry of Magic and Hogwarts. Suffice it to mention Harry's exposure of Fudge's incompetence, proneness to bribes, and the resulting complicity in allowing Voldemort and Death Eaters to take control over the magical world. Furthermore, the author mentions Fudge's policies and propaganda aimed at diverting public attention from the threat posed by Voldemort. The crisis also affects Hogwarts, which is presented as an old-fashioned institution whose standards lag behind those of foreign schools. As the French Ambassador bitingly comments in a

---

6   I want to thank Agnieszka Muc, a 2009-2011 MA student of mine, for suggesting fics to be analyzed in this chapter.

conversation with Fudge:

> [S]urely you don't think your provincial little school is the only one in the world… How many potions masters has England produced in the last decade? Three. How many has Peru created? Forty-eight. And the Peruvian test is much more challenging than the English version. Really, Minister, you're not very well up to date on educational matters and methods, I think. I've heard about your plan to place Dolores at Hogwarts. In real schools, teachers are required to demonstrate their qualifications in the subjects they teach. Political connections are irrelevant.

The overall chaos in the British magical world is averted by European Magical Union emissaries, who arrest Death Eaters and nominate Sirius Black as Interim Minister for four and a half months. The author concludes the political commentary by presenting Black as "shaking things up a bit" and effecting such far-reaching changes as sinking the dementors into the ocean, revoking most laws passed by passed by the Wizengamot, "particularly anything that had to do with pureblood grandfathering," and making the wizard high court "an elected body, rather than a hereditary one."

In "Padfoot's Proclamations," the subsequent chapter on the changes in the wizarding world following the defeat of Voldemort, DisobedienceWriter elaborates on specific reforms introduced by Sirius in a series of Ministerial Proclamations. The most important goal of Sirius's decisions, however humorous, witty and prankish he seems, is to abolish traditional administrative, class, and social hierarchies and ensure that the value of every individual to the community and individual rights will be respected within the democratic system of consensual decisions. With this goal in mind, Sirius introduces laws enabling all sentient magical creatures to vote, thereby restructuring the Wizengamot to include "merfolk, centaurs, house-elves, goblins, werewolves, vampires, Crumple-Horned Snorkacks…" with the provision that "[a] minimum of ten percent of the vacant seats are reserved for non-human creatures." Moreover, the election reforms introduced by the wizard also result in the liberation of house-elves, who create "a new company to do spot cleaning and cooking work on a paid basis for a large number of families" and are very happy about the newly gained independence. As DisobedienceWriter explains, the extended suffrage invalidates "any master-servant bond." Sirius also attempts to improve relationships with Muggles by enabling Muggle-born children "or magical children from squib lines" to "learn of their heritage, including how to access further resources in Diagon Alley" and to attend a school of magic. Finally, Sirius extends the Muggle Relations division "as the Ministry began to work more and better with the larger world outside it."

Dealing with problems at Hogwarts, Sirius makes sure that its Board of Governors will now be "elective," which in turn will eliminate favoritism:

> Board members will serve two-year terms, be eligible for reelection, and will step down from the board during the period when their own children or wards attend Hogwarts or when they are appointed to teach or administer at the school.

Of particular interest is also the author's idea of an "educational revolution" aiming at raising the standards of education at Hogwarts, for example by careful assessment of teachers' competence and the supervision of the curriculum and classes, as well as by providing graduates with the opportunity to either enter apprenticeships or continue their schooling at Balliol College, Oxford. Equally significant is the transformation of Hogwarts' inner organization into a more democratic one:

> the houses were now being randomized and the Sorting Hat was brought out a couple of times per year to chat with the students and also studied in the new seventh year course on Enchanting;...,the prefects and Head students were being abolished as obsolete;... there were age-group common rooms throughout the castle.

The ideal outcome of reading socially and politically critical fiction is the awakening of readers in the hope that they will extrapolate from the world of the text to the actual problems in the real world and actively face them. As the above example indicates, fan fiction may be a transitory stage of practical thinking that will lead from the reflection on the institutions and laws of the wizarding world to the ability to comprehend social and political mechanisms of the real world. Far from the abstract discussions of rights or liberty, DisobedienceWriter has engaged in an autonomous rediscovery of the genuine meaning of such ideas as justice, freedom or solidarity. Moreover, complex and detailed as the description of Sirius's reforms is, the text is far from boring as Sirius is skillfully depicted as having both a humorous and thoughtful approach to the rectification of the social and political problems of the magical world. Significantly, the chapter concludes with Sirius reflecting that "change was good! Change was fun. That was the last message Sirius wanted to leave behind," which may be seen as highlighting the fact that even if political structures organizing individual and social life are concepts that people create and develop over the ages, they can be transformed both through collective intellectual labor and as redefined as personal struggles, in the context of moral commitment, pluralism, and non-violence, so rare in contemporary political structures and institutions.

New World Order in the Wizarding World

The theme of race inequality is addressed in fics by Elenillor and Wyrmskyld. In "Remus defined," the former presents the Ministry's humiliating procedures of branding animagi with numbers, which, as is shown on the example of the young Remus, does indeed make them feel acutely that they have lost their humanity and irrevocably turned into animals.[7] The young Sirius, in love with Remus, empathizes with him, speculates about the possibility of changing ministerial regulations, and even wishes to get a number, himself which, ironically happens when he is sentenced to Azkaban.

In "Registration," Wyrmskyld focuses on the obligatory annual check-up for animagi at the Ministry. A frightened young male wererabbit meets the elderly Lupin, who has become President of the Werewolf Coalition. Although the story is not developed beyond this brief meeting, the formation of the Coalition suggests the emergence of an organized oppositional movement questioning the ministerial segregationist policies. Admittedly, neither of the stories contains the all-pervasive utopian optimism of DisobedienceWriter's fics, but they nevertheless point out the possibility of the solidarity of those disempowered by institutionalized racial intolerance in their rejection of subjugation.

The corresponding theme of the rebellion against the institutionalized intolerance at Hogwarts also appears in "Prejudice," a Second Generation Fic by BookNerd7. Defying her father's exhortations on the day she left for her first year at Hogwarts, and not caring about other students' reactions, Rose Weasley, a Ravenclaw, repeatedly eats her breakfast by the Slytherin table. Also Albus, Rose's cousin and a Slytherin, sits at the Ravenclaw table during dinners. As Scorpius Malfoy reflects on Rose's rebellious behavior:

> [She] had started something. No matter how much better House Unity had been since the Battle of Hogwarts, students had never dared to sit at another table for more than a couple of minutes, not even the offspring of the Golden Trio.

Rose's initiative is so successful that when the children are in their seventh year, as Scorpius remarks, it became "pretty useless to even have the house tables anymore. He was sitting at the Gryffindor table next to Albus, and talking to Hugo Weasley from Hufflepuff about Quidditch." Rose's radical stance testifies to the author's belief that young people perfectly realize the crucial role they play in improving the world. Significantly, as Rose also falls in love with Scorpius, she makes other students understand that he cannot be blamed for his father's misdeeds, which in turn indicates the author's conviction that adolescents respond to challenges of current crises with creative and clear-

---

7   As Remus is not an animagus, it can be assumed that the author means all witches and wizards who can transform into an animal.

headed decisions that enable them to deal with problems created by the adult generation.[8]

CONCLUSION

> We do not need magic to transform the world. We carry all the power
> we need inside ourselves already. We have power to imagine better.
> - Rowling, 2008

The sample fan fiction texts analyzed above testify to their young authors' ability to find and express their own stances on the wizarding world's status quo. These individual visions of the Ministry of Magic and Hogwarts reflect their critical appraisals of real life social and political processes, even if their radicalism and progressiveness is at time utopian. Positioned in a broader context, these fan fictions belong to the Harry Potter fandom, within which its participants, young and old, share common interests and build political alliances. Most importantly, Harry Potter fandom has also generated a space "where children teach one another and where, if they would open their eyes, adults could learn a great deal" (Jenkins 2006: 205).

The Internet has become a new means of building and developing communities and solidarity; therefore it is quite likely that, as Marina Umaschi Bers (2008: 152) remarks, "youth who are more active on-line will also grow into more engaged citizens." These young citizens will soon become members of cyberdemocracy, which as Pierre Lévy (2005) argues, will bring both unprecedented creative freedom that may result in the shaping of a new reality, and the obligation to critically assess the possibilities before any concrete decisions may be taken. This responsibility necessitates the operation of what Hector Raul Solis-Gadea (2005: 117) calls the sociological imagination of the New Millennium: a multi-perspective and ever-scrutinizing understanding of the current reality, as well as "a creative form on inquiry more than a source of definite answers" and "corpus of knowledge." The virtual communities of Harry Potter fandom, focused on collective creation linking one's own fate and with the future of others, as well as on discussion and dissemination of alternative social visions, seem to herald a possibility of the emergence of a

---

8   Interestingly, John Granger argues for a similar future scenario for the development of the relationships between the Houses, which he reads in the context of Rowling's allusions to Dante: "But there is a third wave of generations that we meet on the Epilogue platform. I think we can expect, just as Hermione was the infolding into the Inner Triumvirate of the Lily figure of Harry's father generation, that Draco's son Scorpius will be the inclusion of the Slytherin foe into Albus Severus' trio. Albus, Rose and Scorpius won't battle Voldemort, but they will, as the third generation and "white rose," enter the Paradise of Love and the end of the Four Houses metanarrative, which divides and causes the prejudices of all wizards and witches at Hogwarts" (Granger 2008: 149).

new world, freer of prejudice, conflicts and differences.

REFERENCES

Bers, Marina Umaschi. 2008. "Civic Identities, Online Technologies: From Designing Civic Curriculum to Supporting Civic Experiences." Pp. 139-160 in *Civic Life Online: Learning How Digital Media Can Engage Youth.* Edited by W. Lance Bennett. The John D. and Catherine T. MacArthur. Foundation Series on Digital Media and Learning. Cambridge, MA: The MIT Press.

Bennet, Lance. W, ed. 2008. "Changing Citizenship in the Digital Age." Pp. 1-25 in *Civic Life Online Learning How Digital Media Can Engage Youth.* The John D. and Catherine T. MacArthur. Foundation Series on Digital Media and Learning. Cambridge, MA: The MIT Press.

Bond, Ernest, and Nancy Michelson. 2003. "Writing Harry's World: Children Coauthoring Hogwarts." Pp. 109-124 in *Harry Potter's World: Multidisciplinary Critical Perspectives.* Edited by E. E. Heilman. New York: RoutledgeFalmer.

BookNerd7. 2011. "Prejudice." 2011. Retrieved February 20, 2011 (http://www.fanfiction.net/s/6615032/1/Prejudice).

Chappell, Drew. 2008. "Sneaking Out After Dark: Resistance, Agency, and the Postmodern Child in JK Rowling's Harry Potter Series." *Children's Literature in Education.* 39: 281–293.

Derecho, Abigail. 2006. "A Definition, a History, and Several Theories of Fan Fiction." Pp. 61-78 in *Fan Fiction and Fan Communities in the Age of Internet: New Essays.* Edited by K. Hellekson and K. Busse. Jefferson, NC and London: McFarland.

DisobedienceWriter. 2007. "A Bad Week at Wizengamot" (2007). Retrieved February 20, 2011 (http://www.fanfiction.net/s/3639659/1/A_Bad_Week_at_the_Wizengamot).

Downes, Daragh. 2010. "Harry Potter and the Deathly Hollowness: A Narratological and ideological Critique of J.K. Rowling's Magical System." *International Research in Children's Literature.* 3.2: 162-173.

Dresang, Eliza T. 2002. "Hermione Granger and the Heritage of Gender." Pp. 211-242 in *The Ivory Tower and Harry Potter: Perspectives on a Literary Phenomenon.* Edited by L. A. Whited. Coumbia MO: University of Missouri Press.

Ellenilor. 2007. "Remus defined" Retrieved February 20, 2011 (http://www.fanfiction.net/s/3402321/1/Remus_Defined).

Gilsdorf, Ethan. 2009. *Fantasy Freaks and Gaming Geeks. An Epic Quest for Reality among Role Players, Online gamers, and Other Dwellers of*

Imaginary Realms. Guilford, CT.: The Lyons Press.

Granger, John. 2008. *The Deathly Hallows Lectures: The Hogwarts Professor Explains Harry's Final Adventure*. 2nd Edition. Allentown, PA: Zossima Press.

Busse, Kristina and Karen Hellekson. 2006. "Introduction: Work in Progress." Pp. 5-32 in *FanFiction and Fan Communities in the Age of Internet: New Essays*. Edited by K. Hellekson and K. Busse. Jefferson, NC and London: McFarland.

Jenkins, Henry. 2006. *Convergence Culture: Where Old and New Media Collide*. New York: New York University Press.

—. 2009. "How Fictional Story Worlds Influence Real World Politics." Retrieved February 20, 2011 (http://henryjenkins.org/2009/12/how_fictional_story_worlds_inf.html).

Ito, Mizuko et al. 2008. "Foreword." Pp. in *Civic Life Online: Learning How Digital Media Can Engage Youth*. Edited by W. Lance Bennett. The John D. and Catherine T. MacArthur Foundation Series on Digital Media and Learning. Cambridge, MA: The MIT Press.

Lévy, Pierre. 2005. "Collective Intelligence, A Civilisation: Towards a Method of Positive Interpretation." *International Journal of Politics, Culture, and Society*. 18: 189–198.

Mendlesohn, Farah. 2002. "Crowning the King: Harry Potter and the Construction of Authority." Pp. 159-181 in *The Ivory Tower and Harry Potter: Perspectives on a Literary Phenomenon*. Edited by L. A. Whited. Columbia, MO: University of Missouri Press.

Mills, C. Wright. 1959. *The Sociological Imagination*. New York, NY: Oxford University Press.

Miéville, China. 2002. "Editorial Introduction." *Historical Materialism*, 10(4): 39-49.

Natov, Roni. "Harry Potter and the Extraordinariness of the Ordinary." Pp. 125-139 in *The Ivory Tower and Harry Potter: Perspectives on a Literary Phenomenon*. Edited by L. A. Whited. Columbia, MO: University of Missouri Press.

Prinzi, Travis. 2009. *Harry Potter and Imagination: The Way between Two Worlds*. Allentown, PA: Zossima Press.

Pugh, Sheenagh. 2005. *The Democratic Genre: Fan Fiction in a Literary Context*. Brigend: Seren.

Rowling, J.K. 2006. "The Fringe Benefits of Failure, and the Importance of Imagination." Retrieved 17 February 12, 2011 (http://www.npr.org/templates/st77ory/story.php?storyId=91232541).

Rheingold, Howard. 2008. "Using Participatory Media and Public Voice to Encourage Civic Engagement." Pp. 97-118 in *Civic Life Online:*

Learning How Digital Media Can Engage Youth. Edited by W. Lance Bennett. The John D. and Catherine T. MacArthur Foundation Series on Digital Media and Learning. Cambridge, MA: The MIT Press.

Slack, Andrew. 2007. "Harry Potter and the Muggle Activists." *In These Times.* Retrieved March 01, 2011 (http://www.inthesetimes.com/article/3365/harry_potter_and_the_muggle_activists/).

Solis-Gadea, Hector Raul. 2005. "The New Sociological Imagination: Facing the Challenges of a New Millennium." *International Journal of Politics, Culture, and Society.* 18: 113–122.

Tosenberger, Catherine. 2008. "Homosexuality at the Online Hogwarts: Harry Potter Slash Fanfiction." *Children's Literature.* 36: 185-207.

Urbanski, Heather, ed. 2010. *Writing in the Digital Generation: Essays on New Media Rhetoric.* Jefferson, NC: McFarland.

Van Someren, Anna. 2009. "On Chuck and Carrot Mobs: Mapping the Connections Between Participatory Culture and Public Participation." Retrieved February 17, 2011 (http://henryjenkins.org/2009/12/on_chuck_and_carrot_mobs_mappi.html).

Wyrmskyld. "Registration." 2006. Retrieved February 17, 2011 (http://www.fanfiction.net/s/3024448/1/Registration).

"A world that's entirely our own"

INDIAN RESPONSE TO THE BRITISH WIZARDING WORLD

RAVINDRA PRATAP SINGH

The wizarding world that the chapters in this volume have been discussing has captivated the minds of young and old across the globe. One of the pleasures of reading J.K. Rowling's Harry Potter series is discovering the playful references to history, legend and literature that she uses in her books. The locale of the wizarding world is set in Great Britain, with the clear influence of European culture and dominance of primarily an Anglican society. The surface analysis gives the feel that magic and all other things are considered in the very western way, almost 'othering' non-western ontological and epistemological versions of magic and witchcraft. But a careful analysis of the nuances and connotations establish a healthy connection and compatibilities between Harry's world and the modern Orient.

In 2010 I conducted an exploratory study, in association with Mahendra Pratap Singh, seeking to understand why the Harry Potter series, and a magical society in Europe, managed to secure a successful fan following in India. Our hypothesis, developed from reading the books ourselves, was that Indian readers would notice similarities between Indian culture and myths and the British wizarding world. We surveyed 500 school children between the ages of 9 and 14 in different elite schools of Uttar Pradesh, North India. Sixty per cent of the respondents reported that they do in fact find elements in Harry Potter familiar due to commonalities with Indian stories, legends and culture.

In this chapter I will elaborate upon three elements that I believe enable Indian children to relate to the British wizarding world. First, I believe one factor in the positive reception of Harry Potter in India is due to the fact that Indian society has an established fascination with various supernatural and paranormal elements. Second, many characters (humans and beasts) which are present in the British wizarding world have, in some way or the other, already existed in Indian society. Finally, the social structure of the British wizarding world parallels the Indian caste system. These three elements, I believe, are why Indian children find such familiarity in story set in Great Britain.

INDIAN MAGIC

India has a rich tradition of magic and witchcraft of her own which dates back even to the earliest history of human civilizations. India has been the land of the *Panchtantra, Jataka Tales* and *Amarchitra Katha* series in which witchcraft (para human) and human civilizations are shown to co-exist. These traditions still affect the collective public consciousness and consequently desires for the supernatural are already rooted in a larger population of Indian origin.

The oeuvre and spectacle in the British wizarding world are closely related to similar patterns in India. Michael Naas (2007: 6), who speaks of the power of phantasm, writes that:

> [Phantasm] does not exist but that we believe exists. A phantasm that would be nothing other than a belief in a phenomenon that transcends itself, that spontaneously gives rise to itself – like an Immaculate Conception. For in any consideration of the phantasm, one must be interested less in the ontological status of the phantasm than in its staying power, its returning power, I would be tempted to say its regenerative power. In a word, one must be interested in the fact that, to cite an English idiom, the phantasm has "legs."

The whole of the British wizarding world creates a phantasm (of magic) before the Indian reader; and the minds of Indian readers are already acculturated to sustain pleasure from something supernatural and phantasmal.

INDIANS IN WIZARDING BRITAIN

According to census data, Indians are the largest ethnic minority group in United Kingdom (Office of National Statistics 2005). During Harry Potter's tenure at Hogwarts there were two Indian British witches: twins Parvati and Padma Patil. The Patil twins were smart and "the best-looking girls in the year" (GOF 411). They attended the Yule Ball with Harry and Ron in fourth year, joined Dumbledore's Army during their fifth year, and fought during the ensuing Second Wizarding War.

I believe that Parvati and Padma Patil by their commendable tasks become role models for Indian children, especially girls. In Indian society gender roles are quickly changing. Now women are not shown as damsels in distress but like partners who equally fight with similar determination. As such, I believe Indian readers were more attracted the Patil twins as they exemplified their changing social and gender constructs.

Moreover, by directing our attention to nomenclature and its contextual association, we see that when we semantically analyse the name of "Parvati" we find her name is the name of Hindu Goddess Parvati, the better half of Lord Shiva, who is known for her bravery and courage. Etymologically,

"Parvati" originates from Sanskrit/Hindi word *Parvat* which means mountain, connoting something bold and strong, in determination. Parvati was in Gryffindor, the house which selects only those students who are brave, determined and courageous.

Similarly, "Padma" refers to goddess Saraswati. She is the goddess of intellect. Unlike her sister, Padma was selected for Ravenclaw house, which values intelligence, learning, creativity and wit. Since the names relate to Indian mythologies and base themselves to the potent beliefs, the common reader can relate himself /herself in a better way. It clearly shows that Rowling had knowledge of Hindu mythology and as such constructed a well-connected maze for the Indian readers to solve and link. We all are aware of the fact Rowling writes in such a manner as to create more mystery for all her readers to solve while the plot is happening at parallel. The names of the Patil twins contributed to this effort and I believe is one reason why Indian readers were attracted the British novels.

The twins' personalities likewise reflect a psyche that Indian children can related to. One reason why Parvati's favourite subject was Divination can be attributed to the fact that a significant portion of Indian society, especially the followers of Hindu religion, believe in "Kundali." This a document which is said to contain all the details and secrets of a person's past, present and future, similar to Linda Goodman's books on astrology. The main aim of Divination is also to find out the secrets of future life, therefore I believe Indian readers would perfectly relate to Parvati's love of this subject.

FANTASTIC BEASTS AND WHERE IN INDIA TO FIND THEM

Creatures from Western mythology are readily recognizable in the wizarding world. For instance, the Sphinx in the maze during the Triwizard Tournament asks a riddle, just as the Sphinx of ancient Greek mythology did. Hagrid's pet dog, Fluffy, is actually another famous beast from Greek mythology, Cerberus. Draco, Harry's nemesis, gets his name from the Latin word for dragon or snake. Dumbledore's pet phoenix, Fawkes, gets his name from a historical figure linked to bonfires just as phoenixes are said to be reborn in fire.

Less often recognized, however, are the many magical creatures in the British wizarding world that have their origin in India. Indian society is a strong believer in supernatural elements and magical creatures; consequently, I believe readers were excited to see creatures they recognized (the manticore, snakes, and unicorns) in the British wizarding world.

A manticore is a monstrous creature which was said to inhabit the forests in Asia, especially those of India. It has a body of lion and a head with human resemblance. The mouth is filled with three rows of razor sharp teeth and the scaled tail ends in a ball of poisonous darts. The monster was believed to stalk through the forest in search of humans. Anthropologists now believe that the ancient Greek travellers in India mistook a tiger for a manticore when they saw the animals for the first time. I believe that whereas Western readers agreed with Harry that the creature he encountered during the third task of the Triwizard Tournament, a creature that "had the body of an over-large lion: great clawed paws and a long yellowish tail ending in a brown tuft" with the head of a woman was a sphinx (GOF 628), Indian readers identified Harry's interrogator as the familiar Indian manticore.

Nagini is another creature that I believe contributed to the positive Indian response to Harry Potter. Nagini was Lord Voldemort's green snake and was roughly 12 feet long and thick as a man's thigh (GOF 122; DH 9). She was known to be venomous and her venom was used to sustain her master prior to his return to the true physical form (GOF 9). The last of her master's Horcruxes, Nagini was beheaded during the Battle of Hogwarts by Neville Longbottom wielding the sword of Gryffindor. Indian readers would know that *naga* means a male snake in Sanskrit, and the word *nagin* is used for the female snake in Hindi and Urdu. This creature parallels many a *naag* characters in Indian mythology and I believe this is familiar to Indian children.

The unicorn is the third mythical creature that I believe Indian readers were able to strongly appreciate. As per the records of Greek writers, unicorns were animals found in India. Unicorns were described as having a straight, long horn that extends from its forehead. It was also said to have goat's beard, cloven hooves and a lion's tail. In the British wizarding world they are seen as pure animals which are gold when babies then turn sliver and ultimately white as they grow into adulthood (GOF 484). Witches and wizards use unicorn horns and tail hairs, and unicorn's silvery blood is lifesaving to one who drinks it, but at the cost of the life becoming cursed (SS 258).

In ancient India, a unicorn was used on one of the seals from Indus Valley Civilization. Cosmas Indicopleustes, a sixth-century merchant of Alexandria who made a voyage to India, subsequently wrote works on cosmography, which describe a figure of the unicorn, not from actual sight of it, but as reproduced from four figures of it in brass contained in the palace of the King of Ethiopia. He stated, that "it is impossible to take this ferocious beast alive; and that all its strength lies in its horn. When it finds itself pursued and in danger of capture, it throws itself from a precipice, and turns so aptly in falling, that it receives all the shock upon the horn, and so escapes safe and sound" (*Christian Topography* 1897: 358). I believe that the existence of the unicorn in Indian mythology made it another magical creature that ingratiated Indian readers to the British wizarding world.

Parallel Social Structure

The most spectacular feature of British wizarding world is the blood based division of society. In this social structure, we witness a tri-layered social structure: wizards belonging to wizarding families (purebloods) are supposedly superior to wizards belonging to partial – or non-wizarding families (half-bloods and Muggle-borns respectively). Harry learned of this notion of social hierarchy when Draco Malfoy said to Ron Weasley and then to Harry:

> No need to ask who you are. My father told me all the Weasleys have red hair, freckles, and more children than they can afford… You'll soon find out some wizarding families are much better than others, Potter. You don't want to go making friends with the wrong sort. (SS 108)

Similar stratification is also prevalent in Indian society. India is famous for its caste system, which has become a strong institution in its society. Under this institution the Hindus have been divided into four *Varnas*: Brahmans, Kshtriyas, Vaishyas and Shudras. As per social hierarchy, the Brahmans are the most superior followed by the Kshtriyas and the Vaishyas. The Shudras have been treated as the outcastes. This system has been so rigid that even inter-caste marriages and inter-dining were prohibited. Initially based on choice of profession, this practice, at later stage, became hereditary. Even today, it has not completely subsided in the Indian society.

In a stratified social system, one's location in the hierarchy affects access to goods and services. For example, Harry and his friends learn that that Slytherin chooses its students partially based having "great ambition" (GOF 177) but also only selects "those whose ancestry is purest" (OOTP 205). Indian traditional social system shows the illustrations of similar discriminatory practices in education in literature as well. For example in the Indian epic the *Mahabharata*, we see the example of Eklavya who went to Guru Drona to learn archery but was refused on the grounds that he was not a prince of the Brahmin or Kshtriyas castes, and Guru Drona only taught those of these higher castes. Determined Eklavya, however, created a mud bust of Guru Drona and started practicing on his own in front of it. In time he became the world's best archer, even surpassing legendary Arjuna who was a student of Drona.

When the Hindus were first divided into four *Varnas*, it was based on the work of the person concerned. Only over time did the classification become rigidly rooted in birth. We see the influence of occupation in the wizarding world as well. Mr. Weasley, for example, is considered by other purebloods to be "a disgrace to the name of wizard" (COS 62) for his personal interactions with Muggles and for his professional work with Muggles in the Misuse of Muggle Artefacts Office at the Ministry of Magic. Squibs (non-magical persons born into wizarding families) are another example of the status-occupation link. Squibs often have the worst jobs in the wizarding world, where they are seen as outcasts. Mr. Filch the caretaker at Hogwarts is an example. This also happened in India where people belonging to the lower rung of the caste system were assigned jobs usually considered unclean. They were also outcasted from society.

Another feature of the British wizarding world to which Indian fans could relate is inter-caste conflict, exemplified by purebloods' torture of Muggle-borns and the latter fighting back. Some of these rivalries mirror the scene of Indian society where people belonging to high castes misbehave and assault the people of the lower castes. One of the Big Trios of Indian English novel writers, Mulk Raj Anand, makes a very lively description of the issue in question in his short story, "The Barber's Trade Union," where a "low caste barber's son" Chandu is humiliated several times for wearing fine clothing and behaving like members of the upper caste. The narrator of the story finds one day that the protagonist of the story Chandu, who happened to be his classmate, invites unfavourable situations for him when he wears a nice outfit. He writes:

> One day I was thrilled to find Chandu at the door of my house in the morning. He was dressed up in a white turbon, a white rubber coat (a little too big for him, but nevertheless very splendid), a pair of pumpsin which I could see my face reflected in clear silhouette, and he had a leather bag in his hand. He was setting off on his round and had come to show me how grand he looked in his new new rig-out (Singh 2000: 31-32).

Although the narrator was excited and exclaimed, "Marvellous" at his friend's attire, the traditional gentry of the village was all set to denounce it. One burly landlord yells, "Go away you swine, go away and wear clothes befitting your low status as a barber, and don't let me see you practising any of your new fangled notions, or else I will have you flogged"(32).

Although this tale is some three or four decades old, still the ideology is found in the national psyche. This often takes a violent turn resulting in bloodshed. Similarly in the British wizarding world, purebloods like Draco Malfoy often are set to "get that jumped up Mudblood" when Muggle-borns "act above" their station (HP3).

Finally, in India there has been a great chain of scholars, leaders, and social workers who worked for eliminating caste system. Raja Ram Mohan Roy, Mahatma Gandhi, B.R. Ambedkar and many more worked in this direction. The untouchability and disparity based on caste system has been almost eliminated, but the castes still exist. In the twenty-first century, some

Indians want to write off even the existence of castes from the social structure. They are working to change the caste system. Consequently, the final correlate I find between the Indian social system and the British wizarding world is that Indian readers could identify with the Harry's and others' efforts to fight against Voldemort's caste system and bring about a more equal society.

CONCLUSION

Though the British wizarding world created by JK Rowling is fictional, it grows from a deep foundation of myths and folklore that have endured across time and space. The world wide popularity of Harry Potter books testifies to the breadth of cultures from which she draws many of her images, characters and themes. Sometimes she creates something entirely new from the fragments gleaned from different cultures, collating a postmodern collage, yet she remains remarkably true to the essence of each.

The results of my survey suggest that Harry Potter has enjoyed a great reception in India because readers find familiarity in certain characters, creatures, and other elements of the British wizarding world. In this chapter I have presented three such elements that I believe underlay these feelings – Indian's affinity for the supernatural, the Patil twins and many magical creatures, and the caste-like social structure of the society. Future research on Pottermania in India could address these and other social elements to discover which are most important and influential to children readers.

Despite being set in the United Kingdom, Harry Potter has enjoyed great success in many countries, including those that, at first glance, appear very different culturally and socially. However, as I have tried to show, Harry Potter was immensely successful in India because, in short, when readers opened the book about a British school boy, they, nonetheless, entered into "a world entirely their own" (HP3).

REFERENCES

Anand, Mulk Raj. 1944[2000]. " The Barber's Trade Union." Pp. 29-42 in *An Anthology of English Short Stories*. Edited by R. P. Singh. New Delhi: Oxford University Press.

Encyclopedia Britannica. "Naga." Retrieved 3 November 2011 (http://www. britannica.com/EBchecked/topic/401527/naga).

Indicopleustes, Cosmos. 1897[2003]. *The Christian Topography*. Transcribed by R. Pearse. Retrieved 3 November 2011 (http://www.tertullian.org/ fathers/index.htm#Cosmas_Indicopleustes).

Naas, Michael. 2007. "*Comme si comme ca*: Phantasm of Self, State, and a Sovereign God." *Mosaic: A Journal for the Interdisciplinary Study of Literature* 40(2): 1-26.

Office of National Statistics. 2005. "UK Snap Shot: Ethnicity and Identity Population Size."

"Either Must Die at the Hand of the Other"

RELIGIOUS REACTIONS TO HARRY POTTER

LEO RUICKBIE

A man stood by the window, arms folded, a dark silhouette against the light. In front of him, a girl with eyes reddened and puffy from crying. "Tell me, Samantha," he began, "how did you and Holly get into the craft?" The girl looked up at him. "Through the Harry Potter books! We wanted his powers, so we called for spirit guides. Then *they* came into us." She sank onto the sofa, the man standing over her. "They led us into stuff we found in the Harry Potter books – Tarot cards, Ouija boards, crystal balls..." The man interrupted her, "Samantha, the Potter books open a doorway that will put untold millions of kids into hell."[1]

This scene never took place. It is based on a comic strip by Jack T. Chick called "The Nervous Witch" (2002). It does, however, reflect the real concerns of many Christians, despite the fact that there were no Tarot cards or Ouija boards in J.K. Rowling's Harry Potter series, and crystal balls were presented in nothing but the poorest light. That in itself tells us much about the Christian Fundamentalist reaction to Harry Potter. Why was the religious reaction to Harry Potter so strong? Why did it seem like we were again about to relive the witch hunts of the late sixteenth and seventeenth centuries?

Intended as an innocent and educative tale for children (and adults), Harry Potter clearly became a battleground for certain expressions of religiosity that reignited pre-established antagonisms towards paganism and magic. Rowling's liberal messages of equality and the necessity of fighting tyranny were supplanted by a focus on magic, a magic that was purportedly rooted in evil. What is surprising is how much force this backlash could assume in our supposedly globalised, multicultural world.

Nor is it simply a question of Christianity's reaction to Harry Potter. Perceptions of the multimedia series have become a nexus of competing conflicts ranging from Islam to atheism to Wicca. Then we have a shift in some religious reactions that seemed to bear out the old adage that 'if you can't beat 'em, join 'em.' Harry Potter was suddenly being co-opted and resold as a Christian message. How could that come about and is it sustainable? Is this assimilation, by its distortion of the original material, yet another form of persecution?

Is it the case that in the conflict between certain elements of current religiosity and Harry Potter that "either must die at the hand of the other?"

Are these same elements positioning themselves as Voldemort – the man who died – against Harry Potter – the boy who lived?

The classic interpretation, following Marwick (1964), is of witchcraft as a social strain gauge. Could even literary witchcraft be a social strain gauge? And in this case, of what social groupings? Of broader society, or of the denouncing parties? Could it be the case that the groups demanding the destruction and/or assimilation of Potter were in fact exhibiting symptoms of their own crises? As well as this, wider problems and cultural shifts are also brought into focus and/ or being. What does a multivocal debate on magic say about the secularisation thesis, for example? What does the conceptual conflict arising out of modes of entertainment tell us about the condition of modern social interaction?

"POTTER STINKS": PERVERTING POTTER

In 2006 a stout, bleach-bottle blonde stood in front of a group of children and shouted "Warlocks are enemies of God! And I don't care what kind of hero they are, they're an enemy of God and had it been in the Old Testament, Harry Potter would have been put to death!" A small voice in the audience called out "Amen!" Applause followed. Stabbing the air with an accusatory figure, she continued "You don't make heroes out of warlocks." Pastor Becky Fischer was addressing the Pentacostalist Kids on Fire prayer camp in North Dakota, USA. At the end of the session many were in tears (Ewing and Grady 2006).

According to figures from the American Library Association (ALA 2006), the Harry Potter series constitute the most frequently challenged books of the 21st century. For the decade 1990-1999 the Harry Potter series was ranked 48th out of a 100 (ALA n.d.: a), when only the first three books had been published and none of the films, which undoubtedly raised awareness, were on release. For the decade 2000-2009 the series was ranked first (ALA n.d.: b). Reasons for challenging the series included violence, religious viewpoint and anti-family values, but the perceived promotion of occultism or Satanism was the most common accusation. These were mostly challenges made by parents against schools (ALA n.d.: c).

Among the many attempts to ban the books from school libraries, especially in the USA, one particular case has attracted notable international attention. In the long-running 'Mom vs Potter' case, Laura Mallory has tried to have Harry Potter banned from school libraries in Georgia, USA, claiming that they promote "evil themes, witchcraft, demonic activity, murder, evil blood sacrifice, spells and teaching children all of this" (Madan 2006). Usually identified in press reports as a "mother of four," she added that the books "have been shown to be harmful to some kids" (Daily Mail 2006). She first made her complaint in September 2005 against the use of the books at J.C. Magill Elementary School, taking her claim to successively higher authorities through 2006 and into 2007 before finally stopping short of the federal court.

There have been several recorded public destructions of Harry Potter books, all of them conducted by Protestants. Rev George Bender, leader of the Harvest Assembly of God Church, near Pittsburgh, Pennsylvania, organised a book burning in 2001 in which copies of the Harry Potter books were fed to the flames, saying "We believe that Harry Potter promotes sorcery, witchcraft-type things, the paranormal, things that are against God" (ABC 2001). The Jesus Party in Lewiston, Maine, attempted to burn Harry Potter books in a public park, again in 2001, but being denied a fire permit resorted to "book cutting" 12 copies in its place. Their leader, Rev Doug Taylor, said "We think these books are dangerous" (Sun Journal 2001). He repeated the book cutting in 2002 (Serchuk 2006). Also in 2001, Pastor Jack Brock told members of the Christ Community Church in Alamogordo, New Mexico, that "Harry Potter is the Devil and he is destroying people" before leading his congregation to burn copies of Rowling's novels (BBC 2001). In 2003, T.D. Turner, Sr, and his son T.D. Turner, Jr, both pastors, burnt a copy of one of the novels outside their Jesus Non-Denominational Church, Greenville, Michigan (Serchuk 2006). In 2009 Taylor publicly ripped pages out of another Harry Potter book on the opening night of the film *Harry Potter and the Half-Blood Prince* (Hannon 2009) and wrote to the local paper, the *Sun Journal*, with the plea "Burn, Harry, burn" (Taylor 2009).

A number of books, information packs, audio CDs and videos have been produced carrying the same arguments against Harry Potter. Books include Steve Wohlberg's *Exposing Harry Potter and Witchcraft* (2005) and Richard Abanes's *Harry Potter and the Bible: The Menace Behind the Magick* (2008). Most recently, Candy Gwen Lopitz (2011: 215) made the extraordinary claim that "Harry Potter films are prevalently used in satanic ritual abuse cults" in her self-published *Spiritual Battery*. Family Life Center International had its 'Harry Potter Kit,' consisting of a twelve page newsletter, audio tape and a PowerPoint presentation sheet. Probably the most influential was *Harry Potter: Witchcraft Repackaged* (Matrisciana 2001) with promotion via the Christian Broadcasting Network's *The 700 Club*, presented by the controversial Pat Robertson. Chick's (2002) 'The Nervous Witch' footnotes the video during Samantha's 'confession' scene. On the product page at chick.com we are told that through Harry Potter "millions of children are being desensitized to the dangers of the occult spirit world." The battle against Potter is compared to that being fought against the teaching of evolutionary theory in schools.

The reaction against Harry Potter was neither restricted to Fundamentalist Protestant Christianity, nor to the USA. According to letters published by the Canadian religious news service LifeSiteNews.com, then Cardinal Joseph Ratzinger, now Pope Benedict XVI, endorsed Gabriele Kuby's critical book *Harry Potter: Gut oder Böse?* ('Harry Potter: Good or Evil?'), saying "It is good that you enlighten people about Harry Potter, because those are subtle seductions, which are unnoticed and by this deeply distort Christianity in the soul, before it can grow properly" (LifeSiteNews 2005). Although this was widely reported as papal opposition to the series, there has been no official statement from the Vatican. Kuby condemns the series for, among other things, having "no positive transcendent dimension" and using "emotional manipulation and intellectual confusion" to make "an assault upon the young generation, seducing it playfully into a world of witchcraft and sorcery" (Kuby 2011). Father Gabriele Amorth, honorary life-president of the International Association of Exorcists and exorcist of the Diocese of Rome, was characteristically forthright in his view: "Behind Harry Potter hides the signature of the King of Darkness, the Devil," adding that there could be no distinction between black and white magic "because magic is always a turn to the Devil" (Lawler 2002).

In the UK, reactions were less extreme. The Church of England response was mixed. Canterbury Cathedral refused permission to film on location for *Harry Potter and the Philosopher's Stone*, citing inappropriate pagan imagery, and Carol Rookwood, headmistress of St Mary's primary school, Chatham, Kent, banned the books from the school library (Petre 2001). The Very Reverend Nicholas Bury, Dean of Gloucester Cathedral, came in for criticism from Anglicans, including a public demonstration, for allowing filming to take place in the cathedral (Rosenthal 2005).

Members of the Eastern Orthodox church in Greece and Bulgaria have spoken out against Harry Potter (Ekathimerini 2003; Leviev-Sawyer 2004). Notably, the See of Didymoteicho, Thrace, whilst making the familiar accusations, also denounced Potter's "Christ-like attributes" (Ekathimerini 2003). Following Stanislav Ianevski's casting as Quidditch ace Viktor Krum (HP4), posters appeared across Sofia proclaiming "God hates magic" and the Bulgarian Orthodox Church ran a front-page story in its official newspaper warning that "magic is not a children's game" (Leviev-Sawyer 2004).

Harry Potter has also incensed Muslims, largely for the same reasons. The United Arab Emirates Ministry of Education and Youth banned *Harry Potter and the Philosopher's Stone* from use in private schools (BBC 2002); a move later echoed by Muslim schools in the UK (Hall 2009). When Iran's Culture and Islamic Guidance Ministry approved Harry Potter, Ayatollah Ali Khamenei spoke out against the decision and the daily newspaper *Kayhan* castigated the series as a Zionist project intended to pervert the minds of the young (Memri 2007). Hours before *Harry Potter and the Deathly Hallows* went on sale in Karachi, Pakistan, police found 10kg of RDX explosives following an anonymous tip-off (The Nation 2007). It was also reported that a fatwa had been issued against JK Rowling (Abbot 2007).

The intense controversy pushed Rowling onto the defensive as interviewers repeatedly questioned her on the accusations. "I don't believe in witchcraft" (Woods 2000), she has said, adding on another occasion, "Practicing Wiccans think I'm also a witch. I'm not" (Jensen 2000). Speaking to Katie Couric (2003) she was more forthright: "I absolutely do not believe in the occult, [or] practice the occult". Rowling has repeatedly stated that none of her readers has ever told her that her books have led them to take an interest in the occult (Weeks 1999; BBC 2001; Couric 2003). Newspapers also report similar statements from readers themselves (e.g., Madan 2006), whilst Christian sources offer supposed exposés, such as David Meyer's 'Former Witch Exposes Harry Potter' in which he claims that "the Harry Potter books are training manuals for the occult" based on his own alleged experience as a 'witch' (Meyer n.d.).

In many cases the negative outburst to the Harry Potter series was a reflex reaction exhibiting little familiarity with the novels, films, or opinions of JK Rowling. Both Brock (BBC 2001) and Mallory (Madan 2006), for example, revealed that they not read any of the Harry Potter novels. Outrage coalesced around the presentation of magic as a real and potentially positive force, re-drawing the old battle-lines of Christian outrage against the occult in general. In particular, many Christians expressed the fear that they were losing control over their children through exposure to what was perceived as occult propaganda. This was a multi-faith, multi-denominational assault, although expressed more forcefully and vocally by Fundamentalist groups. The extreme presentations of this fear in book burning and bombing attest to a social strain gauge effect comparable to classic witchcraft accusations.

"A Fresh Attempt to Seize Power": Subverting Potter

In 2002 Dutch priest Pastor Joris Ridderbos pulled on a conical hat and in front of a group of children dressed as Harry Potter characters celebrated what the media dubbed as "a Harry Potter mass". Speaking to the *Haagse Courant* newspaper he said "The story of Harry Potter starts with an alternative reading of the story of the three kings, there is a speaking snake and, like Jesus, Harry Potter was a very obedient boy" (BreakingNews 2002). He was not alone. Connie Neal's three books (2001, 2002, 2007) on the subject trawled J.K. Rowling's series looking for allusions, however contrived, to Christian teachings – she received death threats from Christians for her efforts (Bailey 2011). Similarly, Presbyterian minister Dr John Killinger turns Potter into an "often unwitting Christ figure" (2002). Another recent attempt is Derek Murphy's *Jesus Potter Harry Christ* (2011).

The Rev Dr Francis Bridger, principal of Trinity College, member of the Church of England's General Synod, argued that the Harry Potter books were "opening the door to the Gospels" (Petre 2001). Himself an author of Potter apologia, Bridger used *A Charmed Life: The Spirituality of Harry Potter* (2008) to downplay the role of magic in the series and highlight "intrinsic human goodness, love and friendship" as part of his argument that the books are "firmly based in [sic] Christian values." Bury defended his decision to allow Warner Brothers to use Gloucester Cathedral as a location for Hogwarts (HP1) by stating that "I've no evidence that these books have done any harm or led any children astray." Instead he found that "the lessons are positive. Good defeats evil" (Rosenthal 2005). The then Archbishop of Canterbury and leader of the Church of England, Dr George Carey, called Harry Potter "great fun" in his New Year message broadcast on BBC Radio 2. Again, he found the differentiation between good and evil to be the central message (ACNS 2002). To coincide with the publication of the final book (DH), the Church of England published a guide for youth groups (Smith 2007) using Harry Potter to illustrate Christian principles in an intentional effort to harness the popularity of Harry Potter for its own ends (Sugden 2007).

Reversing its position of the previous year on Harry Potter, the official Vatican newspaper, *L'Osservatore Romano,* was notably positive about the film adaptation of *Harry Potter and the Half-Blood Prince*: "There is a clear line of demarcation between good and evil and [the film] makes clear that good is right. One understands as well that sometimes this requires hard work and sacrifice" (Squires 2009). The paper (2011) essentially restated this comment for the release of *Harry Potter and the Deathly Hallows*, Part 2, leading Deacon Greg Kandra (2011) to announce that it had given the film the "thumbs up." Rev Peter Fleetwood, a member of the Vatican's council for culture, said that the books "help children to see the difference between good and evil" and that Rowling was Christian "in her way of writing" (Guardian 2003). The United States Conference of Catholic Bishops website (USCCB 2004; 2009) placed two of the Harry Potter films in its top ten family films category (HP3 and HP6), noting in particular how "good and evil are clearly delineated" in the latter.

The Orthodox Church also has its Potter apologists. American Orthodox writer John Granger claimed that there was "a profoundly Christian meaning at the core of the series" (2004: xviii). Similarly, Russian Orthodox writer Deacon Andrei Kuraev (2003) noted the presence and importance of Christian values in the books.

The final word must go to Rowling herself, who said about her avowed Christian faith in an interview that "I think you can see that in the books" (Lindell 2007), which led to headlines such as 'Christianity Inspired Harry

Potter' (Petre 2007). However, she has also made it clear that her "faith is sometimes that my faith will return" (Petre 2007) and, more directly, "I did not set out to convert anyone to Christianity" (Bailey 2011).

For much of the pro argument it is the differentiation between good and evil that makes Harry Potter religiously acceptable. It is a differentiation that is not always clear in the storylines, something that critics, such as Fr Amorth (Lawler 2002), have made much of. The character of Severus Snape is morally divided: he appears evil, but works for the good. Even the character of Potter struggles with the connection between himself and Voldemort, fearing that he is becoming like him and being perceived as being like him by the other pupils, as "the heir of Slytherin" (COS: 198-199), for example. That said, the storyline over the series clearly resolves into the choice between presentations of what is intended to be 'good' and 'evil.'

However, the polarisation of good versus evil is not an exclusively Christian theme. Even if the character of Harry Potter, like Jesus, does sacrifice himself for his believers, that is not an exclusively Christian theme either. The widespread idea of the sacrificial god can be studied at length in Sir James George Frazer's monumental *The Golden Bough* (1890 and other editions), although, admittedly, few people are going to be aware of the commonality of this theme. Rowling is right to distance herself from Wicca and it is unlikely that any Wiccans, despite her claims, would see her imaginative world as in any way Wiccan. Steve Paine, speaking for the Pagan Federation, noted the stories were popular amongst Pagans but were "taken as fantasy entertainment" (BBC 2000). Where Wicca is a nature religion expressed as the veneration of fertility through engendered duality (Goddess and Horned God) with an eightfold ritual calendar celebrating seasonal change, the 'wizarding world' is essentially a secular construct revolving around pedagogic (Hogwarts) and bureaucratic (the Ministry of Magic) constellations. For Rowling magic is a technology, albeit a supernatural one, but not a faith. The Harry Potter series remains, if anything, religiously neutral, playing out its conflicts within the context of modern liberal ideology rather than theology. With the obvious parallels between Voldemort's reign and the Nazi regime, the choice between 'good' and 'evil' takes a political, rather than a religious cast. Positive religious responses are, therefore, just as guilty of distorting the Harry Potter series as negative ones.

"YOU CAN'T GIVE A DEMENTOR *THE OLD ONE-TWO*": CONCLUSION

Jack T. Chick is believed to have sold more than 500 million copies of his comic book 'tracts' promoting his polemical interpretation of Christianity and earning him the title of "the world's most published author" (Ito 2003: 56).

His sales have even beaten the astonishing success of the Harry Potter series, currently at 450 million copies sold (BBC 2011), but "The Nervous Witch," although reproduced in full on the website, is no longer stocked by Chick Publications (Chick 2002).

Even ten years ago, before the release of the film adaptations, awareness of Harry Potter was extremely high with Gallup (Jones 2000) finding that 71 per cent of American adults had heard of the books. Amongst them, 52 per cent approved of the books, 41 per cent had no opinion and only seven per cent disapproved. What these figures would suggest is that it is only a vocal minority who are pushing the anti-Potter agenda. Yet we have seen that that minority was able to bring the Harry Potter books to the forefront of public debate.

However, attempts to ban the book were either ineffectual, as in the Mallory case, or produced only temporary and localised censure, as in the Rookwood case. Destruction of the book was a symbolic gesture, headline grabbing to be sure, but one that was ultimately more futile – after all, the protesters had to buy the copies they destroyed and arguably made Harry Potter more appealing through such controversy. Notably, amongst the lists of books burnt and complained of there was no mention of actual books about Wicca or the occult. Given the non-religious context of the 'wizarding world,' the presentation of magic by itself was no challenge to secularisation, instead being perceived of as a threat to particular religious outlooks. The sales figures alone show that the anti-Potter lobby has had little or no negative impact on the popularity of the franchise.

'Harry Potter' became an empty phrase in the ongoing conflict over the Western mind. Christians such as Chick appear to have little or no knowledge of the content of the Harry Potter books or films, but simply use the phrase as a magnet and focusing point for a constellation of ideas inimicable to the 'anything goes' direction of post-modern, post-industrial, post-Christian, pro-consumer society. The flawless packaging, distribution, marketing and consumption of Harry Potter in multiple media configurations attest to its successful integration into that society.

However, it is not simply the case that "either must die at the hand of the other, for neither can live while the other survives" (OOTP 741). Harry Potter was also praised. Attempts to subvert Harry Potter as a Christian story have been almost as widespread and numerous as attempts to censure Harry Potter, yet it is the case that a religiously neutral story is innocent on both charges of either promoting the occult or championing Christianity. Instead, it could be argued that the groups demanding the destruction or assimilation of Potter were in fact exhibiting symptoms of their own crises in line with Marwick's (1964) social strain gauge theory, although in a different, globalised context.

Notably, Rowling herself was not accused of being a witch, [2] although she found it necessary to deny that she was one. The 'occult' within the Harry Potter series is simply a fantasy milieu, whilst the 'occult' functions within religious extremism as a socially cohesive force, an 'enemy' that the faithful can face together, but at the same time the intense concern demonstrates fears of social disintegration ('strain') in the face of a dominant culture that has left religious certainties behind.

NOTES

[1] This is a reconstructed narrative based on Chick, 2002.

[2] The few sources making this accusation are web based, such as the 'God Hates Harry Potter' page on the godhatesgoths.com website (http://godhatesgoths.com/godhatesharrypotter.html, retrieved July 15, 2011), and such accusations have not been reported in the media nor in the published anti-Potter literature as far as I am aware.

REFERENCES

Abanes, Richard. 2008. *Harry Potter and the Bible: The Menace Behind the Magick*. Camp Hill, PA: Christian Publications.

Abbot, Sebastian. 2007. "'New Media' Fatwas Rankle Islamic Establishment." *USA Today*. August 12.

ABC News. 2001. "Purging Flame: Pa. Church Members Burn Harry Potter, Other Books 'Against God.'" March 26.

ACNS (Anglican Communion News Service). 2002. "Archbishop of Canterbury's New Year Message." January 2. Retrieved July 11, 2011 (http://www.anglicancommunion.org/acns/news.cfm/2002/1/2/ACNS2810).

ALA (American Library Association). 2006. "Harry Potter Tops List of Most Challenged Books of 21st Century." September 21. Retrieved July 12, 2011 (http://www.ala.org/ala/newspresscenter/news/pressreleases2006/september2006/harrypottermostchallenge.cfm).

—. N.d. (a). "100 Most Frequently Challenged Books: 1990-1999." Retrieved January 26, 2011 (http://www.ala.org/ala/issuesadvocacy/banned/frequentlychallenged/challengedbydecade/1990_1999/index.cfm).

—. N.d. (b). "Top 100 Banned/Challenged Books: 2000-2009." Retrieved January 26, 2011 (http://www.ala.org/ala/issuesadvocacy/banned/frequentlychallenged/challengedbydecade/2000_2009/index.cfm).

—. N.d. (c). "Number of Challenges by Year, Reason, Initiator & Institution (1990 – 2010)." Retrieved January 26, 2011 (http://www.ala.org/ala/issuesadvocacy/banned/frequentlychallenged/challengesbytype/index.cfm).

Anelli, Melissa. 2008. *Harry, A History: The True Story of a Boy Wizard, His Fans, and Life Inside the Harry Potter Phenomenon*. New York, NY: Pocket Books.

Bailey, Sarah Pulliam. 2011. "How Christians Warmed to Harry Potter." *Wall Street Journal*, July 15.

BBC News. 2000. "Buffy Draws Children to Witchcraft." August 4. Retrieved July 15, 2011 (http://news.bbc.co.uk/2/hi/entertainment/864984.stm).

—. 2001. "'Satanic' Harry Potter Books Burnt." December 31. Retrieved July 11, 2011 (http://news.bbc.co.uk/2/hi/entertainment/1735623.stm).

—. 2002. "Emirates Ban Potter Book." February 12. Retrieved July 11, 2011 (http://news.bbc.co.uk/2/hi/entertainment/1816012.stm).

—. 2011. "Harry Potter Series to be Sold as E-Books." June 23. Retrieved July 15, 2011 (http://www.bbc.co.uk/news/entertainment-arts-13889578)..

BBC TV. 2001. "Harry Potter and Me." December 28.

Bosmajian, Haig A. 2006. *Burning Books*. Jefferson, NC: McFarland.

BreakingNews.ie. 2002. "Dutch Priest Celebrates Harry Potter Mass." January 13. Retrieved July 6, 2011 (http://www.breakingnews.ie/archives/2002/0113/entertainment/mhgbcwqlmh/).

Bridger, Francis. 2002. *A Charmed Life: The Spirituality of Potterworld*. Garden City, NY: Image Books.

Chick, Jack T. 2002. "The Nervous Witch." Ontario, CA: Chick Publications.

Chick.com. N.d. Retrieved January 26, 2011 (http://www.chick.com/catalog/videos/0127.asp).

Couric, Katie. 2003. "Interview with JK Rowling." *Dateline NBC*. June 20.

Daily Mail. 2006. "Ban Harry Potter or Face More School Shootings." October 4.

Ekathimerini. 2003. "Church: Harry Potter Film a Font of Evil." January 14.

Ewing, Heidi, and Rachel Grady (dirs). 2006. *Jesus Camp*. Loki Films and A&E IndieFilms.

Frazer, Sir James George. 1890. *The Golden Bough: A Study in Comparative Religion*, 2 vols. London: Macmillan and Co.

Granger, John. 2002. *The Hidden Key to Harry Potter*. Wayne, PA: Zossima Press.

—. 2004. *Looking for God in Harry Potter*. Carol Stream, IL: Tyndale House Publishers.

Guardian. 2003. "Catholic Church Stands Up for Harry Potter." February 4.

Hall, Macer. 2009. "Muslim Schools Ban Our Culture." *Express*. February 20.

Hannon, Andie. 2009. 'Jesus Party Rips "Harry Potter" on Eve of New Movie'. *Sun Journal*. July 15.

Ito, Robert. 2003. "Fear Factor: Jack Chick is the World's Most Published Author – And One of the Strangest." *Los Angeles*. May, 56-63.

Jensen, Jeff. 2000. "'Fire' Storm." *Entertainment Weekly*. September 7.

Jones, Jeffrey M. 2000. "Even Adults Familiar with Harry Potter Books." *Gallup*. July 13. Retrieved January 26, 2011 (http://www.gallup.com/poll/2740/Even-Adults-Familiar-Harry-Potter-Books.aspx).

Kandra, Greg. 2011. "Vatican Paper: Thumbs Up for Last 'Harry Potter' Film." Patheos.com. July 12. Retrieved July 13, 2011 (http://www.patheos.com/community/deaconsbench/2011/07/12/vatican-paper-thumbs-up-for-last-harry-potter-film/).

Keim, David. 2000. "Children's Literature: Parents Push for Wizard-Free Reading." *Christianity Today*. January 10.

Killinger, John. 2002. *God, the Devil, and Harry Potter: A Christian Minister's Defense of the Beloved Novels*. New York, NY: Thomas Dunne Books.

Knuth, Rebecca. 2006. *Burning Books and Leveling Libraries: Extremist Violence and Cultural Destruction*. Westport, CT: Praeger.

Komschlies, Jacqui. 2000. "Matters of Opinion: The Perils of Harry Potter." *Christianity Today*. October 23.

Kuby, Gabrielle. 2003. *Harry Potter: Gut oder Böse?* Kißlegg-Immenried: Fe-Medienverlags.

—. N.d. "Ten Arguments Against Harry Potter." Retrieved July 11, 2011 (http://www.gabriele-kuby.de/buecher/harry-potter/).

Kuraev, Andrei. 2003. *Гарри Поттер в Церкви: между анафемой и улыбкой* ["Harry Potter in the Church: Between an Anathema and a Smile"]. CPb: Neva.

Lawler, Phil. 2002. "Famed Exorcist Sees Dangers in Harry Potter." *Catholic World Report*. January 2.

Leviev-Sawyer, Clive. 2004. "Bulgarian church warns against the spell of Harry Potter." *Ecumenica News International*. June 28.

LifeSiteNews.com. 2005. "Pope Opposes Harry Potter Novels – Signed Letters from Cardinal Ratzinger Now Online." July 13. Retrieved July 6, 2011 (http://www.lifesitenews.com/news/archive/ldn/2005/jul/05071301).

Lindell, Karen. 2007. "Magical Experience for Harry Potter Fans." *Ventura County Star*. October 21.

Lopitz, Candy Gwen. 2011. *Spiritual Battery: Hope for Cult Casualties – Help for Those Assisting Their Recovery*. Longwood, FL: XulonPress.

Madan, Rubina. 2006. "Hearing to Determine Fate of 'Harry Potter' Books in GCPS." *Gwinnett Daily Post*. April 18. Retrieved 13 July, 2011 (http://www.gwinnettdailypost.com/archives/headlines/79807052.html).

Marwick, Max G. 1964. "Witchcraft as a Social Strain Gauge." *Australian Journal of Science*. 26: 263-8.

Matrisciana, Caryl. 2001. *Harry Potter: Witchcraft Repackaged, Making Evil Look Innocent*. Westminster, CA: Jeremiah Films.

The Memri Blog. 2007. "Iranian Daily: Harry Potter, Billion-Dollar Zionist Project." Retrieved July 11, 2011 (http://www.thememriblog.org/blog_personal/en/2269.htm).

Meyer, David J. N.d. "Former Witch Exposes Harry Potter." Jesus-is-Savior.com. Retrieved July 13, 2011(http://www.jesus-is-savior.com/False%20Religions/Wicca%20&%20Witchcraft/former_witch_exposes_harry_potter.htm).

Murphy, Derek. 2011. *Jesus Potter Harry Christ: The Fascinating Parallels Between Two of the World's Most Popular Literary Characters*. Portland, OR: Holy Blasphemy.

The Nation. 2007. "Terrorist Attack at the Potter Book Launch Site Foiled in Pakistan." August 4. Retrieved January 26, 2011 (http://www.

nationmultimedia.com/2007/07/21/headlines/headlines_30041840. php)

Neal, Connie. 2001. *What's a Christian to Do with Harry Potter?* Colorado Springs, CA: Waterbrook Press.

—. 2002. *The Gospel According to Harry Potter: Spirituality in the Stories of the World's Favourite Seeker.* Louisville, KY: Westminster John Knox Press.

—. 2007. *Wizards, Wardrobes and Wookies: Navigating Good and Evil in Harry Potter, Narnia and Star Wars.* Nottingham: IVP Books.

Olsen, Ted. 1999. "Opinion Roundup: Positive About Potter." *Christianity Today.* December 6.

L'Osservatore Romano. 2011. "Harry Potter's Last Battle." Retrieved July 13, 2011 (http://www.osservatoreromano.va/portal/dt?JSPTabContainer. setSelected=JSPTabContainer%2FDetail&last=false=&path=/ news/cultura/2011/159q11-L-ultima-battaglia-di-Harry-Potter. html&title=Harry%20Potter's%20last%20battle&locale=en).

Petre, Jonathan. 2001. "Wizard Harry 'has Magic Key to the Christian Life.'" *The Telegraph.* September 9. Retrieved July 11, 2011 (http:// www.telegraph.co.uk/news/uknews/1339986/Wizard-Harry-has-magic-key-to-the-Christian-life.html).

Petre, Jonathan. 2007. "JK Rowling: 'Christianity Inspired Harry Potter.'" *The Telegraph.* 20 October. Retrieved July 16, 2011 (http://www. telegraph.co.uk/culture/books/fictionreviews/3668658/J-K-Rowling-Christianity-inspired-Harry-Potter.html).

Rosenthal, Elisabeth. 2005. "Don't Count Pope Among Harry Potter Fans." *New York Times.* July 16. Retrieved July 11, 2011 (http://www.nytimes. com/2005/07/15/world/europe/15iht-pope.html).

Serchuk, David. 2006. "Harry Potter and the Ministry of Fire." *Forbes.* January 12.

Smith, Owen. 2007. *Mixing It Up With Harry Potter: 12 Sessions on Faith for 9-13s.* London: Church House Publishing.

Squires, Nick. 2009. "Harry Potter and the Incredibly Positive Review from the Official Vatican Paper." *Independent.* July 15. Retrieved January 26, 2011 (http://www.independent.ie/entertainment/news-gossip/harry-potter-and-the-incredibly-positive-review-from-the-official-vatican-paper-1821926.html).

Sugden, Joanna. 2007. "Use Harry Potter to Spread Christianity Says Church." *The Times.* July 17. Retrieved July 16, 2011 (http://www. timesonline.co.uk/tol/comment/faith/article2092321.ece).

Sun Journal. 2001. "Lewiston Christian Group to Protest Potter." *Sun Journal.* November 15.

Taylor, Doug. 2009. "Potter Mania is Back." *Sun Journal.* July 12. Retrieved

July 12, 2011 (http://www.sunjournal.com/node/29539/category/product-sections/lifestyle/category/product-sections/connections/nuptials).

USCCB.org. 2004. "Ten Best List for the Year 2004." Retrieved January 26, 2011 (http://www.usccb.org/movies/topten/topten2004.shtml).

USCCB.org. 2009. "Ten Best List for the Year 2009." Retrieved January 26, 2011 (http://www.usccb.org/movies/topten/topten2009.shtml).

Weeks, Linton. 1999. "Charmed, I'm Sure." *The Washington Post*. October 20. Retrieved July 7, 2011 (http://www.washingtonpost.com/wp-srv/style/books/features/rowling1020.htm).

Winseman, Albert L. 2004. "'Born-Agains' Wield Political, Economic Influence." Gallup. April 13. Retrieved January 26, 2011 (http://www.gallup.com/poll/11269/BornAgains-Wield-Political-Economic-Influence.aspx).

Wohlberg, Steve. 2005. *Exposing Harry Potter and Witchcraft*. Shippensburg, PA: Destiny Image.

Woods, Aubrey. 2000. "Harry Potter and the Magic Key of JK Rowling." *Associated Press*. July 6. Retrieved July 7, 2011 (http://www.accio-quote.org/articles/2000/0700-ap-woods.html).

HOGWARTS

DEPARTMENT OF SOCIOLOGY

Dr. Drew Chappell is a performance studies scholar with interests in play, cultural representation, and childhood studies. He is the editor of *Children Under Construction: Critical Essays on Play as Curriculum* (Peter Lang 2010) and teaches in the department of theatre and dance at California State University Fullerton. He earned an MFA in theatre for youth from the University of Texas and a PhD in theatre from Arizona State University. Dr. Chappell has been traveling the world studying the intersections of magic, performance, and history. Along the way, he has visited some fascinating places, including the ruins of Stonehenge (where he could still feel magic flowing) and the ocean reefs off Maui (where he cast a spell to speak with the fish, who had much to say about the rise of the tourist industry). In addition to teaching and research, he is an award winning playwright whose work focuses on issues that affect both children and adults. He is a member of Ravenclaw House and his favorite character is housemate Luna Lovegood. His wand core contains a selkie claw.

Dr. Anna Chilewska was born in Poland and lives in Edmonton, Canada. She has a Master of Arts degree in Slavic Linguistics and a PhD in Translation Studies from the University of Alberta. She specializes in the translation of children's literature, with a focus on the influences of politics and ideologies on the translation processes of children's books. Her other interests include animal rights, the role of women in horror films, Aboriginal literature, and Death Metal music. She currently teaches English literature and Writing Studies and is working on a book about images of Lucifer in Death Metal music. Dr. Chilewska is a member of Slytherin House and Severus Snape was her mentor. Her boggart is a leech (any kind, they all make her scream). Her favourite Harry Potter character is Ron, but she is far too old to be thinking about him.

Katie Christie is a graduate from the College of Charleston in South Carolina where she studied Sociology and African Studies. She is currently working towards her Master's degree in Social Work from the University of South Carolina. Her professional research interests include narrative therapy with adolescents, Native Americans and grief, rural poverty, social network analysis, and the sociology of literature. Katie has traveled extensively and her research and work interests have taken her to such places as eastern Montana, where she collaborated with the Rocky Mountain Tribal Epidemiology Center on a study of women's health issues on the Crow Reservation. Her favorite *Beedle the Bard* tale is "The Wizard and the Hopping Pot." Katie is a Gryffindor and enjoys chats with Hagrid and eating chocolate frogs.

Tanya Cook is an advanced graduate student in the department of Sociology at the University of Wisconsin-Madison. A Wisconsin native, Tanya was thrilled to be sorted into Hufflepuff House with its badger mascot. Tanya participated in the U.S. National Science Foundation's Summer Institute in Japan for graduate students where she gained access to a survey about the nuclear power accident in 1999 at Tokai-mura. She used this data to develop her Master's thesis titled "The Symbolic Politics Spiral: Transcending the Divide between Sociological Approaches to the Study of Risk," which compared the accidents at Tokai-mura and Three Mile Island. For her dissertation, currently titled "Exploring Childbirth Outcomes: An Analysis of Mother-Birth Professional Interaction," Tanya is interviewing expecting mothers and their doctors or midwives as well as observing interactions between mothers and birth professionals at prenatal visits. According to her three children, her boggart would be a particularly messy kid's room; but in truth it is similar to Molly Weasley's vision of dead family members. Known to channel Mrs. Weasley's "howler voice" on occasion, Tanya's patronus is a rabbit.

Dr. Justyna Deszcz-Tryhubczak is an Assistant Professor of Literature and member of the Center for Young People's Literature and Culture at the Institute of English Studies, University of Wrocław, Poland, where she teaches British literature, contemporary children's and young adult fantasy, ecocriticism, and theory or literature. She is the author of *Rushdie in Wonderland: "Fairytaleness" in Salman Rushdie's Fiction* (Peter Lang 2004). With Marek Oziewicz she co-edited *Towards or Back to Human Values: Spiritual and Moral Dimension of Contemporary Fantasy* (Cambridge Scholars Press 2006), *Considering Fantasy: Ethical, Didactic and Therapeutic Aspects of Fantasy in Literature and Film* (Atut 2007) and *Relevant Across Cultures: Visions of Interconnectedness and World Citizenship in Modern Fantasy for Young Readers* (Atut 2009). Her current research interests include interventions of a utopian problematic in recent fantasy for children and young adults. Dr. Deszcz-Tryhubczak is a member of Ravenclaw House and her patronus is a dolphin.

Shruti Devgan is a PhD candidate in the department of Sociology at Rutgers, The State University of New Jersey. She also has degrees in Sociology and Social Anthropology from Lady Shriram College and Jawaharlal Nehru University, both in New Delhi, India. Shruti is interested in collective memories, commemoration, trauma and violence. She focuses on Sikhs in the United States in her research. She has won awards from the Sociology department at Rutgers and the Sikh Studies Program at U.C. Berkeley for her papers on India's partition and Sikh religious symbols. She teaches courses in the Sociology department including Contemporary Theory and Sociology of

Women. She has also been involved in S.P.E.W. since her time at Hogwarts and is working in close association with Hermione Granger to fight for equal rights for house-elves. Together, Hermione and Shruti have extended S.P.E.W. from the confines of Hogwarts to the wizarding world at large. S.P.E.W. currently has 25 active members and is recruiting and growing in strength consistently. In a recent interview to the *Daily Prophet* Shruti revealed that she shares Hermione's passion for knitting socks for house-elves in addition to Ancient Runes being her favorite subject while she was at Hogwarts.

Mya Fisher is a doctoral candidate in the Department of Sociology at the University of Wisconsin-Madison. She received her BA in Sociology and Psychology from Williams College in 2000, and her MA in International Education from New York University in 2006. Her research is on student pathways and study abroad, and her dissertation focuses on the factors that influence study abroad decision-making for African-American students. Additionally, Mya speaks Japanese and was the recipient of a U.S. Department of Education Foreign Language Area Studies grant to study in Japan. As an exchange student at Hogwarts, she was sorted into Hufflepuff House. Her patronus is a penguin and her boggart is a black hole, which represents her fear of emptiness swallowing her whole. Mya loves to travel, cook and host dinner parties and always says no when offered some Bertie Bots Every Flavor Beans. Upon completion of her Muggle PhD, she aspires to teach a Foreign Language Charms class at Hogwarts in which students will learn to recognize and use charms in different languages.

Ty Hayes is a doctoral researcher at the University of Warwick, dissertating on a topic of Negotiating Stigmatized Identities with Cyborg Subjectivities. His main topics of interest are the sociology of the internet and sexuality, queer and gender studies. While at Hogwarts, he was in Ravenclaw House after the Sorting Hat gave him the choice between there and Hufflepuff. He could often be seen sporting wacky coloured hair after experimenting with hair-dyeing potions as part of his N.E.W.T. studies which could have landed him many galleons in fines had the Ludicrous Patents Office not acknowledged his priority over a deceitful Slytherin contemporary who stole his recipe and made minor adjustments. After completing his Muggle PhD he hopes to get a job in the Ministry, researching love in the Department of Mysteries.

Dr. Marcia Hernandez is an Associate Professor of Sociology at the University of the Pacific. Her scholarship interests include Black Greek-Letter organizations, higher education, popular culture and media studies in sociology. A member of Gryffindor House, she learned to produce her lion patronus from her favorite professor, Remus Lupin. Dr. Hernandez is currently working on projects that focus on the intersection of social class, body politics and images of beauty within African American communities. Other projects include assessing service-learning pedagogy, and community based research examining social cohesion and civic engagement in California's Central Valley. Her research is featured in the Journal for Civic Commitment, Social Indicators Research and the anthology *Black Greek Letter Organizations in the Twenty First Century: Our Fight Has Just Begun.*

Kristen Kalz is an Adjunct Professor of Sociology in the St Louis Metro Area. She earned her Master's Degree in Sociology at Southern Illinois University Edwardsville. She attended Hogwarts, taking her black cat Gonzo with her, and was sorted into Gryffindor House. While at school she once checked out a library book that, unbeknownst to her, Madam Pince had put a spell on to cause the book to write on her when she tried to write in it. Kristen's research interests include gender studies and social movements/change, and Minerva McGonagall is her favorite professor.

Dr. Dustin Kidd serves as Associate Professor of Sociology at Temple University in Philadelphia where he teaches courses on popular culture and social theory. He is a member of Ravenclaw House and his favorite class at Hogwarts was History of Magic. He has published on the Harry Potter phenomenon in the Journal of Popular Culture. In addition, he has published articles on W.E.B. Du Bois' theories about art, the Robert Mapplethorpe photography controversy, and management practices in the non-profit arts. His book *Legislating Creativity* (Routledge 2010) examines the intersections of art and politics in the arts controversies of the late 1980s, centering on the National Endowment for the Arts. He holds a bachelor's degree in religious studies from James Madison University, an MA in English from the University of Virginia and a PhD in sociology, also from the University of Virginia. Dr. Kidd's Patronus is an otter and his boggart is a pile of rubbish because he fears clutter.

Rachel LaBozetta resides in Baltimore, Maryland with her husband, Nick. She graduated from Towson University with a Bachelor of Science degree in Anthropology, where her main focus was on cultural anthropology, sociology, and archaeology. Rachel also has a previous degree in biology. While at Towson University, she was the vice president of their Anthropological Society in 2009. Her academic interests are quite varied from environmental conservation to issues of racism and researching Southwestern Native Americans and the Inuit. She has written editorials for mugglenet.com titled

"Sociology of Harry Potter 101" (2008) and "Severus Snape in Love?" (2005). Rachel was sorted into Gryffindor House.

Dr. Florence C. Maätita is an Associate Professor of Sociology at Southern Illinois University Edwardsville. She earned her doctorate at the University of Connecticut. Her research and teaching interests include motherhood, gender, race-ethnicity, social psychology and family. Currently, she is conducting research on homophobia and anti-gay sentiments among undergraduate Sociology majors and the status/inclusion of issues related to gays and lesbians throughout Sociology curricula. A Gryffindor, Dr. Maätita's patronus is a monkey, which she learned to produce in her favorite class, Defense against the Dark Arts, with her favorite professor, Remus Lupin. In that class, she also learned how to turn her boggart, a snake, into a slinky.

Jelena Marić is an elementary school teacher in Sisak, Croatia. In 2008 she received her Masters degree in Elementary Education and Information and Communication Technology in Zagreb. Her professional interests are educational software and children's literature and she has written several articles for Croatian Magazines. During her schooling at Hogwarts, she was a proud member of Slytherin House, though she was never a pure blood fanatic, and Severus Snape was her favourite teacher. Jelena was a book worm, not an athlete, and she found Quidditch to be a childish game. She also absolutely adores all products from Weasleys' Wizard Wheezes.

Alice Nuttall of Ravenclaw House is a part time PhD student in English Literature at Oxford Brookes University. She is studying how American Indian characters are represented in children's literature particularly in fantasy and sci-fi. She has presented papers at the Global Youth Culture conference held at the University of Kent in 2009, and the Worlds of Violence conference at the University of Essex in 2010. She is also involved in the Oxford Children's Literature and Youth Culture Colloquium. Alice is quite fond of Acid Pops, despite the risk of burns. Her wand is birch and unicorn hair, and Charms is her favourite class.

Grainne O'Brien is a hardcore Slytherin who's on a mission to rid the wizarding world of the propaganda that Harry Potter was a saint. She is a graduate of University of Limerick with a BA in English and History and has studied the history of medieval restorative architecture, with a focus on Bunratty Castle, an Irish monument, and its reconstruction, as part of her undergraduate program. She is currently undertaking a Masters program in Gender Culture and Society at the same university. She is interested in the topic of "messaging" as it has been transmitted over time through the medium of utopian and alternative worlds in children's writing. She has chosen the topic of Queer Theory within the Harry Potter series as the principle focus of her thesis and expects to pursue a career in children's literature. She argues that Voldemort, or more specifically the child Tom Riddle Jr., is a "queer child," in her paper "Queering the Half Blood Prince" presented at The Age of Sex Event conference in Prato, Italy. Her patronus is a snow leopard and her boggart would be a giant mushroom that would try to eat her. Grainne was Head Girl in her 7th year but turned down a chance to work at the Ministry of Magic to become an academic.

Meredith Railton of Ravenclaw House is an undergraduate student at the University of Louisville, Kentucky. She is majoring in History, with a concentration in the Social Sciences, with a minor in Women's & Gender Studies. Upon graduation she plans to pursue her Master's in History with the hopes of becoming a high school History teacher. She worked as writer at accio-potter.com, a fan-run website devoted to Harry Potter, from 2009 until it closed in 2011. In July 2010 she presented an informal paper (expanded from one of her editorials on the site) entitled "The Sociology of Harry Potter: Gender Issues in Early Childhood Socialization" at the Harry Potter Symposium Infinitus 2010 in Orlando, Florida. Harry is her favorite character and her patronus is an albatross.

Sheruni "Sher" Ratnabalasuriar is a doctoral student at Arizona State University in the School of Social Transformation. Her current dissertation research focuses on examining the experiences of non-traditional students, specifically educational trajectories of women of color in various higher education computer science programs in both traditional face-to-face and primarily online and distance learning contexts. As a Ravenclaw, she tends to spend her time sneaking around the restricted section more than the Quidditch field, looking up new charms and spells, though she enjoys a good butterbeer at the Hogshead when she gets the chance. Sher has been known to write a column or two for the *Quibbler* on the many uses of dirigible plums and the garden gnome conspiracy connection. Her patronus is a Squirrel Monkey.

Dr. Leo Ruickbie is a scientist who has been investigating and writing about the darker side of life - from magic to haunted houses - for most of his professional career. What began as a philosophical discussion on re-enchantment (MA with distinction, Lancaster University) led to his being awarded a PhD from King's College, London, for his research into modern witchcraft and magic. As well as being a regular contributor to *Paranormal* magazine, amongst others, he is also the author of several academic books such as *Witchcraft Out of the Shadows* (Robert Hale, 2004, 2011), *Faustus: The Life and Times of a Renaissance Magician* (The History Press, 2009) and *A Brief Guide to the Supernatural* (Constable & Robinson, 2012). Other scholarly work includes a chapter on black magic and cryptography for *Science and the Occult* (Cambridge Scholars Press, forthcoming) and spirit communication in the Golden Dawn for *The Spiritualist Movement* (Praeger, forthcoming). He is a member of Societas Magica, the European Society for the Study of Western Esotericism, the Society for Psychical Research and the Ghost Club. Currently, he lives in a small village in Germany, overlooked by a castle suspiciously reminiscent of Hogwarts School of Witchcraft and Wizardry, where, over a glass of beer (non-dairy variety), he might be heard discussing defence against the dark arts. To read more about Leo's research, log on to www.ruickbie.com

Jenn Sims is a doctoral candidate in the Department of Sociology at the University of Wisconsin-Madison. She has a BA in Sociology with a minor in Spanish from Hampton University, and an MA in Sociology from Vanderbilt University. Her research focuses on race/ethnicity, identity, human transfiguration and charms. Her dissertation explores the role that ambiguous physical appearance, and its alteration, plays in mixed race Muggles' lives with regard to racial identity and the micro-politics of social interactions. Jenn was an exchange student at the University of Seville in Spain and at Hogwarts School of Witchcraft and Wizardry. At the latter, she was sorted into Ravenclaw House and received a Time-Turner so that she could take concurrent classes (though she also sometimes used it to squeeze in an evening run at the end of a particularly busy day). Her patronus alternates between a seahorse and a peacock depending on whether she is conjuring it for communication or protection respectively. Upon completion of her PhD she plans to move to the UK and hopes to find a post teaching sociology at a Muggle university in London.

Dr. Ravindra Pratap Singh teaches English in the Department of English and Modern European Languages, University of Lucknow in India. He specializes in Canadian Literature, Translation Studies and Technical Communication. His other areas of interest are Children's Literature, folk and Indology. He has contributed more than 30 papers to journals and magazines and presented 42 papers in different national and international seminars and conferences besides working on different projects/ fellowships / and programmes of the University Grants Commission, Indian Council of Cultural Relations, Indian Council for Social Science Research, Indian Council for Philosophical Research, and Indian Institute of Advanced Studies.

Dr. Singh has 7 published books, including two anthologies: *An Anthology of English Essays (2000)* and *An Anthology of English Short Stories (2000)* and two books: *Professional Communication (2001) and Functional Skills in Language and Literature (2005)*. He is also a creative writer and has one collection of English poems, *Banjaran and other Poems,* four Hindi plays, *Shakespeare ki Saat Raatein ,Dugdhika aur anya naatak, Adrishya* and *Samvedna* and one travelogue *Patheya* to his credit. Currently he is giving finishing touches to his collections of one act plays, *Five Virgins* and *Curtain Raisers.* Dr. Singh is a member of Gryffindor House and his patronus is a tiger.

Daniel Smith is currently studying for a PhD in sociology in at the University of Exeter. His research is on the transformation of English identity and understandings of "Englishness" through material artifacts. Daniel works as a research assistant and graduate teaching assistant, and is interested in interdisciplinary scholarship on the history of consumption, studies in material culture and theories of recognition. He discovered the Harry Potter novels at seven years old when they first arrived in Muggle bookstores, and is so excited to be twenty-two (a technical "adult") and writing about them in his professional job! His favourite of the book series is *Chamber of Secrets* (or *Half Blood Prince*). He was happily sorted into Ravenclaw House, which he believes is the best of all houses because books are honored and cleverness is a virtue. Plus, he believes solving a riddle is much more fun than remembering a boring password to enter the common room! In the unfortunate event that he ever encountered a Dementor in his little English-Muggle town, he would have to defend himself with his falcon patronus. Or, if he were cleaning out the spare room and discovered a boggart, it would take the shape of his old history Professor – a Muggle version of Snape if there ever was one!

INDEX

institutionalized, 4, 91, 94
manipulation of, 27
ownership of, 21
safe, 2, 19-20, 22-24, 121
social relevance of, 18
unsafe, 22-23
spaciality, 18
specieism, 172-173
Sports
coed nature of, 160-161
international competitions, 134-135, 144
Muggle sports, 52, 134-135, 156-157, 160-161
professioanlism and careers, 85, 127, 156-157, 161
regulating bodies, 128
unifying goal of, 134-135, 143-144
see also Quidditch
see also Social institutions
Squibs (see Race)
see also Prejudice
see also Stigma
Stigma, 2, 4, 99
against half-breeds, 119
against Muggle-borns, 115-116
against Squibs, 119
against the mentally ill, 95
against werewolves, 117- 118,
definition, 95, 114
management strategies, 119-123
Normals, 114, 116, 118-119, 121-123
professionals, 121-122
the Wise, 117-118, 123
transmission, 116-117
Study abroad/student exchange, 4,

134-135, 141-144
see also Triwizard Tournament
Symbolic interactionism, 10-11, 114, 125
Symbols
as contents of culture, 51-52
in Symbolic Interactionism, 11
objects as, 53, 74-75, 114, 116, 149-150, 186
words and language, 11, 81

T
Technological determinism, 28
Technology
and socialization, 12, 28
as innovation, 63
magical, 26, 219
Muggle, 10, 26-30, 32
see also Social Shaping of Technology
Time-Turner, 27, 95
Transportation, 2, 138, 151
cars, 33, 72, 80-81
Floo Network, 51
Thestrals, 105
Trauma
personal, 111, 183
cultural, 146-152
see also Memory
Trelawney, Sybil, 157
Triwizard Tournament, 4, 106, 137, 139-140, 143-144, 164, 174, 185, 207-208
see also Study abroad/student exchange

U
Umbridge, Dolores, 14, 20, 33, 73, 83, 87, 96, 103, 105, 110, 130,

OTHER BOOKS OF INTEREST

C. S. Lewis

C. S. Lewis: Views From Wake Forest - Essays on C. S. Lewis
Michael Travers, editor

Contains sixteen scholarly presentations from the international C. S. Lewis convention in Wake Forest, NC. Walter Hooper shares his important essay "Editing C. S. Lewis," a chronicle of publishing decisions after Lewis' death in 1963.

"Scholars from a variety of disciplines address a wide range of issues. The happy result is a fresh and expansive view of an author who well deserves this kind of thoughtful attention."
Diana Pavlac Glyer, author of *The Company They Keep*

The Hidden Story of Narnia:
A Book-By-Book Guide to Lewis' Spiritual Themes
Will Vaus

A book of insightful commentary equally suited for teens or adults – Will Vaus points out connections between the *Narnia* books and spiritual/biblical themes, as well as between ideas in the *Narnia* books and C. S. Lewis' other books. Learn what Lewis himself said about the overarching and unifying thematic structure of the Narnia books. That is what this book explores; what C. S. Lewis called "the hidden story" of Narnia. Each chapter includes questions for individual use or small group discussion.

Why I Believe in Narnia:
33 Reviews and Essays on the Life and Work of C. S. Lewis
James Como

Chapters range from reviews of critical books, documentaries and movies to evaluations of Lewis' books to biographical analysis.

"A valuable, wide-ranging collection of essays by one of the best informed and most accute commentators on Lewis' work and ideas."
Peter Schakel, author of *Imagination & the Arts in C.S. Lewis*

C. S. Lewis Goes to Heaven: A Reader's Guide to The Great Divorce
David G. Clark

This is the first book devoted solely to this often neglected book and the first to reveal several important secrets Lewis concealed within the story. Lewis felt his imaginary trip to Hell and Heaven was far better than his book *The Screwtape Letters*, which has become a classic. Clark is an ordained minister who has taught courses on Lewis for more than 30 years and is a New Testament and Greek scholar with a Doctor of Philosophy degree in Biblical Studies from the University of Notre Dame. Readers will discover the many literary and biblical influences Lewis utilized in writing his brilliant novel.

C. S. Lewis & Philosophy as a Way of Life
Adam Barkman

C. S. Lewis is rarely thought of as a "philosopher" per se despite having both studied and taught philosophy for several years at Oxford. Lewis's long journey to Christianity was essentially philosophical – passing through seven different stages. This 624 page book is an invaluable reference for C. S. Lewis scholars and fans alike

C. S. Lewis: His Literary Achievement
Colin Manlove

"This is a positively brilliant book, written with splendor, elegance, profundity and evidencing an enormous amount of learning. This is probably not a book to give a first-time reader of Lewis. But for those who are more broadly read in the Lewis corpus this book is an absolute gold mine of information. The author gives us a magnificent overview of Lewis' many writings, tracing for us thoughts and ideas which recur throughout, and at the same time telling us how each book differs from the others. I think it is not extravagant to call C. S. Lewis: His Literary Achievement a tour de force."
 Robert Merchant, *St. Austin Review*, Book Review Editor

Mythopoeic Narnia: Memory, Metaphor, and Metamorphoses in C. S. Lewis's The Chronicles of Narnia
Salwa Khoddam

Dr. Khoddam, the founder of the C. S. Lewis and Inklings Society (2004), has been teaching university courses using Lewis' books for over 25 years. Her book offers a fresh approach to the *Narnia* books based on an inquiry into Lewis' readings and use of classical and Christian symbols. She explores the literary and intellectual contexts of these stories, the traditional myths and motifs, and places them in the company of the greatest Christian mythopoeic works of Western literature. In Lewis' imagination, memory and metaphor interact to advance his purpose – a Christian metamorphosis. *Mythopoeic Narnia* helps to open the door for readers into the magical world of the Western imagination.

Speaking of Jack: A C. S. Lewis Discussion Guide
Will Vaus

C. S. Lewis societies have been forming around the world since the first one started in New York City in 1969. Will Vaus has started and led three groups himself. *Speaking of Jack* is the result of Vaus' experience in leading those Lewis societies. Included here are introductions to most of Lewis' books as well as questions designed to stimulate discussion about Lewis' life and work. These materials have been "road-tested" with real groups made up of young and old, some very familiar with Lewis and some newcomers. *Speaking of Jack* may be used in an existing book discussion group, to start a C. S. Lewis society, or to guide your own exploration of Lewis' books.

George MacDonald

Diary of an Old Soul & The White Page Poems
George MacDonald and Betty Aberlin

The first edition of George MacDonald's book of daily poems included a blank page opposite each page of poems. Readers were invited to write their own reflections on the "white page." MacDonald wrote: "Let your white page be ground, my print be seed, growing to golden ears, that faith and hope may feed." Betty Aberlin responded to MacDonald's invitation with daily poems of her own.

"Betty Aberlin's close readings of George MacDonald's verses and her thoughtful responses to them speak clearly of her poetic gifts and spiritual intelligence."
     Luci Shaw, poet

George MacDonald: Literary Heritage and Heirs
Roderick McGillis, editor

This latest collection of 14 essays sets a new standard that will influence MacDonald studies for many more years. George MacDonald experts are increasingly evaluating his entire corpus within the nineteenth century context.

"This comprehensive collection represents the best of contemporary scholarship on George MacDonald."
     Rolland Hein, author of *George MacDonald: Victorian Mythmaker*

In the Near Loss of Everything: George MacDonald's Son in America
Dale Wayne Slusser

In the summer of 1887, George MacDonald's son Ronald, newly engaged to artist Louise Blandy, sailed from England to America to teach school. The next summer he returned to England to marry Louise and bring her back to America. On August 27, 1890, Louise died, leaving him with an infant daughter. Ronald once described losing a beloved spouse as "the near loss of everything". Dale Wayne Slusser unfolds this poignant story with unpublished letters and photos that give readers a glimpse into the close-knit MacDonald family.

A Novel Pulpit: Sermons From George MacDonald's Fiction
David L. Neuhouser

"In MacDonald's novels, the Christian teaching emerges out of the characters and story line, the narrator's comments, and inclusion of sermons given by the fictional preachers. The sermons in the novels are shorter than the ones in collections of MacDonald's sermons and so are perhaps more accessible for some. In any case, they are both stimulating and thought-provoking. This collection of sermons from ten novels serve to bring out the 'freshness and brilliance' of MacDonald's message."
     From the author's introduction

Through the Year with George MacDonald: 366 Daily Readings
Rolland Hein, editor

These page-length excerpts from sermons, novels and letters are given an appropriate theme/heading and a complementary Scripture passage for daily reading. An inspiring introduction to the artistic soul and Christian vision of George MacDonald.

Pop Culture

To Love Another Person: A Spiritual Journey Through Les Miserables
John Morrison

The powerful story of Jean Valjean's redemption is beloved by readers and theater goers everywhere. In this companion and guide to Victor Hugo's masterpiece, author John Morrison unfolds the spiritual depth and breadth of this classic novel and broadway musical.

Through Common Things: Philosophical Reflections on Popular Culture
Adam Barkman

"Barkman presents us with an amazingly wide-ranging collection of philosophical reflections grounded in the everyday things of popular culture – past and present, eastern and western, factual and fictional. Throughout his encounters with often surprising subject-matter (the value of darkness?), he writes clearly and concisely, moving seamlessly between Aristotle and anime, Lord Buddha and Lord Voldemort…. . This is an informative and entertaining book to read!"
Doug Bloomberg, Professor of Philosophy, Institute for Christian Studies

Spotlight:
A Close-up Look at the Artistry and Meaning of Stephenie Meyer's Twilight Novels
John Granger

Stephenie Meyer's *Twilight* saga has taken the world by storm. But is there more to *Twilight* than a love story for teen girls crossed with a cheesy vampire-werewolf drama? *Spotlight* reveals the literary backdrop, themes, artistry, and meaning of the four Bella Swan adventures. *Spotlight* is the perfect gift for serious *Twilight* readers.

Virtuous Worlds: The Video Gamer's Guide to Spiritual Truth
John Stanifer

Popular titles like *Halo 3* and *The Legend of Zelda: Twilight Princess* fly off shelves at a mind-blowing rate. John Stanifer, an avid gamer, shows readers specific parallels between Christian faith and the content of their favorite games. Written with wry humor (including a heckler who frequently pokes fun at the author) this book will appeal to gamers and non-gamers alike. Those unfamiliar with video games may be pleasantly surprised to find that many elements in those "virtual worlds" also qualify them as "virtuous worlds."

Memoir

Called to Serve: Life as a Firefighter-Deacon
Deacon Anthony R. Surozenski

Called to Serve is the story of one man's dream to be a firefighter. But dreams have a way of taking detours – so Tony Soruzenski became a teacher and eventually a volunteer firefighter. And when God enters the picture, Tony is faced with a choice. Will he give up firefighting to follow another call? After many years, Tony's two callings are finally united – in service as a fire chaplain at Ground Zero after the 9-11 attacks and in other ways he could not have imagined. Tony is Chief Chaplain's aid for the Massachusettes Corp of Fire Chaplains and Director for the Office of the Diaconate of the Diocese of Worcester, Massachusettes.

Harry Potter

The Order of Harry Potter: The Literary Skill of the Hogwarts Epic
Colin Manlove

Colin Manlove, a popular conference speaker and author of over a dozen books, has earned an international reputation as an expert on fantasy and children's literature. His book, *From Alice to Harry Potter*, is a survey of 400 English fantasy books. In *The Order of Harry Potter*, he compares and contrasts *Harry Potter* with works by "Inklings" writers J.R.R. Tolkien, C.S. Lewis and Charles Williams; he also examines Rowling's treatment of the topic of imagination; her skill in organization and the use of language; and the book's underlying motifs and themes.

Harry Potter & Imagination: The Way Between Two Worlds
Travis Prinzi

Imaginative literature places a reader between two worlds: the story world and the world of daily life, and challenges the reader to imagine and to act for a better world. Starting with discussion of Harry Potter's more important themes, *Harry Potter & Imagination* takes readers on a journey through the transformative power of those themes for both the individual and for culture by placing Rowling's series in its literary, historical, and cultural contexts.

Repotting Harry Potter: A Professor's Guide for the Serious Re-Reader
Rowling Revisited: Return Trips to Harry, Fantastic Beasts, Quidditch, & Beedle the Bard
James W. Thomas

In *Repotting Harry Potter* and his sequel book *Rowling Revisited*, Dr. James W. Thomas points out the humor, puns, foreshadowing and literary parallels in the Potter books. In *Rowling Revisted*, readers will especially find useful three extensive appendixes – "Fantastic Beasts and the Pages Where You'll Find Them," "Quidditch Through the Pages," and "The Books in the Potter Books." Dr. Thomas makes re-reading the Potter books even more rewarding and enjoyable.

Deathly Hallows Lectures:
The Hogwarts Professor Explains Harry's Final Adventure
John Granger

In *The Deathly Hallows Lectures*, John Granger reveals the finale's brilliant details, themes, and meanings. *Harry Potter* fans will be surprised by and delighted with Granger's explanations of the three dimensions of meaning in *Deathly Hallows*. Ms. Rowling has said that alchemy sets the "parameters of magic" in the series; after reading the chapter-length explanation of *Deathly Hallows* as the final stage of the alchemical Great Work, the serious reader will understand how important literary alchemy is in understanding Rowling's artistry and accomplishment.

Hog's Head Conversations: Essays on Harry Potter
Travis Prinzi, Editor

Ten fascinating essays on Harry Potter by popular Potter writers and speakers including John Granger, James W. Thomas, Colin Manlove, and Travis Prinzi.

Harry Potter, Still Recruiting:
An Inner Look at Harry Potter Fandom
Valerie Frankel, editor

Chapters include a wide variety of topics such as social networking, Pottermore, college Quidditch, fan art, fan fiction, conferences, exhibitions, Wizard Rock, websites, and fan locations such as the Wizarding World of Harry Potter. The book includes photographs and interviews with prominent Harry Potter community members. Frankel emphasizes the recent effects on society ranging from the Simpsons to Facebook.

Poets and Poetry

Half-Blood Poems: Inspired by the Stories of J.K. Rowling
Christine Lowther

Like Harry Potter's life, Christine's poetry can soar above the tragic to discover the heroic and beautiful in such poems as "Neville, Unlikely Rebel," "For Our Wide-Armed Mothers," and "A Boy's Hands." There are seventy one poems divided into seven chapters that correspond with the seven book series. Fans of Harry Potter will experience again many of the emotions they felt reading the books - emotions presented most effectively through a poet's words.

In the Eye of the Beholder: How to See the World Like a Romantic Poet
Louis Markos

Born out of the French Revolution and its radical faith that a nation could be shaped and altered by the dreams and visions of its people, British Romantic Poetry was founded on a belief that the objects and realities of our world, whether natural or human, are not fixed in stone but can be molded and transformed by the visionary eye of the poet. Unlike many of the books written on Romanticism, which devote many pages to the poets and few pages to their poetry, the focus here is firmly on the poems themselves. The author thereby draws the reader intimately into the life of these poems. A separate bibliographical essay is provided for readers listing accessible biographies of each poet and critical studies of their work.

The Cat on the Catamaran: A Christmas Tale
John Martin

Here is a modern-day parable of a modern-day cat with modern-day attitudes. Riverboat Dan is a "cool" cat on a perpetual vacation from responsibility. He's *The Cat on the Catamaran* – sailing down the river of life. Dan keeps his guilty conscience from interfering with his fun until he runs into trouble. But will he have the courage to believe that it's never too late to change course? (For ages 10 to adult)

"Cat lovers and poetry lovers alike will enjoy this whimsical story about Riverboat Dan, a philosophical cat in search of meaning."
Regina Doman, author of *Angel in the Water*

CPSIA information can be obtained
at www.ICGtesting.com
Printed in the USA
LVHW032254181222
735495LV00003B/416

9 781936 294183